Working with adolescents
Supporting families, preventing breakdown

Working with adolescents
Supporting families, preventing breakdown

Nina Biehal

British Association for Adoption & Fostering
(BAAF)
Skyline House
200 Union Street
London SE1 0LX
www.baaf.org.uk

Charity registration 275689

British Library Cataloguing in Publication Data
A catalogue record for this book is available
from the British Library

ISBN 1 903699 78 9

Editorial project management by Shaila Shah
Cover photographs posed by models;
John Birdsall Photography
Designed by Andrew Haig & Associates
Typeset by Avon DataSet, Bidford on Avon
Printed in Great Britain by Creative Print
and Design Group
Trade distribution by Turnaround Publisher
Services, Unit 3, Olympia Trading Estate,
Coburg Road, London N22 6TZ

BAAF is the leading UK-wide membership
organisation for all those concerned with
adoption, fostering and child care issues.

For Max, Rosa, Sam,
Anna and Joe

Contents

Tables

Acknowledgements

I would like to thank the Department of Health for sponsoring this project under its research programme on the costs and effectiveness of services for children and, in particular, Dr Carolyn Davies and Dr Caroline Thomas for their support throughout. I also benefited from the advice of our Advisory Group throughout the course of the study. Thanks are due to Professor David Berridge, Dr Jeni Beecham, Dr John Coleman, Janet Grauberg, Tessa Ing, John Rowlands and Kevin Woods.

I owe a major debt to everyone in the eight participating local authorities who helped and advised me during the course of this study and I would like to thank the staff of support teams, the social workers and the managers who helped with this study. I would also like to thank my colleagues at SWRDU (the Social Work Research and Development Unit). In particular, thanks are due to Ian Sinclair for his advice on statistical analysis and general support, to Ian Gibbs, who also helped with statistical analysis, and to Sarah Ellison and Suzy Alcock, who managed the fieldwork at different stages of the study. Thanks too to Claire Baker, who advised on the research on children with disabilities, to Jim Wade, who helpfully commented on draft chapters, to Helen Jacobs and Dawn Rowley for their unstinting secretarial support, and to Jo Dixon, Fiona Mitchell and Emilie Smeaton for help with the fieldwork. Colleagues at the University of York's Centre for Health Economics also collaborated on the study and I would therefore like to thank Helen Weatherly and Sarah Byford.

Above all, I am extremely grateful to the many young people and parents who agreed to take part in the study. Without their willingness to talk about what were often very difficult experiences, this book could not have been written.

Nina Biehal

Note about the author

Nina Biehal is a senior research fellow at the Social Work Research and Development Unit at the University of York and editor of the journal *Child and Family Social Work*. Building on her previous experience as a social worker, Nina has been involved in child care research for many years. Her research interests focus particularly on social work with older children and adolescents. She has completed studies on leaving care, runaways from care, family support and missing persons. Her current research interests include the rehabilitation of looked after children, adoption, long-term fostering and treatment foster care. Publications include Biehal, N, Clayden, J, Stein, M and Wade, J (1995) *Moving On: Young People and leaving care schemes*, London: HMSO; Wade, J and Biehal, N with Clayden, J and Stein, M (1998) *Going Missing: Young people absent from care*, Chichester: Wiley; and Biehal, N, Byford, D and Clayden, J (2000) *Home or Away? Supporting young people and families*, London: National Children's Bureau.

1 Introduction

This book is about services which aim to prevent the placement of young people in residential or foster care. Placement rates are high for older children and adolescents. During 2003–2004, 44 per cent of children who started to be looked after in England were aged 10–16 years and there had been little fluctuation in the preceding five years. Around one-third had started to be looked after as a result of abuse or neglect and a further third for reasons of family dysfunction or because their families were in acute stress (Department for Education and Skills (DfES), 2005).

Historically, fluctuations in the number of teenagers in care have for the most part been due to legislative changes. The abolition of the system of approved schools by the Children and Young Persons Act 1969 led many teenage young offenders to enter the care system. As a result, between 1962 and 1987, the proportion of children admitted who were aged 14 years or over increased from 3 per cent to 25 per cent (Bebbington and Miles, 1989; Rowe et al, 1989). Yet, although the Children Act 1989 removed offending, truancy and moral danger as specific grounds for a care order, the proportion of teenagers among new admissions to substitute care has remained high.

Concerns about high rates of admission to substitute care or accommodation for older children and young people, as well as the high cost of accommodating them, has led to the establishment of specialist support teams in many local authorities, which are variously known as community support teams, adolescent support teams, young people's support services or family support teams. Support teams for adolescents have developed rapidly since the late 1980s. Typically, they offer an intensive, short-term preventive service aimed at diverting adolescents from the care system. Most of these teams have been set up in tandem with a reduction in residential provision and many of their staff have been re-deployed from residential units. Indeed, a survey of community support teams around the country found that *all* had been created in order to reduce the rate of admission to local authority accommodation, although some had additional aims (Brown, 1998).

This book describes the findings of a research study into the effectiveness of these specialist support teams in their work with young people at imminent risk of family breakdown. It compares outcomes for young people referred to support teams with those for others receiving a mainstream social work service. It also explores the reasons why older children and teenagers may come to the brink of placement, the circumstances in which some of them are placed and patterns of placement for these young people. The findings from this study are discussed in the context of an analysis of relevant policy and research in order to draw out important implications for policy and practice.

This study is unusual since, unlike most other research on family support services, it focuses specifically on services for 11–16-year-olds. It is also unusual in its attention to the *effectiveness* of family support services, and to the circumstances in which interventions appear to be helpful to young people.

Plan of the book

The first three chapters situate support services for adolescents within a policy and research framework. Accordingly, Chapter 2 focuses on the policy and conceptual frameworks underpinning the current provision of family support services to young people and their families. Chapters 3 and 4 then review the relevant research literature on interventions with older children and adolescents in the UK and the USA.

The remainder of the book focuses on a research study on the effectiveness of family support services for young people who appear to be on the brink of placement. This study focuses on three main issues:

The young people and families
- What are the characteristics, histories, needs and circumstances of young people and families who receive a family support service?

The nature of the service
- What kind of service is provided by specialist support teams and how does it differ from that provided by mainstream social workers?

Outcomes
- Are specialist support teams for adolescents more successful in

achieving positive outcomes for young people at risk of family break-down than mainstream social work services?

- Are these specialist support teams effective in reducing the likelihood of placement, in comparison with mainstream services?
- How, why and in what circumstances do these interventions help to bring about positive change in the lives of young people?

2 From prevention to early intervention: policy and concepts

From prevention to family support

Since the passing of the Children Act 1948 there has been a continuing tension between state paternalism and the defence of the birth family. In some periods policy has favoured a legalistic, protectionist approach to children while in others there has been a stronger focus on providing support to families with a view to preventing entry to care wherever possible (Packman and Jordan, 1991; Packman, 1993). This has been characterised as an ongoing conflict between protagonists of the "state as parent" and the "kinship defenders", with the latter arguing for greater support to families in order to prevent admission to substitute care (Fox-Harding, 1991). Although the pendulum swings in state policies towards children are said to have commenced as far back as the Poor Law Amendment Act of 1834,[1] they appear to have intensified since the early 1970s (Parker, 1990).

The concept of prevention was not explicit in the Children Act 1948, although some have argued that it was implicit (Marsh and Triseliotis, 1993). Certainly, questions were raised in parliament as early as 1949 regarding the wisdom of removing neglected children from their families rather than supporting families to prevent cruelty and neglect. In 1950, the Home Secretary issued a circular, jointly with the Ministries of Health and Education, which was the first government statement explicitly to link the prevention of neglect and ill-treatment with the prevention of removal of children from their homes (Heywood, 1978). As the 1950s progressed, a number of factors converged to focus attention on the need to prevent unnecessary admission to care: the increase in the number of children entering care, mainly for reasons of neglect; the rising costs associated with this increase; and the influence of Bowlby's work on the psychological consequences for children of separation from their parents

---

[1] This was the first legislation to require parishes to provide some rudimentary education for the destitute children looked after in workhouses (Heywood, 1978).

(Bowlby, 1951; Packman, 1975). There was increasing recognition of the link between material deprivation and neglect and increasing pressure from children's officers, appointed by the local Children's Committees, for wider powers to undertake preventive work (Heywood, 1978).

As Parker has observed, what changed in the years after the 1948 Children Act were views about what it was necessary to prevent – 'namely the disruption or breakdown of families that led to children having to be looked after by a corporate body' (Parker, 1990, p. 98). These concerns led the government to set up a Committee of Inquiry chaired by Lord Ingleby in 1956 to inquire into the working of the law in respect of children brought before the courts as being in need of care or protection or as delinquents.

The conclusions of the Ingleby Report in 1960 informed the Children and Young Persons Act 1963. This marked a new departure in that it was the first legislation to set out a statutory duty to provide assistance to families 'to promote the welfare of children by diminishing the need to receive children into or keep them in care'. It marked a new attitude on the part of government, indicating a shift from a paternalistic, protective, child-centred attitude to a greater emphasis on work to support families in caring for their children (Heywood, 1978). The concept of prevention embodied in the 1963 Act encompassed not only the prevention of admission to care but also the restoration of children to their families, the prevention of neglect and cruelty in the home and the prevention of juvenile offending. The aim was to promote the welfare of children, particularly those experiencing neglect, by helping the family as a whole, and it resulted in a reduction in the number of children with less serious problems entering substitute care (Packman, 1993). The focus on preventing admission to care was reinforced by studies of the foster care service, which identified a number of problems, including high breakdown rates (Trasler, 1960; Parker, 1966; George, 1970). Preventive work was also broadened by the introduction of Intermediate Treatment by the Children and Young Persons Act 1969, which led to a great deal of preventive activity with teenagers until criticism of its labelling and net-widening effects led to its decline (Thorpe et al, 1980).

During the 1970s, researchers identified the problem of children who "drifted" in care due to a lack of proper planning and concern was expressed about the possible consequences of long-term care for the psycho-social development of children (Goldstein *et al*, 1973; Rowe and Lambert, 1973; Fanshel and Shinn, 1978). These concerns contributed to the emergence of the permanency planning movement in both the UK and the USA. The permanency planning approach encouraged a focus on ensuring continuity of care for children, preferably within their own families but, if this was not possible, through adoption or long-term foster care (Maluccio and Fein, 1983). In the UK, the emphasis of permanency planning was primarily on planning for children in care rather than on keeping them with, or returning them to, their birth families.

The work of Goldstein and colleagues (1973) was influential during this period. This promoted the idea that state intervention in family life should be minimal but, once parenting was found to be severely impaired, decisive action should be taken by the state. This action might include the severance of ties with the biological family and encouragement of the development of new psychological ties to substitute parents. Hence, preventive and rehabilitative work came to be viewed as less important. In the UK, though, perhaps the major factor which contributed to concern over child care policy and practice during this period was a series of child abuse inquiries, in particular the Maria Colwell Inquiry which reported in 1974 (Secretary of State for Social Services, 1974; Parton, 1991). The combined impact of the permanence movement and of panics over child abuse led to a decline in preventive activity as the 1970s progressed (Holman, 1988; Parton, 1991).

However, by the early 1980s renewed interest in prevention was evident in the Barclay Report. This argued for the development of community social work, which would tap into local networks of formal and informal support to families (Barclay Working Party, 1982). Shortly afterwards, the House of Commons Social Services Committee report, known as the Short Report, complained of a lack of commitment to preventive work and a lack of understanding of where preventive effort should be targeted (House of Commons Social Services Select Committee, 1984). This was followed by the Review of Child Care Law, which questioned the distinction between the needs of the child and the needs of the family (Department of Health and Social Security (DHSS), 1985a). In the same period, a number of studies argued for greater attention to supporting families in order to prevent family breakdown and the collection of pressure groups which constituted the parents' rights lobby, such as the Family Rights Group, campaigned to re-establish a commitment to preventive work (Parker, 1980; Fisher *et al*, 1986; Holman, 1988). This renewed concern with preventing admission to care was reinforced by a series of research studies in the mid-1980s which identified a lack of planning for children in care and poor outcomes for young people leaving care (DHSS, 1985b; Stein and Carey, 1986).

These developments helped to shape the Children Act 1989, which placed a duty on local authorities, under Section 17, to safeguard and promote the welfare of "children in need" and to promote their upbringing by their families. The Act represents a shift in emphasis from the old negative conception of prevention to a more positive, proactive duty of family support with the broader aim of promoting the welfare of children. Parents of "children in need" were encouraged to look to local authorities for non-stigmatising support services, without fear of a loss of parental responsibility. Indeed, the continuity of parental responsibility was emphasised by the Children Act, thus satisfying both conservative and liberal commentators. The focus on supporting families and the promotion of parental responsibility reflected the contemporary Conservative anti-collectivist policies aimed at reducing the role of the welfare state and a concomitant reassertion of the role of the family in taking responsibility for its members. In line with this philosophy, the emphasis was on reducing state intervention in the private sphere of family life (Jack and Stepney, 1995). At the same time, this policy satisfied those with more liberal views regarding the need for support to disadvantaged families to enable them to care adequately for their children. Thus, for different reasons, policy on family support appealed to "kinship defenders" across a wide political spectrum.

The Act sought to integrate the duty to protect children from harm and the duty to support families, so that the aims of preventive services would no longer be focused on the narrow goal of preventing children being looked after, but on preventing harm, or the need for compulsory intervention, or offending. The Children Act 1989 also abolished the use of Care Orders in criminal proceedings and in response to truancy, thus increasing the pool of young people who might potentially require family support services instead. However, within a few years of the Children Act's implementation, concern was being expressed at the continuing prioritisation of child protection work and the marginalisation of family support services (Audit Commission, 1994). A review of a series of Department of Health-funded studies into the operation of the child protection system found that too many families were drawn into the child protection net without receiving any services to meet their needs. It called for a rebalancing of services to shift the focus of attention from investigation to support to families with children in need. The intention was to lower the threshold for the provision of services from the identification of significant harm to the identification of the needs of children (Department of Health (DH), 1995). The aim was that a refocusing of services would ensure that family support became the context within which child protection interventions might take place, rather than an alternative to them.

Despite these intentions, a subsequent inspection report found that social services continued to give little attention to supporting the families of children in need and suggested that, to some extent, this was due to pressures on public expenditure and reduced local authority spending on personal social services (Social Services Inspectorate (SSI), 1997). It has also been argued that the increase in numbers of children looked after during the late 1990s demonstrated that there was still little evidence of a shift in social work policy and practice from investigation and protection to prevention and support (House of Commons Health Committee, 1998; Walby and Colton, 1999).

Prevention and the concept of need

Attempts to conceptualise prevention have centred on the concept of need and the question of where interventions should be targeted. Although an apparently simple notion, prevention can be a slippery concept which can have a variety of meanings, depending on who is using it. As Hardiker and colleagues observed, a key question is 'preventing what?' and the answers to this question are likely both to reflect a variety of value positions and require a variety of practice strategies (Hardiker *et al*, 1991; Tunstill, 1996). As we have seen, in the early years after the 1963 Children and Young Persons Act, prevention came to refer not only to the prevention of admission to care but also to the prevention of abuse, neglect and delinquency. While official views of prevention tend to be fairly narrowly focused in this way, others have taken a broader view of the needs of children and hence of what should be prevented. For example, Holman addressed the question 'preventing what?' with a seven-point typology. This included not only preventing admission to care, preventing children being abused and neglected, and preventing young people appearing before the courts but also the prevention of poor parenting, the prevention of lengthy episodes in care, the prevention of the isolation of children in care from their families and preventing children suffering the effects of severe socio-economic disadvantage (Holman, 1988). He also argued that prevention may be either a reactive activity, for example, to prevent children being unnecessarily separated from their parents when problems arise, or a positive support to promote the well-being of children in their families and so forestall the development of severe problems. Like Packman, he argued for a wider perspective on prevention, one that is broader than a solely problem-focused approach (Packman, 1986; Holman, 1988).

Drawing on the classifications of preventive medicine, Parker highlighted the need to view preventive activity as a continuum of provision ranging from universal services to those targeted at children in greatest need (Parker, 1980). Accordingly, prevention has been categorised in terms of three levels of need, each of which requires a particular model of service characterised as primary, secondary or tertiary prevention (Parker, 1980; Hardiker et al, 1991; Gardner, 1992; Sinclair et al, 1997). Primary interventions are intended to prevent the emergence of problems and normally involve provision of universal services on an open access basis, such as nursery education. Secondary preventive services address problems in their early stages, for example, neighbourhood services located in areas of social disadvantage whose users are self-selected. Tertiary prevention aims to limit the damaging effects of a problem already established and normally involves provision targeted at particular individuals who are referred to specialist services (Sinclair et al, 1997).

This conceptualisation of prevention has led to debates about the most effective levels at which to intervene and, associated with this, to discussion of the right balance between universal and targeted services. For example, Holman has argued that universalist provision would reduce the need for coercive intervention in family life and make state intervention unnecessary in all but extreme cases (Holman, 1988). Similarly, Gibbons advocated a strategy of neighbourhood-based family support services delivered by independently run voluntary and informal groups, with local authority intervention only in situations where serious problems are identified (Gibbons, 1990). Within local authorities, different family support services may intervene at different levels of prevention, for example, some family centres may target families at high risk of losing their children while others may be concerned with community initiatives reaching out to a broader spectrum of families (Packman and Hall, 1998).

With the passing of the Children Act 1989, the debate shifted from a discussion of levels of prevention to an examination of the concept of "children in need", but at the heart of this new debate lie the same concerns about the merits of universal or targeted services, of early intervention or later reaction to problems which have become more serious. Although the Children Act 1989 has expanded the duties and powers of local authorities to provide services, it has at the same time stipulated that these services are to be available only to children "in need". The concept of family support could conceivably imply that a wide range of children might be entitled to universal services, which potentially has enormous resource implications for local authorities. The concept of children in need serves to narrow the focus of service provision, so that services are targeted at those "in need", as defined in Section 17 of the 1989 Children Act. A child is considered to be "in need" if:

- he/she is unlikely to achieve or maintain, or to have the opportunity of achieving or maintaining, a reasonable standard of health or development without the provision for him/her of services:
- his/her health or development is likely to be significantly impaired, or further impaired, without the provision for him/her of such services; or
- he/she is disabled.

Implicit in the Act, therefore, is the notion of targeting, the precise nature of which is to be determined through local discretion.

Concern has been expressed about the way the deliberately wide definition of need in the 1989 Children Act is translated into operational definitions at local level. Some have argued that the Children Act's aim of developing a positive and proactive family support service – whose purpose would be to identify and meet a wide range of needs rather than simply prevent a narrow range of outcomes – is not being fulfilled. For example, a study of the implementation of Section 17 of the Children Act found that, instead of attempting to ascertain the particular needs of children in their local areas, most local authority policy statements went little further than the definitions provided in the Children Act and its Guidance (Aldgate and Tunstill, 1995). This study of 82 English local authorities found that many had established a hierarchy of access to services for children in need, with the highest priority given to children at risk of abuse or neglect and children "looked after". Similarly, Colton and his colleagues' study of English and Welsh authorities found that social workers continued to think in terms of protection rather than prevention (Colton *et al*, 1995). They were also reluctant to identify needs which could not be met and so tended to define children as being "in need" only if resources were available to meet that need (Colton *et al*, 1995). Several commentators have argued that local authority discretion in this matter has led to the category "children in need" being interpreted too narrowly and to insufficient resources being allocated to family support work (Gibbons, 1991; Tunstill, 1992; Colton *et al*, 1995; Tunstill, 1996). The concern is that the targeting of family support at "children in need" is likely to be sensitive to financial pressures and will therefore serve as a means of rationing services.

Underlying these debates are broader value positions. Government and local authority definitions of need tend to frame the concept in terms of individualised social and health-related difficulties, whereas proponents of more comprehensive definitions of need and of greater provision of universal services are generally working with a concept of need framed in terms of social justice (Gardner and Manby, 1993). The latter have argued that concepts of need should include attention to the impact of economic disadvantage on children and families as well as to health, development and disability, pointing to research evidence showing that poverty is a major factor associated with family stress and with the separation of children from their families (Packman *et al*, 1986; Holman,

1988; Bebbington and Miles, 1989; Rowe *et al*, 1989). As the Short Report put it, 'children in care are the children of the poor' (House of Commons Social Services Select Committee, 1984). Accordingly, the Children Act 1989 has been criticised for not locating its discussion of need within a wider social, political and economic analysis of the circumstances of children and families under stress (Parton, 1997). The implications of the social justice model are that areas of high social need should have an infrastructure of enhanced universal services (Gardner and Manby, 1993).

If the category of "children in need" is narrowly defined, local authorities are unlikely to provide a wide range of universal, open-access services to ensure children's needs are met and to avoid stigmatisation. In these circumstances, family support becomes a residual service targeted at those deemed to be in the greatest need. Yet needs are not attributes of individuals, waiting to be discovered by policy makers and professionals. Instead, policy makers bring to their construction of local definitions of "children in need" concepts derived from the legal framework of the Children Act 1989 together with concern about the management of limited resources and hence the management of demand. These national and local political concerns are also articulated with an assessment of the specific needs of local children and with professional social work theories about child welfare, to produce definitions of children in need which underpin both service development and assessments of eligibility for family support services. In this way, definitions of need are socially constructed within politically negotiated boundaries. In a context of limited resources it is likely that thresholds for service provision will be high and that definitions of children in sufficient need to meet those thresholds will be narrow. These issues of need, resources and demand management were very much in evidence in this study and will be discussed in the chapters which follow.

Changing policy under New Labour

Following the election of the Labour government in 1997, new policy initiatives took centre stage and the language changed, with a shift from debates about the relative merits of investigative or family support approaches to a focus on targeting and on performance indicators to ensure quality in service delivery. The *Quality Protects* initiative abandoned the issue of refocusing in favour of setting specific targets for the support, protection and care of children (DH, 1998a). There was little direct attention to family support services in the *Quality Protects* framework, with objectives relating to family support integrated within broader objectives on referral and the care of children. The initiative contained requirements for local authorities to identify children in need, assess different levels of need and produce a timely response, which has direct implications for access to family support services. It also required authorities to ensure that children living with their families, as well as those who are looked after, are provided with safe and effective care for the duration of their childhood. The requirements pertinent to family support services were pitched at a greater level of generality than the far more precise targets set for services for children at risk of significant harm, looked after children and care leavers.

However, the *Assessment Framework* demonstrated a sharper emphasis on support to families and reiterated the central principle of the refocusing debate that safeguarding children should not be seen as a separate activity from promoting their welfare (DH, 2000a). It also emphasised the importance of a whole family – rather than child-focused approach, reminding readers that Section 17 of the Children Act 1989 makes provision for services to be 'provided to any members of the family in order to assist a child in need' (DH, 2000a). The ecological approach underpinning the *Assessment Framework* is also conducive to a broadly-based vision of family support work, with its emphasis on the need to focus not only on child development but also on work which aims to enhance parenting capacity and which takes account of the impact of environmental factors. These three dimensions of the *Assessment Framework* have since been incorporated into the *Integrated Children's System* in an attempt to underpin work with children both in and out of the care system with a common conceptual framework and to develop a more coherent approach to ensuring good outcomes for children (DH, 2003a).

Other key policy developments have focused primarily on issues related to the care system, notably the Children (Leaving Care) Act 2000, the Adoption and Children Act 2002, the *Choice Protects* policy initiative and, in the Children Act 2004, on child protection. The Children Act 2004 provides the legislative basis for the wider programme of reform in children's services (including social care, health and education services) set out in the *National Service Framework for Children's, Young People's and Maternity Services* and the *Every Child Matters* Green Paper (DfES, 2003; DfES/DH, 2004).

Both the *National Service Framework* and the *Every Child Matters* programme emphasise the importance of early intervention with children. The *National Service Framework* sets out a number of core service standards, which are intended to underpin *all* services for children. The first five of these could potentially contribute to improvements in family support services, through their focus on early intervention and parenting support. The standards highlight the importance of identifying needs at an early stage in their development and intervening early; offering age-appropriate services to children and young people that are child and family centred; safeguarding and promoting the welfare of children and supporting parenting.

The *Every Child Matters* programme is underpinned by five outcomes which represent the broad components of well-being for children: being healthy, staying safe, enjoying and achieving, making a positive contribution and economic well-being. Achievement of these outcomes is the rationale for service provision. This outcomes framework underpins the Children Act 2004 and is intended to serve as a basis for local policy development.

Every Child Matters proposes a three-pronged strategy for supporting parents and children in order to achieve these outcomes, one which, to use an older terminology, intervenes at different levels of prevention. This strategy encompasses both early intervention to prevent the emergence or worsening of problems, offered on a voluntary basis, and compulsory intervention with families whose children's behaviour brings them within the remit of the Anti-social Behaviour Act 2003. First, there is a focus on primary prevention through the integration and improvement of universal services in the fields of health, education and early years provision. Second, more targeted, specialised help is offered in the form of both secondary preventive services in areas of high social need and tertiary preventive services for families where problems have already emerged. In the third prong of the strategy, compulsory action with the parents of children who display anti-social behaviour or are persistent truants, the attempt to integrate child welfare and youth justice policy results in the somewhat contradictory conflation of the notion of *compulsory* intervention with the concept of *support*.

The principal concern of the Children Act 2004, emerging as it did from the government's response to Lord Laming's inquiry into the murder of Victoria Climbié, is on arrangements for the better protection of children. This is accompanied by an emphasis on the value of universal services to improve outcomes for all children. There is a dual focus on opposite ends of a spectrum, with universal provision for all children (for whom, in most cases, there are no serious concerns) at one extreme, and targeted services for those at risk of harm at the other. Falling somewhere between the two, the question of family support services for children in need is notable by its absence.

The attention to early intervention evident in recent policy developments could, in theory, provide a rationale for developing family support services, just as Section 17 of the Children Act 1989 did, but as always in the context of limited resources for public services, actual provision is determined by decisions about which areas of service should be prioritised. There has been no commitment of increased government expenditure to fund the proposed reform of children's services, despite local authorities' highlighting of the tension between demand and capacity and their concerns that cost pressures represented a key risk to the development of services (Platt, 2004).

Much of the emphasis in the *Every Child Matters* programme, the *National Service Framework* and the Children Act 2004 is on organisational arrangements, with a view to breaking down professional "silos" and developing a multi-agency, and multi-disciplinary approach, consistent with Labour's focus on joined-up government. Together they aim to promote the greater integration of services both to safeguard children at risk of harm and to achieve positive outcomes for a wider group of children, for example, through the development of the *Common Assessment Framework* and the development of local Children's Trusts arrangements for the commissioning of services.

However, there is a danger that the focus on organisational arrangements is seen as a panacea for a wider set of problems, such as the shortage of adequately trained and experienced staff and, in the context of limited resources, the perennial difficulty of balancing children's needs against agencies' needs to manage the demand on their services. In this context children who are in need, although not visibly at risk of harm, are likely to lose out whatever the administrative arrangements. *Every Child Matters* makes only brief mention of support to parents 'who are facing particular difficulties because of their, or their children's, experiences' (DfES, 2003, p. 42) and it seems likely that for families in these circumstances, only a residual service will continue to be available from social services.

Restructuring the welfare state

The residual nature of most family support services for teenagers and their families is to some extent a product of the more wide-ranging restructuring of the welfare state which has taken place since 1979. This has involved a greater centralisation of state control alongside a decentralisation and dispersal of service provision (Clarke *et al*, 2000). The managerial state inherited from the Conservative administration has been transformed under New Labour's modernising agenda into the enabling state, in which partnership, brokerage and regulation are key. Joined-up government, in which partnership is emphasised, has drawn community groups, voluntary sector organisations and local businesses into delivering public policy alongside statutory services ((Lister, 2003; Newman, 2001).

In recent years, greater central control has been exercised not only through the Best Value requirements for all public services but, specifically, through the *Quality Protects* objectives and the *Performance Assessment Framework Indicators* (Department of the Environment, Transport and the Regions, 1998; DH, 1998a, 2002a). While tightening its central control on public services, the Government has at the same time dispersed the provision of secondary preventive services through promoting and supporting local private and voluntary sector partnerships in areas of high social need, for example, through the Sure Start and Children's Fund initiatives. A mixed economy of welfare had already been envisaged by the Children Act 1989 in its commitment to a corporate approach to service provision, and this vision had been further developed by the Audit Commission some years later (Audit Commission, 1994). In this development of a mixed economy of children's services, however, the scope of public sector services was reduced. Although the Children Act 1989 set out a broad vision of the family support services to be commissioned or provided by social services, in practice a retrenchment in statutory preventive services and an expansion of voluntary sector services took place (Walker, 2002).

Preventing social exclusion

The shifts in the structure of service provision under New Labour also need to be understood within the context of the government's wider policy on combating social exclusion. Social exclusion, a relatively new term in British policy, refers not only to poverty and low income but also to some of their wider causes and consequences. The government has defined social exclusion as what can happen when people or areas suffer from a combination of linked problems such as unemployment, poor skills, low incomes, poor housing, high crime, bad health and family breakdown (Batty, 2002). Its ambitious national programmes have aimed to tackle not only social exclusion but also the associated issues of child poverty and health inequalities.

For New Labour, the objective of preventing both family breakdown and the need for children to become looked after by local authorities is nested in a much wider set of objectives related to the prevention of social exclusion. The government's cross-cutting approach to social exclusion has resulted in a broad preventive strategy aimed at children at risk of abuse, neglect, school failure, disaffection and offending. This wider strategy has involved the promotion of community development through supporting local partnership and regeneration.

In relation to family support, other policy has become more important than the Children Act 1989. While a plethora of area-based initiatives have offered open-access support services to a broad group of children living in areas of high socio-economic deprivation, provided by partnerships set up between the statutory, voluntary and private sectors, for those children in greatest need the role of social services in delivering family support has become more narrowly defined. Social services provide a narrowly-targeted residual service as their resources continue to be directed primarily at services for children at risk of harm or those in substitute care, and there is nothing in the *Every Child Matters* programme to suggest that this is likely to change.

More recently there has been some evidence of a shift away from a focus on local community partnerships and parental participation towards a greater emphasis on local authority responsibility. The original emphasis on both community and child development in the Sure Start programme has been replaced by a focus on the provision of child care to enable mothers of young children to return to work. The prevention of child poverty and social exclusion is to be achieved by means of supporting maternal employment. The end to ring-fencing, the "capture" of these early years services by the employability agenda and the folding back of local Sure Start programmes into local authority control marks a shift in priorities – from the provision of family support to the provision of child care and from community participation back to local government control (Coote, 2005; Glass, 2005).

Throughout this period, much of the emphasis of policies on both parenting and family support has been on services to support families with younger children, for example, through the Sure Start and the Children's Fund initiatives. Although the Connexions programme is aimed at teenagers, it is qualitatively different from the other two initiatives as its principal focus is on education and the prevention of school failure and disaffection. While all three of these initiatives are underpinned by a broader policy concern with the prevention of social exclusion, Connexions focuses principally on children within their schools and local communities, rather than within their families. There is little support available for teenagers and their families when other difficulties arise. A study of services for children in need in seven local authorities commented on the dearth of age-appropriate family support services and community facilities for children in middle childhood and adolescence, which meant that few received early intervention with emerging mental health or substance abuse problems (Tunstill and Aldgate, 2000).

There is perhaps an assumption that, as a result of initiatives aimed at younger children, fewer problems will occur during adolescence. It is too soon to tell, however, whether the Sure Start and Children's Fund initiatives will indeed have a longer-term impact of this kind, but it is undoubtedly the case that some teenagers and their families will continue to need support. Research reviewed in the next chapter indicates that children may continue to experience difficulties as they grow older and for some young people problems will emerge for the first time during adolescence.

The focus on parenting

Since 1997, there has also been a shift in the thinking of policy-makers from the concept of children "in need" towards the increasingly dominant concept of parenting. Policies on parenting have had a somewhat different focus in relation to families with younger or older children. As the question of parenting has moved up the policy agenda, there has at the same time been renewed attention to the perennial question of troublesome youth. The two are connected by political concerns over the link between perceived failures in parenting and anti-social behaviour by young people.

The current political discourse on parenting has two strands: the need for support to parents and the need for parental accountability. When these political concerns are translated into policy, however, the strands begin to separate, with policies concerning *support* principally targeted at families with younger children and policies grounded in concerns about parental *accountability* principally directed at parents of older children and teenagers.

Although group-based parenting programmes have become more widely available in recent years, most are targeted at parents of younger children. However, while there are few parenting programmes available to parents of teenagers who may want them, some parents may be *obliged* to attend such programmes under the Anti-social Behaviour Act 2003. Under the terms of this Act, youth offending teams may enter into parenting contracts with parents of children who have engaged, or are likely to engage, in criminal conduct or anti-social behaviour, and education authorities may similarly draw up such contracts with children excluded from school for disciplinary reasons or who fail to attend school regularly. The latter group of parents may subsequently be served with a parenting order by the courts if they fail to comply with the terms of a parenting contract. Both parenting contracts and parenting orders may include a requirement for parents to attend a counselling or guidance programme, either on a voluntary or compulsory basis. Although these programmes may be compulsory, many parents who attend have been anxious to receive help in managing difficult behaviour by their children (Ghate and Ramella, 2002). This provision is only available to parents of children whose behaviour has an impact outside the family environment, in their schools or local communities. For other families with older children and teenagers there are few support services, apart from telephone helplines such as Parentline.

Although there is clearly an emphasis on *prevention* in the legislation on anti-social behaviour, this refers solely to preventing young people committing further criminal actions and is not accompanied by any reference to the children's welfare. As Goldson has observed, there has been a conceptual shift in recent years which has resulted in children in trouble increasingly being viewed, and treated, as "offenders" first and "children in need" second, if at all (Goldson, 2000). While older discourses of parental responsibility and of young people's threat to the moral and social order have acquired a renewed emphasis, for example, in the Crime and Disorder Act 1998 and the Anti-social Behaviour Act 2003, there continues to be little parenting support available to families with teenagers (Brannen, 1996).

Investing in children?

New Labour's focus on early intervention, embodied in its wider policies on social exclusion as well as in the *Every Child Matters* programme, may be evidence of a recent trend towards the social investment state (Williams, 2004). The social investment state is characterised by attempts to prevent long-term social exclusion through an investment in the citizens of the future, with the emphasis on investing in children and families now in order to achieve better behavioural and educational outcomes and to reduce both social problems and public expenditure in the long term. The notions of investing in 'human capital' (Giddens, 1998), and in particular investing in children, are central. It has been argued that the current focus on investment in children involves greater attention to children "becoming" citizens-workers in the future than to their well-being in the present (Prout, 2000; Fawcett *et al*, 2004).

The social investment state focuses on particular stages of childhood, such as early years, and on particular groups of children, such those engaged in anti-social behaviour. Prevention, to be achieved partly through early intervention with certain groups, is conceptualised as the prevention of children becoming socially excluded and, in some cases, becoming a threat to the social order. However, the government's policy objective of eradicating child poverty in two decades would, if successful, clearly improve the quality of children's lives in the present as well as help to prevent social exclusion in the future. Similarly, the Sure Start initiative is likely to bring present as well as future benefits to children and families.

As always in policy and politics, there are contradictory forces at play. A genuine concern with improving the well-being of children through the creation of more holistic, accessible and less stigmatising services for all and offering better protection to the most vulnerable, co-exists with an unsurprising government preoccupation with both fiscal imperatives and social order. Policies on improving child behaviour, for example, may be the product *both* of concerns with the welfare of children *and* concerns regarding their threat to the social order. Similarly, policies concerned with the welfare of children co-exist with a drive to reduce public expenditure in the medium term by initiatives to reduce parental dependence on benefits and, through improving both child behaviour and educational outcomes, the future dependence on benefits of today's children. Accordingly, discourses of need, care, support and protection, which construct some children as vulnerable or troubled, are traversed by the discourses of social order and fiscal prudence which construct others as troublesome and potentially costly to society.

Conclusion

There have been a number of shifts in policy on prevention and family support in the years since the late 1980s. As we have seen, the Children Act 1989 brought a policy shift from the negative concept of prevention towards a positive and proactive vision of family support, but pressure on resources meant that, in practice, work on child protection continued to be prioritised at the expense of family support services. The election of the New Labour government in 1997 brought a massive expansion of services to support families, provided by local voluntary, private and public sector partnerships, as a result of a wide-ranging strategy on preventing social exclusion. These services were, however, predominantly targeted at families with very young children in areas of high social deprivation. The unprecedented expansion of voluntary sector services to support families during recent years has, for the most part, been evident in the development of services for families with younger children (Henricson *et al*, 2002). In relation to family support, other policy became more important than the Children Act 1989 and the mid-1990s concern with refocusing social services for families with serious difficulties away from child protection and in favour of family support appeared to dissipate.

More recently, the *Every Child Matters: Change for Children programme*, the *National Service Framework* and the Children Act 2004, have together brought a positive emphasis on early intervention with children to improve child well-being and prevent social exclusion. Early intervention is to take place, for the most part, through the provision of universal services to a wide range of children. However, early intervention appears to mean early in the life of a child rather than at an early stage in the development of problems, since much of the emphasis here is on services for younger children. Specialist services are situated within this framework of universal provision, but the focus is primarily on child protection and early years services.

Families with troubled or troublesome adolescents, who turn to social services for support because there is little other support available, are therefore unlikely to be eligible for a service unless their children are considered to fall within a fairly narrow conceptualisation of children "in need", or they cause difficulties outside the family environment. Where services *are* targeted at older children, the principal focus appears to be on anti-social behaviour and offending rather than on young people at risk of family breakdown. As for social services provision to young people, in the absence of new funding to underpin the *Every Child Matters* programme, and in the context of a quite proper concern with child protection and emphasis on improving services for children who are looked after, it seems likely that services to support young people on the brink of family breakdown may, for the time being, remain the poor relation of children's services.

3 Family support and young people: research in the UK

The next two chapters review the research relevant to work with young people on the brink of the care system. First of all, this chapter outlines the evidence from the field of psychology on emotional and behavioural problems in adolescence and on the risk and protective factors associated with these. It then considers the research on preventive work with young people at risk of placement and on family support services in the UK. The following chapter considers family preservation services in the USA and some interventions developed by psychologists, such as Multisystemic Therapy and Cognitive Behavioural Training. Finally, the research evidence from both countries is summarised at the end of Chapter 4.

Emotional and behavioural problems in adolescence

The last chapter showed that, for the most part, recent policy on supporting families has focused on families with younger children. Yet as they grow older, children may continue to display emotional and behavioural problems or, alternatively, these may emerge during adolescence. In addition to the continuing impact of family problems, which may bring distress, separation or loss, with the onset of adolescence, peer groups begin to exert a greater influence on behaviour, and this may be a negative influence for some young people (Rutter et al, 1998). There is also an increased risk of involvement in drug and alcohol abuse, offending and running away (Graham and Bowling, 1995). Mental health problems, which are uncommon among younger children, are more likely to emerge during adolescence (Coleman and Hendry, 1999; Meltzer, 2000, 2001). Running away and youth homelessness are also indicators of family problems for young people, as they are often associated with abuse, neglect and unresolved conflicts between teenagers and their parents (Pleace and Quilgars, 1999; Safe on the Streets Research Team, 1999; Biehal and Wade, 2000).

The research evidence suggests that the need for support to families with teenagers may have grown, since over the past 50 years there has been a rise, in real terms, in the prevalence of psychosocial disorders among young people (Rutter and Smith, 1995). Rutter and Smith's comprehensive review of the research shows that increasing numbers of young people exhibit conduct disorders, eating disorders, depression and suicidal behaviours or misuse drugs and alcohol.

More recently, another study has assessed the extent to which conduct, hyperactive and emotional problems have become more common among 15–16-year-olds between 1974 and 1999 (Collishaw *et al*, 2004). It found that the proportion of adolescents with conduct problems had doubled during this 25-year period, and this was true for both males and females and across all family types and social classes. However, although there was a marginal increase in aggressive problems for boys, the increase in conduct disorder was largely due to an increase in non-aggressive behaviour such as disobedience, lying and stealing. This study also found evidence of a rise in emotional problems since the mid-1980s, but the evidence relating to changes in the rate of hyperactive behaviour was mixed.

These trends were not the result of changes in the reporting of these difficulties over this period. Instead, the authors concluded that these changes were likely to be the product of environmental influences on the psychosocial development of young people. They suggest that changes in the family contexts in which children grow up may have contributed to this trend, for example, rising divorce rates, increasing numbers of single-parent and stepfamilies, changing patterns of child care and possible changes in parenting practices and family dynamics. Changes in the wider social context may also have been influential, such as the stress resulting from the increasing emphasis on educational attainment, a lengthening of transitional period between childhood and adulthood, the greater availability of drugs and changes in youth culture and in social cohesion.

Risk and protective factors for emotional and behavioural difficulties

Research in the field of developmental psychology has been highly influential in its identification of the stresses associated with the development of emotional and behavioural problems in children. A number of longitudinal studies investigating the developmental outcomes of children have, despite their frequent preoccupation with juvenile delinquency, provided more widely relevant evidence on the correlates of social and emotional difficulties in children and young people. The key studies in the UK have been the National Child Development Study, the Newcastle study and the Cambridge study, all of which followed up cohorts of children into adulthood (West and Farrington, 1973; Fogelman, 1983; Kolvin, 1990). Cumulative evidence from these studies has indicated that risk and protective factors for developmental problems may be located in the individual child, the family, the school and the local neighbourhood. Studies of this kind in the UK and elsewhere have informed the ecological model of child development, which suggests that outcomes for children are influenced by the interaction between factors in the individual child, the family context, the child's peer group, the school and the wider community. Individuals are nested in this set of inter-connected domains, so that any difficulties they experience are likely to be due to the interaction of multiple factors (Bronfenbrenner, 1979).

In each of these domains both risk and protective factors for children's well-being may be identified. Both Buchanan and Little and Mount have helpfully summarised the key risk and protective factors identified by a range of longitudinal studies (Buchanan, 1999; Little and Mount, 1999). Risk factors in the individual child include temperament, impulsiveness, physical illness, physical or learning disabilities and genetic factors. Good health and development, a continuous engagement with school, high IQ and a resilient temperament, manifest in a positive outlook on life, have all been identified as protective.

There has been much debate about the impact of genetic factors on developmental outcomes but it is now widely thought that, although genetic factors may have moderate effects on both internalising and externalising behaviour, environmental factors create the conditions whereby these effects either do or do not become manifest (Rutter *et al*, 1998; Buchanan, 1999). The implications of this are positive, since it may be possible to intervene in a child's environment to prevent the emergence of problems or to assist recovery from difficulties which have emerged.

The principal risk factors for emotional and behavioural problems located in the domain of the family are family adversity, mental illness, alcoholism and criminality in parents, marital conflict, weak and inconsistent discipline or harsh and erratic discipline. A lack of domestic tensions, good relationships with parents, support from grandparents and family involvement in activities have all been identified as protective for children. At the level of the school and the neighbourhood, bullying at school, schools with low rates of achievement and disadvantaged communities with high levels of crime appear to be risk factors (Buchanan, 1999). Furthermore, as mentioned earlier, peer groups become increasingly influential during adolescence, so peer group affiliation may have either positive or negative effects depending on the nature of the peer group (Rutter *et al*, 1998).

It is important to bear in mind that the influence of risk and protective factors on the child is not always one way, as qualities in the child, such as their temperament or behaviour, may have an impact on parenting style as well as *vice versa*. Also, risk factors do not usually operate singly. Instead, it is the cumulative interaction between them that can produce the most harmful effects (Rutter, 1979). Furthermore, other factors may operate indirectly to mediate or moderate the risk. Mediating factors may transform the risk factor in such a way as to lead to a particular outcome. For example, poverty may be a risk factor for anti-social behaviour but only insofar as it operates indirectly, through making parenting more difficult. On the other hand, moderating factors may change the strength or direction of risk factors. For example, a pro-social peer group may moderate the negative effects of poor parenting on children's behaviour, while anti-social peers and school failure may intensify these effects. However, other factors may be protective. Variables such as intelligence, good problem-solving skills, a supportive school environment, consistency in parenting or pro-social peers may moderate the potentially harmful effects of accumulated risk factors (Rutter *et al*, 1998).

In recent years, an appreciation of risk and protective factors has begun to inform approaches to child welfare. The concept of resilience is important here, defined as the capacity of children to develop positively despite experiencing adversity (Rutter, 1987). Resilience should not be seen as a trait since it involves environmental factors as well as qualities such as temperament or IQ which are intrinsic to the child (Little *et al*, 2004). This means there is scope for professional intervention in children's social environments to enhance children's strengths and supports and promote their resilience. There has been increasing recognition of the importance of promoting resilience in children, through attempting to reduce the number of risk factors and increase compensatory protective factors (Sinclair and Burton, 1998; Gilligan, 2001; Newman and Blackburn, 2002; Flynn *et al*, 2004). Either explicitly or implicitly, an understanding of risk and protective factors has informed a number of the interventions discussed below, particularly those in the USA that are explicitly based on ecological approaches, as well as some of the work undertaken by support workers and social workers in this study.

Preventive work with older children and adolescents

Since the 1980s, a variety of researchers have questioned the necessity of "looking after" so many children and have called for improved preventive services. In the mid-1980s, a series of studies funded by the DHSS and the Economic and Social Research Council (ESRC) highlighted the lack of emphasis on services to prevent admission. *Who Needs Care?* found few sharply-identifiable differences between those who were admitted to care and those who were not, although those admitted tended to have somewhat more severe relationship and behaviour problems, or problems in their parents' behaviour were more extreme (Packman, 1986). Admission to care was frequently unplanned and traumatic, with care often used as a last resort rather than as a planned service to support families in difficulty. "Prevention" was often little more than the refusal to admit a child, which was experienced as neglectful and unhelpful by families.

In and Out of Care reported that preventive services were rarely offered unless families were in crisis, so that families had to plead desperation or imminent abuse in order to receive a service (Fisher *et al*, 1986). *In Care:*

A study of social work decision-making similarly found that social workers admitted children to care with great reluctance and often only after sustained pressure from families or other agencies (Vernon and Fruin, 1986). An overview of these and other contemporary studies commented that, while none of them were specifically concerned with prevention, their findings directly or indirectly highlighted the importance of preventive services (DHSS, 1985b).

Other studies conducted at around the same time considered the consequences of admission to care and raised questions about the value of admission. *Trials and Tribulations*, a study of young people returned "home on trial" to their families after a period in substitute care, found that removal had done little to change their troublesome behaviour and that any changes were not sustained once they returned home, so admission to care had brought few lasting changes. Paradoxically, behaviour that had originally led to admission to substitute care was not considered sufficient grounds for removing children a second time. Admission to care of troublesome young people had achieved little more than to exacerbate the disruption in their lives (Farmer and Parker, 1991). Furthermore, research on young people leaving care at the age of 16 and over highlighted the poor outcomes for care leavers (Stein and Carey, 1986). The cumulative findings from these studies of the care system, several of them government funded, undoubtedly contributed to strengthening the emphasis on family support in the Children Act 1989.

Since the Children Act 1989, there have been few studies which have focused specifically on support services to prevent the placement of older children and teenagers. However, in the mid-1990s, three studies of social work with teenagers were funded by the Department of Health and later summarised in a useful overview report (Biehal *et al*, 1995; Sinclair *et al*, 1995; Triseliotis *et al*, 1995; DH, 1996). There have also been a few modest evaluations of specialist teams working to prevent the accommodation of young people.

Teenagers and the Social Work Services (Triseliotis *et al*, 1995) was a follow-up study of 116 young people aged 13–17 years referred to social work services in Scotland. Just over half of the sample had just been admitted to care at the start of the study, so this was a rather mixed group. *Social Work and Assessment with Adolescents* was a critical case study of a specialist adolescent assessment service in one London local authority (Sinclair *et al*, 1995). The 75 young people in this study had all experienced a "transitional event", namely, consideration of admission to care, admission to care or placement breakdown, so again the focus was wider than simply the prevention of placement.

Both studies followed up the young people one year later, but it is difficult to draw firm conclusions about the effectiveness of different interventions from these studies since neither was designed with the evaluation of effectiveness as its principal aim. However, both are valuable since they consider social work with teenagers in considerable depth and provide many useful insights into the objectives and the process of social work with teenagers at risk of entry to long-term care.

These studies found that preventive work with teenagers was afforded only low priority by social work teams. The service these teenagers received was variable and inconsistent, and it was often difficult for families to get help at an early stage, before a major crisis occurred, by which time it was often too late for social workers to deploy preventive strategies which might avert admission. One of these studies noted that part of the problem was the misapprehension that "children in need" were non-statutory cases (Sinclair *et al*, 1995). Due to the lack of consistent work prior to admission, this study found that most admissions of adolescents to substitute care or accommodation were emergency admissions and took place shortly after referral. Those teenagers offered preventive work by mainstream services were likely to be dealt with by less experienced staff with less knowledge of community resources and less experience of working with families in ways which are appropriate to teenagers (Sinclair *et al*, 1995; Triseliotis *et al*, 1995).

There have been only five UK studies of specialist support teams working with teenagers to prevent family breakdown, similar to those in this study, and most of these have been small-scale qualitative studies of single teams. The earliest was an evaluation of the MARS project, a preventive social work team managed by the charity Barnardo's. This study attempted to develop a methodology for evaluating preventive work based on the intensive analysis of 12 cases (Fuller, 1989). Few details of the intervention were provided, other than that the team worked intensively with children age ten and over who were at imminent risk of a breakdown in their living or schooling arrangements. The interventions had multiple objectives and the team's staff were asked to rate their success in meeting these. However, the author acknowledged that the lack of any independent assessment of outcomes plus the lack of a control group made it difficult to set much store by the finding that the team were effective in 75% of cases.

Shortly afterwards, a more broadly-based study of the closure of children's homes in the English county of Warwickshire included some discussion of specialist teams set up to offer direct work to (mainly) older children to prevent admission to care (Cliffe with Berridge, 1991). Again, the principal focus of the discussion of this service was on process rather than effectiveness, so it is difficult to draw clear conclusions about outcomes.

Towards the end of the 1990s, two further small-scale studies of specialist support teams were published. Frost's study of a specialist family support team in the north of England working predominantly with older children and teenagers considered at risk of placement gathered some descriptive data on 327 families and then examined a sub-sample of 30 cases (Frost, 1997). Another small evaluation, with a sample of 16 cases, examined the Adolescent Community Support Team in Stockport. This provided outreach support for children aged 11–15 years and their parents in order to prevent family breakdown (Brodie at al, 1998). The team was based in a small residential unit, which also offered emergency and planned respite care. Again, this was a modest study with a single group design, whose strength lies in its qualitative analysis of process. Another small study of a single support team for adolescents monitored preventive work undertaken by an adolescent support team with 56 young people (Biehal et al, 2000). The focus of this evaluation was on how, why and in what circumstances positive change in child and family functioning occurred rather than on effectiveness in preventing placement. It found that positive change was less likely to occur in families with chronic and severe difficulties and that the adolescent support team was more success-ful in its work with families where difficulties were of more recent onset. These three studies concluded that the specialist teams were helpful in supporting young people at home and so preventing placement, but again the lack of a comparison group meant that it was unclear what proportion of these young people might actually have been placed in the absence of this service.

Family support services

The UK research on family support has principally been concerned with the description of different types of services and few studies have attempted to evaluate outcomes for children. Although a number of such studies have been published since the late 1980s, the literature on family support has paid little attention to social work with older children and adolescents, reflecting the paucity of family support services for this age group as identified in the last chapter.

In the UK, research on family support has tended to take two forms: studies of individual family support organisations (for example, Frost *et al*, 1996 and McAuley, 1999 on *Home-Start;* Oakley *et al*, 1995 on *Newpin*) or studies describing particular types of provision (for example, Aldgate and Bradley, 1999 on respite care; Oakley *et al*, 1990 on home visiting; Sloper, 1999 on services for disabled children and Statham *et al*, 2000 on day care). The descriptive nature of most UK studies of family support is understandable, since these are often formative evaluations of relatively new services. Also, evaluating the impact of *preventive* services is particularly difficult. As Parker acknowledged over twenty years ago, it is hard to show that something has *not* happened as the direct result of an intervention (Parker, 1980).

For example, Gibbons and her colleagues pointed to the difficulty of demonstrating the impact of neighbourhood family centres on the prevention of specific problems (Gibbons, 1990). They found that problems showed greater improvement among the families using family centres compared to those who were not, but found no association between these improvements and the provision of family centre services. They attributed the improvements to the use of day care and the development of better informal support networks. A later review of family support services found little evidence for the effectiveness of open-access family support centres, but this may in part be due to the fact that few of these studies directly addressed the question of the impact of such services (Statham, 2000). Research reviews in both the UK and the USA have, however, found some evidence to support the case for providing intensive, targeted support within a framework of universal provision (Danziger and Waldfogel, 2000; Statham, 2003).

The few UK studies which have focused on measuring the effectiveness of specialist family support interventions have not produced evidence that these are more effective than the usual social work services (Carpenter and Dutton, 2003; McAuley *et al*, 2004; Statham and Holtermann, 2004). However, these and other studies have found that parents of (young) children using a variety of family support services often perceive these services to be helpful in relieving family stress and in supporting their parenting (Tunstill and Aldgate, 2000).

Another strand of research in this area has focused on parenting education and support. Parenting programmes are either behavioural in their approach, drawing on social learning theory, or are relationship-focused and draw on a variety of theories, for example, humanistic, psychodynamic, Adlerian and family systems theory (Barlow, 1999). There is evidence that for younger children, behaviourally-based training programmes can improve children's behaviour and that positive effects can persist over time, whereas programmes which emphasise relationships and communication have been found to have less impact on child behaviour (Statham, 2000). Barlow and Parsons' systematic review of parenting programmes found evidence of their effectiveness, particularly when programmes were group based and helped parents develop strategies for positive reinforcement of desirable behaviour in their children, but the programmes reviewed were all designed for families with very young children (Barlow and Parsons, 2002). Although most such studies have been conducted in the USA, a recent experimental study of the SPOKES project in London, a school-based programme for five- to eight-year-olds with behavioural difficulties which combined a parenting course with support for child literacy, found strong evidence of effectiveness (Scott and Sylva, 2002).

Some reviewers have concluded that parenting programmes are more effective with younger children, for example, Scott suggests that they are most effective in families with children age 10 years or under (Henricson and Roker, 2000; Scott, 1998). One study of a group-based parenting programme for parents of adolescents, in this case young offenders, found a reduction in reconviction rates at one-year follow-up but, without a comparison group, it was unable to assess how far outcomes could be attributed to the programme (Ghate and Ramella, 2002). The authors considered that the parenting programme may have contributed to these outcomes but that it was unlikely to have been solely responsible for them, since it was targeted only at parents while other professionals worked with the young people. They concluded that brief parenting programmes are unlikely to offer a "quick fix" for entrenched anti-social behaviour by young people.

A common theme in the family support literature has been the link between family stress and social disadvantage. For example, both Gibbons and Gardner argued that, for families who come to social services, inter-personal and health problems are combined with stresses arising from socio-economic problems (Gibbons, 1991; Gardner, 1992). Initiatives offering early education and day care services aim to improve the life chances of children from disadvantaged families. It is too early to assess the impact of the Sure Start initiative in this respect, but evidence of the long-term impact of the similar Headstart initiative in the USA suggests that, while early intervention of this kind with families and children in areas of high social need can bring real improvements to children's lives, they cannot overcome the impact of poverty on children's development (Statham, 2003).

Another theme has been the importance of an inclusive, empowering approach. Services working in partnership with parents, using a strengths-based approach and including a social support component, have been found to be more effective than services that do not have these character-istics (Aldgate and Bradley, 1999; Cleaver, 2000). Attention to the *process* of helping has been found to be an important element of successful family support services such as parenting programmes (Statham, 2003). How-ever, one study of family support services commented that workers often considered empowerment as an end in itself and focused on this exclu-sively instead of tackling the substantive issues that were troubling families (Macdonald and Williamson, 2002). This focus on process is evident in many UK studies of family support. Studies of family centres, for example, have paid less attention to their impact on outcomes for children and have instead assessed them principally in terms of their popularity with parents (Holman, 1988; Smith, 1996). Holman, for example, used family centres' ability to engage hard-to-reach families as a measure of their success. He concluded that successful family centres were characterised by open-door policies, the involvement of users in running the centres and an informal atmosphere, and aimed to draw out families' strengths rather than label them as problems (Holman, 1988).

There is also some evidence that an integrated approach offering both child-focused and parent-focused interventions may help to improve outcomes for children. The SPOKES project mentioned earlier is one example of an integrated approach of this kind. Another is the Matrix project targeted at vulnerable 8–11-year-olds, which adopted a whole-family approach and co-ordinated services from a range of agencies. This study reported improved parenting skills and some improvement in children's behaviour, but these promising findings must be treated with some caution as the sample was small (17) and there was no comparison group (McIvor and Moodie, 2002). Cox's review of home visiting services argues that in successful projects practitioners visit often enough to develop an alliance with families and that these projects are based on an ecological framework which takes factors in multiple areas of children's lives into account (Cox, 1997).

Social workers and family support: studies of effectiveness

Few studies have evaluated the impact of social worker support on outcomes for children. A review of studies of social work effectiveness has found that there is a dearth of empirical data about this area of social work activity (Macdonald, 1999). One of the problems in evaluating the impact of social worker support to children is the difficulty of separating the personal qualities of social workers from the activities they undertake, since the relationships they develop with children and parents are intrinsic to much of what they do (Statham, 2000).

Three recent British studies of mainstream family support services, delivered principally by social workers, have had a particular focus on outcomes for children. All three assessed outcomes for children and parents either at six month follow-up (Tunstill and Aldgate, 2000; Carpenter and Dutton, 2003) or when the case was closed (Macdonald and Williamson, 2002), but none compared children studied to a control group receiving an alternative service. Both Tunstill and Aldgate and Macdonald and Williamson examined social services support for children in need. The former had a sample of 93 families with children aged 0–16 years while the latter examined computer records on 249 children, the case records of 152 children and interviewed 72 families. Carpenter and Dutton's study evaluated therapeutic family support services provided either by social services or the voluntary sector to 79 "high risk" families with children in need aged 12 years and under.

All three studies reported that the principal problems at referral were emotional and behavioural problems in the children, stress and low self-esteem in the carers, difficulties in parenting and family relationships and domestic violence. Tunstill and Aldgate observed that behavioural problems were often the result of emotional disturbance and inadequate parenting and were both a cause and effect of family stress. Past events such as domestic violence had a continuing resonance within families and there was a clear association between children's behavioural problems and parents' emotional problems.

These studies all found that the service provided was much appreciated by both parents and children. Around three-quarters of the parents in Tunstill and Aldgate's study felt that social work support had relieved family stress and helped with child development and 41 per cent felt it had brought about an improvement in family relationships. MacDonald and Williamson conducted follow-up interviews with 30 families, of whom 42 per cent felt that their circumstances had improved to some extent, although only 25 per cent attributed this improvement to the social work intervention.

Carpenter and Dutton used a number of standardised measures to assess outcomes and found some improvement in children's pro-social behaviour and peer relationships but no overall change in emotional symptoms and behaviour problems. They also found little change on measures of family functioning, although a more supportive informal support network for carers was associated with improvement in pro-social behaviour for children. The strongest predictor of all outcomes was the severity of difficulties at referral but, once this was adjusted for, the study also found that older children were less likely to show improvement in their behaviour at six-month follow-up. When the three studies are considered together, evidence of the effectiveness of family support services is therefore somewhat mixed, although families clearly appreciate the process of receiving these services. Differences in methods used by each of the studies to assess the impact of services makes it difficult to draw together their findings and arrive at firm conclusions about the impact that mainstream family support services have on children.

Conclusion

Although the majority of UK studies do not offer robust evaluations of services, the recurrence of similar messages gives some weight to their cumulative findings (Statham, 2003). Many studies have drawn attention to the impact of child poverty, the importance of informal support networks, the value of an empowering, strengths-based approach, the need for integrated whole-family interventions and the importance of a co-ordinated inter-agency response. Yet, while the above studies of family support carry individual implications, they do not amount to a coherent set of research findings (Tunstill, 1996). Part of the problem in drawing firm conclusions from this body of literature may lie in the diffuse nature of the family support services themselves, which range from voluntary sector community-based interventions and self-help initiatives to specialist therapeutic interventions. Such a wide, inclusive definition may result in family support, as a concept, losing any useful meaning (Katz and Pinkerton, 2003).

A further problem, in relation to this study, is that the majority of the family support interventions discussed have been aimed at younger children. This is the reason why many of these studies have examined services targeted principally at parents, which aim to improve parenting skills and parent–child relationships with a view to improving outcomes for children. In work with older children and adolescents, however, there is a need to balance attention to the needs and wishes of parents with attention to those of children, whose views may conflict with those of their parents.

4 Interventions with young people: research in the USA

Family preservation services

In the United States, family preservation services (FPS) originated in the 1950s and have been extensively developed since the 1980s. The defining characteristics of FPS are that they are family centred and delivered in the home. They focus on family strengths and empowerment, are community-oriented and use a case management approach to co-ordinate services (Schuerman *et al*, 1994). Intensive family preservation services (IFPS) offer, as might be expected, a more intensive and short-term service. IFPS originated in the development of the *Homebuilders* model by two psychologists in Washington State in 1974, in order to prevent the placement of emotionally troubled children (Kinney *et al*, 1977). Many basic components of IFPS have been adopted from crisis intervention theory, including a response within 24 hours and time-limited services (Staudt and Drake, 2002). Insofar as they provide short-term, intensive services which are crisis-oriented and targeted at children thought to be at imminent risk of placement, IFPS are in some respects similar to the specialist support teams in this study.

However, unlike these support teams, the majority of IFPS have focused on preventive work with younger children and they are also far better resourced, since social workers typically have caseloads of only two to four families. They also offer a more intensive service than British support teams. For example, the *Homebuilders* model, which draws on crisis-intervention and social learning theories, provides an average of 20 hours input into families each week, with staff available 24 hours a day, seven days a week for four to six weeks (Fraser *et al*, 1991). The *Family First* model, which draws on systems theory and an ecological approach, offers a similarly intensive service but over a period of three months (Schuerman *et al*, 1994).

The ascendance of family preservation as an approach in the late 1980s was the product of shifts in policy similar to those in the UK in the post-war years, that is, between a concern with supporting families to care for their children and an emphasis on child rescue/protection (Lindsey, 1994; Berry, 1997). During the 1980s this tension between family-strengthening and child-saving was resolved in favour of an emphasis on maintaining the integrity of families, a policy development influenced not only by politically popular notions of "family values" and by concern about the cost of rising numbers of children in care but also by a backlash by child welfare professionals against the concentration on child protection and the lack of support to families (Lindsey *et al*, 2002). Service development was influenced by the permanency planning movement and also by a number of theoretical approaches, notably ecological theories, social learning theory, family systems theory and brief-treatment models (Reid and Epstein, 1972; Minuchin, 1974; Bronfenbrenner, 1979; Maluccio and Fein, 1983).

Evidence on the effectiveness of intensive family preservation services

Many studies of these services have been undertaken, but the evidence on their effectiveness in placement prevention is mixed. Numerous studies have found no evidence that IFPS were more effective than mainstream services in preventing the placement of children. For example, a meta-analysis of 27 studies of IFPS found that children receiving IFPS were placed almost as often as those in the control groups (Dagenais *et al*, 2004). Another review included 36 studies and found that, of the only four studies identified which used randomised experimental designs, three reported that placement rates were slightly higher for those using IFPS than for those receiving routine social work services (Yuan *et al*, 1990; Schuerman *et al*, 1994; Meezan and McCroskey, 1996; reviewed in Lindsey *et al*, 2002). The findings of the fourth study indicated a positive effect compared to a group receiving no alternative service but the credence that can be given to these findings is questionable due to a number of design problems which are discussed below (Feldman, 1991). Lindsey and colleagues concluded that the only studies which claimed that IFPS were effective in placement prevention were those which used single group designs and were purely descriptive in nature. Even where IFPS were apparently effective, the available evidence suggests that any positive effects dissipated over time. They surmised that this failure in meeting the goal of placement prevention was due to a combination of factors including a reliance on casework intervention which, they argue, has repeatedly been shown to be ineffective in producing positive outcomes; an approach which implies that "one size fits all" interventions can be effective with all families; a limited intervention period and a failure to address the severe problem of poverty.

Despite the lack of conclusive evidence on effectiveness in placement prevention, evaluators have not come to the conclusion that these services are perhaps ineffective in meeting their expressed objectives. Instead, they have suggested that, because of difficulties in identifying who may be at imminent risk of placement, services have not been properly targeted at those most in need. If risk of placement is low for all groups in these studies, then placement rates are unlikely to be significantly lower for children receiving IFPS. The logic of this argument is that it is meaningless to seek to prevent an event that was unlikely to happen anyway.

There has also been much debate as to the validity of placement prevention as a measure of effectiveness, as this may indicate system-based changes as well as, or indeed instead of, family-based changes. The adequacy of the concept of "imminence of risk of placement" has also been questioned as it begs a number of questions. How soon is imminent? How can risk of placement be predicted? What constitutes a placement? Is placement always undesirable? These questions have been addressed in different ways by different studies, so that some, for example, include kinship care or short-term placements under the rubric of out-of-home placement while others do not. For example, Fraser and colleagues have argued that placement taken out of context is a poor indicator of the effects of IFPS since placement may or may not reflect changes in child and family functioning (Fraser et al, 1997). In some cases, planned short-term placements may reflect an understanding of a family's need for respite and support.

These problems led some later studies to turn their attention to other outcomes. There is some evidence that IFPS may bring improvement in some aspects of child functioning (Pecora et al, 1991; Meezan and McCroskey, 1993; Schuerman et al, 1994). Modest improvements in family functioning have also been found by some studies (Pecora et al,

1991; Schuerman *et al*, 1994) but not by others (Feldman, 1991; Meezan and McCroskey, 1993). However, these improvements were usually short-lived. From the limited evidence available on outcomes other than placement, it appears that IFPS may produce modest changes in child and family functioning but that these effects rapidly disappear.

There has also been some attention to the impact of IFPS on different groups. For example, Szykula and Fleischman (1985) found that family preservation services were moderately effective where the presenting problem was child conduct, but this did not hold true for multi-problem families – a serious drawback, since the majority of families who meet thresholds for receiving services tend to have multiple problems. They also found that IFPS were ineffective with families where problems were chronic and severe. Some studies have reported that older children referred for oppositional behaviour were more likely to be placed (Fraser *et al,* 1991; Bath *et al,* 1992). Others have indicated that children referred for reasons of neglect are more likely to be placed than those referred due to physical abuse (Yuan and Struckman-Johnson, 1991; Bath and Haapala, 1993). The review of 27 studies of IFPS mentioned earlier found that three programmes targeted at young people referred for oppositional behaviour or delinquency were more effective at preventing placement (Pecora *et al*, 1991; Schwartz *et al*, 1991; Dagenais *et al*, 2004, referring to Henggeler *et al*, 1992).[1] However, a more recent analysis of data on 6,522 families in the Illinois randomised experimental study of *Family First* has indicated that case characteristics accounted for less than 8 per cent of the variance in outcomes and that the same was true for service characteristics (Littell and Schuerman, 2002). The evidence on the effectiveness of IFPS therefore remains inconclusive.

Family preservation services for adolescents

Just as there have been few studies of family support services for adolescents in the UK, in the USA there have been relatively few studies of family preservation services for this age group. Most of these studies have focused either on projects based on the *Homebuilders* model or on

---

[1] These three studies are discussed later in this chapter.

interventions with specific populations, either young people with severe emotional and behavioural problems or young offenders. Indeed, the *Homebuilders* model was initially developed for work with emotionally disturbed, angry adolescents before being more widely applied.

Evaluations of IFPS using the Homebuilders model with older children and teenagers have assessed the impact of these services on young people with a variety of difficulties who were, in many respects, similar to the young people in this study. Feldman's study of the Homebuilders model used with 117 young people aged 12–17 years and at risk of first-time placement included those referred for a wide range of reasons, including emotional and behavioural problems, abuse, neglect and substance abuse (Feldman, 1991). The majority (71 per cent) of the 678 young people in Haapala and Kinney's sample were aged 13–17 years and were referred for behaviour problems, family conflict, school-related problems, parenting problems, physical violence, running away and substance abuse (Haapala and Kinney, 1988). Pecora and colleagues studied outcomes of the FIT project, a Homebuilders service in Washington state and in Utah. The children in their sample of 446 families, referred to the project because their children were considered to be at risk of placement, were similar to those in the other two studies in terms of their reasons for referral but were somewhat younger, with the majority either pre-adolescent or in early adolescence (Pecora *et al*, 1991).

Although these studies produced some interesting results, the value of these findings is compromised by methodological flaws in all of them. Feldman and colleagues' randomised controlled trial found that initial differences in placement rates between the experimental and control group had dissipated after one year, so the programme appeared to be more successful in delaying placement than in preventing it. Furthermore, the study's findings are undermined by problems in sampling, since 33 families were excluded from the experimental group because the children entered care or the family refused to participate. Within this group of young people who were "turned back", almost twice as many had previous placements, which are known to be a powerful predictor of further placement, so selection bias is likely to have had an impact on the observed differences in placement rates (Fraser *et al*, 1997). Both groups improved on standardised measures of child and family functioning but there were few significant differences between them. Haapala and Kinney's study found that 87 per cent of the sample avoided placement, but since there was no control group it is difficult to know how far they had been at risk of placement at the outset. Pecora and colleagues' study concluded that the intervention was effective in changing behaviours. In Utah, more than twice as many children in the comparison group were placed. However, kinship care placements were not included in the figures for those placed in substitute care and the sample was largely composed of a specific population – Mormons, which limits the generalisability of these findings. Furthermore, this study is compromised by the fact that the comparison group included only 26 families (who were compared to an experimental group of 446), and one-third of these had been lost by follow-up.

The Hennepin County study evaluated an IFPS intervention with seriously emotionally disturbed adolescents (age 12–17 years) which used a structural family therapy model (Schwartz *et al*, 1991). A group of 58 young people using the specialist service delivered by specially trained social workers were compared to a case overflow sample of the same size. Both groups had multiple and serious behavioural, family, school, health and substance abuse problems. Interestingly, only 28 per cent of the young people had a negative attitude to placement. The comparison group were significantly less likely to be placed and the difference in placement rates between the two groups was very large, with 91 per cent of the control group placed compared to 56 per cent of the experimental group, possibly because the comparison group received no service at all rather than an alternative service. However, the fact that over half of the experimental group was nevertheless placed in substitute care led Fraser and colleagues to comment that this model may not be appropriate for many emotionally-disturbed young people (Fraser *et al*, 1997). It might equally be true that placement may have been the optimal outcome for some of these young people.

Many of the family preservation services developed in the USA that have been more directly aimed at teenagers have been targeted at specific subgroups, such as young offenders or young people with serious mental health problems. For example, wraparound services (sometimes referred to as individualised services) are principally aimed at young people with serious emotional and behavioural problems. The best-known wraparound services are Project Wraparound in Vermont, and the Alaska Youth Initiative (Burchard and Clarke, 1990; Van Den Berg, 1993). Both serve children under 18 years old with severe emotional and behavioural problems who are at high risk of residential placement.

These services have been designed to offer greater flexibility in responding to young people's needs and represent an attempt to address problems of poor inter-agency co-ordination. Wraparound services are grounded in an ecological approach to service provision, arguing that adolescent behaviour must be understood in terms of the social contexts in which it occurs: the family, the peer group, the school and the neighbourhood (Scholte, 1992). Inter-disciplinary services offer an individualised response to young people's needs in each of these areas, with a view to preventing placement through "wrapping" tailored services around a child and family (Burchard and Clarke, 1990). The emphasis is on the social context in which young people's behaviour occurs, not solely on the behaviour itself.

One study has found that children receiving wraparound services improved over a one-year period on parent-rated measures of behavioural adjustment, but failed to improve over two years on teacher-rated measures of behaviour (Clarke *et al*, 1992, cited in Bates *et al*, 1997). However, this study used a very small sample and had no comparison group, so its value is limited. Overall, there has been little published evaluation of wraparound services and the studies that exist have been criticised as lacking in methodological rigour, so it is difficult to judge the effectiveness of this potentially promising service approach (Bates *et al*, 1997).

There is no compelling evidence that the key features of IFPS, such as brevity and intensity of services, are necessarily associated with positive outcomes for families. It is also unclear which aspects of services are associated with positive outcomes for particular sub-groups. To sum up, evidence on the effectiveness of these intensive family support services remains inconclusive. However, although few IFPS have been specifically targeted at adolescents, one review of the research evidence in the USA concluded that they may be moderately effective with older children and those in early adolescence, where child behaviour is identified as a major problem (Fraser *et al*, 1997). The authors suggest that the apparently greater effectiveness of these programmes with older children may in part be due to differences in reasons for referral since neglect, often a feature in referrals of younger children, appears particularly intractable.

Psychological interventions with young people

There is also a substantial body of US research on psychological interventions with adolescents with serious behavioural problems, often those with a clinical diagnosis of conduct disorder. Most of these studies have focused on persistent young offenders. A systematic review of family and parenting interventions with 10–17-year-olds with conduct disorder or delinquency assessed the findings of the eight randomised controlled trials which met the review's stringent inclusion criteria (Woolfenden et al, 2003). In seven of these studies the participants were young offenders and only one study was concerned with children/adolescents with conduct disorder who had not had contact with the juvenile justice system. The principal psychological interventions that have been evaluated are multisystemic therapy, cognitive behavioural therapy, behavioural parent training and functional family therapy.

Multisystemic therapy

Multisystemic therapy (MST) was originally designed for juvenile delinquents and young offenders but later extended to a wider group of young people with social, emotional and behavioural problems. MST is grounded in an ecological approach and accordingly intervenes directly in all the systems in which young people are located including the family, the school and the peer group (Borduin, 1999).

Henggeler and colleagues studied a group of 84 seriously emotionally disturbed young people who were serious offenders and were at imminent risk of out-of-home placement comparing outcomes for those (Henggeler et al, 1992). Their average age was 15 years and all came from families with multiple problems. A randomised control trial compared the effectiveness of MST with "usual services". The MST group received interventions which included cognitive-behavioural as well as family systems techniques and which were targeted at individual and family functioning, peer relations, school and the neighbourhood. In contrast, the intervention with the control group consisted of appointments with probation officers in which the need for compliance with requirements for school attendance and contacts with other agencies was emphasised. In comparison with these "usual services", MST was found to be associated with positive results on family cohesion and decreasing peer aggression, recidivism and incarceration. However, a later experimental study of 155 violent and chronic young offenders found that, although the rate of incarceration was lower for the MST group than for the control group receiving only a probation service, there was no effect on either family or peer relations (Henggeler *et al*, 1997).

A subsequent study attempted to determine the effective components of MST (Huey *et al*, 2000). It concluded that there seemed to be a causal pattern in which MST led to improved family functioning (increased parental monitoring, reduction of conflict, improved communication) and to decreased affiliation with delinquent peers, and these two together combined to reduce delinquent behaviour. However, two recent systematic reviews of the research evidence on MST have called into question the claims for its effectiveness. One review concluded that MST had positive effects on a number of criminal justice-related outcomes, such as reducing re-arrest rates and time spent in institutions, but found insufficient evidence that it had a beneficial effect on parenting, child/adolescent behaviour, family functioning, academic performance or peer relations (Woolfenden *et al*, 2003). Another systematic review found that the evidence on MST was inconsistent and that there were no significant effects on behaviour problems, peer relationships or self-reported delinquency (Littell, 2005).

Cognitive behavioural therapy

Cognitive behavioural therapy (CBT) involves the use of certain cognitive techniques which are designed to produce changes in thinking and, as a result, changes in behaviour or mood. This therapy emphasises the process of learning and may focus on improving problem-solving skills or training in social skills and coping with anger. Therapists work with children to change the distorted understandings of social events that children diagnosed with conduct disorder often have which may, for example, lead them to misconstrue benign approaches from adults or peers as hostile in intent. CBT may involve the family or school and usually involves weekly sessions over a period of six months or more (Joughin, 2003). Joughin's brief review of the evidence on CBT suggests that it may have a positive effect in decreasing anti-social behaviour, particularly for older children and adolescents. She also highlights some evidence that CBT works best when administered in intense one-to-one programmes conducted by trained staff but that CBT administered to adolescents in groups may actually make matters worse (Rutter *et al*, 2002).

Although there is strong research evidence as to the efficacy of CBT in improving child behaviour for children with conduct disorder, this does not mean that other interventions are necessarily ineffective. The fact that alternatives have not been systematically evaluated using experimental methods may result in a bias towards evaluated approaches such as CBT. Also, evaluations of CBT have been criticised for focusing predominantly on demonstration projects rather than routine practice (Joughin, 2003).

Behavioural parent training

Behavioural parent training for parents of adolescents teaches parents to use specific behavioural skills based on social learning theory by identifying positive and negative behaviours and observing the situations in which they occur and the typical reactions they elicit. The aim is to systematically reinforce positive behaviours, often through use of concrete privileges (Brosnan and Carr, 2000).

A review of two experimental studies of parent training interventions with repeat adolescent offenders (Bank *et al*, 1991; Dishion and Andrews, 1995) found that intensive behavioural parent training of at least 45 hours over one year reduced recidivism during active treatment (Brosnan and Carr, 2000). For adolescents with significant conduct problems who were at risk of offending, less intensive treatment of 12 sessions over three months improved parent–child interaction in the short term but had little impact on conduct at home or at school. One of the studies reviewed, in which outcomes of highly structured parent training for families of chronically offending delinquents were compared to outcomes of either systemic family therapy (with a behavioural element) or group therapy (with drug counselling), found a similar reduction in offending rates for both groups at follow-up (Bank *et al*, 1991). However, the authors commented that, while parental behaviour had changed in relation to managing the conduct of their children, there were no detectable changes in general family functioning. These remained severely distressed families with multiple problems. This study concluded that the value of the parent training model in work with persistent delinquents was doubtful and suggested that preventive efforts beginning much earlier in the young people's lives were likely to be more effective.

Functional family therapy

Functional family therapy, a behavioural-systems approach to family therapy with a strong emphasis on behavioural and social learning theories, focuses on communication within families and on parental supervision. Therapists work with families to identify patterns of communication and beliefs about problems and solutions within families and then facilitate the development of improved communication, negotiation and problem-solving skills and the reinforcement of positive interaction patterns. Reframing and relabelling are used to encourage parents to recognise that deviant behaviour is maintained by situational factors (Alexander and Parsons, 1982; Gordon *et al*, 1988).

A review of four experimental studies of the impact of behavioural or functional family therapy on adolescent conduct problems found that it was effective in reducing conduct problems and improving family communication and these improvements were maintained 18 months to three-and-a-half years later (Brosnan and Carr, 2000). An important finding was that the therapist's ability to maintain warm, collaborative relationships with families was one of the key ingredients in the success of these interventions.

Summary: research in the UK and the USA

Few studies in either the UK or the USA have focused on the issue of support services for adolescents considered to be on the brink of admission to substitute care. Most studies of family support or family preservation have been concerned with prevention of the abuse and neglect of younger children and have aimed to support families to enable them to care safely for these children. In contrast, in work with adolescents the principal focus is on behavioural and emotional problems rather than abuse and neglect, although there is certainly evidence both from this study and others that adolescents may also be at risk of these (Rees and Stein, 1997; Safe on the Streets Research Team, 1999). For younger children at risk of abuse and neglect, parents are seen as the locus of the problem, whereas for older children it is often the child's behaviour that is seen as the central problem. To use the terminology of an earlier study, younger children may be viewed as "victims", while older children may be viewed as "villains" and may, as a result, be "volunteered" to the care system by their parents (Packman *et al*, 1986). Yet the family circumstances and histories of adolescent "villains" may be little different to those of younger "victims".

Although British studies of the care system and of social work with teenagers have raised the question of preventive work, few studies have taken this issue as their central concern. The few small-scale studies that have done so have largely been descriptive and have provided little evidence on outcomes. This is also true for many of the UK studies of family support services for younger children. While US studies of family preservation *have* focused on outcomes for children, the evidence is inconclusive and, in any case, many of these studies have had serious methodological flaws. In contrast, evidence from a variety of intensive and highly-structured psychological interventions, mainly targeted at young offenders, has shown positive effects on young people's behaviour, at least in the short term, although effects on parenting and on family functioning were either weaker or non-existent. However, disagreement as to the nature of the outcomes that should be measured, inconsistency in the measurement of common outcomes (for example, regarding the inclusion of brief placements or kinship care under the rubric of "placement") and the real difficulty of proving that something has *not* occurred as a direct result of a service, makes it difficult to arrive at clear conclusions as to the effectiveness of services which aim to prevent placement.

Despite the lack of conclusive evidence on the outcomes of services, these studies raise a number of key themes. In both the UK and the USA, researchers have drawn attention to the impact of poverty on child developmental outcomes, the value of informal support networks, the importance of the *process* of service delivery and families' appreciation of a strengths-based approach. Evidence from developmental psychology on risks and protective factors and on the potential of compensatory interventions in different domains of children's lives has underpinned some service developments. There is some evidence that an integrated, well co-ordinated approach that intervenes with both the child and the parent, and in some cases in the child's wider social networks such as the school or peer group, can be effective. Many of these issues will recur during the course of this study.

5 Methodology

Guiding ideas of the research

In order to assess the effectiveness of a service, it is helpful to have some idea of what might happen in the absence of that service. This study compares the outcomes for young people involved with specialist support teams with those for a similar group receiving a "service as usual", referred to below as the mainstream service, from area social workers.

In comparing the effectiveness of two types of service, some clarity is needed about what constitutes a "good" outcome. Lessons from the US studies outlined in Chapter 4 suggest that the prevention of accommodation should not be the sole, or principal, indicator of positive outcomes. As well as considering placement patterns, which may be conceptualised as *service outcomes*, this study also focuses on *outcomes for the young people*, examining changes in child and family functioning and in young people's own perceptions of their well-being. Several outcome measures are used in an attempt to capture change in different aspects of young people's lives and these are described below.

Outcomes for young people are likely to be influenced not only by the services they receive but also by a number of other intervening variables, so the following issues are explored:

- What are the characteristics and histories of the young people using these two services?
- What difficulties have their parents experienced?
- What is the nature and severity of young people's problems at referral?
- What is the nature of the interventions by the specialist teams and mainstream social work services?
- What actions by other agencies affect these young people's lives?

Design of the study

The design of this study was prospective and quasi-experimental. Young people newly referred to specialist support teams were compared to others in similar circumstances referred to mainstream social workers. Young people, parents and support workers from the specialist teams were interviewed as soon as practicably possible after the families' first contact with social services. In most cases, the first interviews took place within two weeks of referral. Follow-up interviews were conducted six months later with as many of the original respondents as possible, although in some cases the workers had changed.

Both quantitative and qualitative methods were used. Quantitative methods were employed to compare young people's histories, difficulties and outcomes. Qualitative methods were used to understand young people and their parents' perspectives on their difficulties and on the services they received. As we have seen in Chapter 4, attempts in the United States to conduct rigorous experimental evaluations of preventive services have proved inconclusive. Either the services studied there were ineffective, or the methods used were not sufficiently sensitive to issues of process and how these may be related to outcomes (Maluccio, 1998). In other words, in order to understand how preventive services work, we need to improve our understanding of how they are delivered, how they are perceived by users and crucially, *how* and *in what circumstances* positive change occurs. Qualitative interviews were therefore undertaken in 50 cases at follow-up to explore how changes occurred in the young people's lives during the six months following the start of the service, in an attempt to tease out what it is about services that helps to bring about positive changes for young people.

Sample recruitment

The principal objective of the specialist teams was to provide family support in such a way as to prevent placement so, in order to compare like with like, it was necessary for the samples recruited both from specialist teams and mainstream services to be equally at risk of placement. However, as we have seen in studies in the USA, imminent risk of placement is hard to define with any accuracy. Inclusion in the study was therefore based on a concrete set of criteria regarding risk of placement. Young people were included in the study if:

- they were 11–16 years old;
- they had just been referred (or re-referred) for a service;
- *either* the parent or the young person had requested accommodation at referral;
- *or* the social worker who first saw them considered the young person was at risk of being accommodated within four weeks of the referral.

Recruitment was difficult because of the prospective nature of the study and because inclusion did not depend on a clear case event (such as placement or child protection registration) that could be identified from agency records. Instead, we had to rely on busy social work staff to inform us of relevant new referrals. The intention was for staff to recruit *every* family who fitted the criteria, until an agreed number per authority had been reached. In practice, there were considerable difficulties in implementing this, particularly in respect of recruiting young people using mainstream services. This accounts for the smaller sample of young people in the comparison group. Very few families who were invited refused to take part, but on the information available from social workers about reasons for referral and circumstances at referral, these did not appear to be dissimilar to those recruited in terms of the nature or severity of their problems. However, it is possible that our difficulties in recruiting a comparison group via field social workers resulted in an element of selection bias, since not all social workers were equally willing to assist with the study. Also, although it was hoped to include both young people and parents in the sample, a few cases were included in the study in which only one of them agreed to take part.

Careful attention was given to research ethics, including obtaining the informed consent of the young people to take part in the research and ensuring confidentiality and the anonymity of the participants.

The sample

Young people referred to specialist teams in six local authorities were compared to others receiving a service from mainstream area social workers in three authorities. A total of eight authorities took part in the study as in one authority, City, a sample of young people using the services of its three specialist teams was compared to a sample of others receiving mainstream social work services alone. This within-authority comparison was possible because City was a very large authority and the specialist teams were unable to offer a service to all young people referred. The authorities which agreed to take part in the study included three counties, a large city, two metropolitan borough councils, a metropolitan district and a unitary. The distribution of the sample between the eight authorities is shown in Table 5.1.

Table 5.1
Sample at referral by case status and local authority (n = 209)

Local authority	Specialist teams	Mainsteam teams	Per cent of total sample
Eastshire	19	–	9
Met East	28	–	13
City	22	33	26
Midshire	–	16	8
Met West	35	–	17
Borough	–	16	8
Northshire	28	–	13
Met North	12	–	6
Total	**144**	**65**	**100**

Only five per cent of the young people recruited to the study were known to come from minority ethnic groups. This was disappointing, as four of the local authorities contained relatively large black and Asian communities and had been expressly selected in order to ensure the inclusion of a reasonable proportion of young people from minority ethnic groups in the study. It was not possible to over-sample young people from minority ethnic groups due to the considerable problems experienced in obtaining *any* referrals to the study.

At follow-up, 195 cases were included in the sample, of which 137 (70 per cent) had received a service from a specialist team and 58 (30 per cent) had received only the mainstream service. It was not possible to obtain full interview sets for all cases at follow-up as sometimes family members or workers could not be contacted. Outcomes in respect of the five key outcome measures (outlined below), and data on young people's and parents' views of the service and of outcomes, could only be gathered where at least one family member was interviewed. Where no family member could be contacted at follow-up, a decision was taken to include worker interviews so that data on case events could at least be collected on issues that workers could be expected to have knowledge of, for example, on placement and on child protection enquiries, registration and contact with the juvenile justice system. In this way, information on interventions and some data on outcomes were collected for 93 per cent of the sample.

At follow-up, a full interview set, including at least one family and one worker interview, was obtained for 62 per cent of the original sample, as shown in Table 5.2.

When sample attrition was examined, it was found that there were no significant differences between the samples at referral and at follow-up in terms of age, sex or the severity of problems.

Table 5.2
Questionnaires received per case at Time 2 (n = 472)

Questionnaires obtained per case	Number of cases	Per cent of original sample
Family member(s) and worker(s)	129	62
Family member(s) only	16	8
Support worker only	22	11
Social worker only	28	13

The qualitative sub-sample of 50 cases included 38 families in contact with support teams and 12 families in contact with mainstream social work teams only.

Data collection and measures

Semi-structured interviews were undertaken with young people, parents and support team workers at both stages of the study and postal questionnaires were completed by social workers. Interviews and questionnaires included a mixture of pre-coded and open-ended questions and some self-completion checklists. The answers to the open-ended questions were, where possible, recorded verbatim by interviewers and provided one source of qualitative data for the study.

Questionnaires at baseline collected data on the characteristics and histories of the young people and details of the referral. Young person, parent and worker assessments of the nature of problems at referral were all obtained. At follow-up, data were collected on events in the intervening period, on how these were viewed by all concerned, on the interventions by workers and other agencies and on outcomes on a range of dimensions. The fieldwork took place between September 2000 and July 2002.

The measures

Some standardised instruments were incorporated into the questionnaires for young people and parents at both stages for use as measures of outcome:

- the Strengths and Difficulties Questionnaire, a measure of emotional and behavioural difficulties in children designed for use with children up to 16 years [used with young people and parents] (Goodman, 1997);
- the General Health Questionnaire (GHQ 12), a measure of psychological distress/mental well-being [used with parents] (Goldberg and Williams, 1988);
- the Family Assessment Device (FAD), a measure of family functioning [used with young people and parents] (Epstein et al, 1983);
- Cantril's Ladder, the general well-being section of the Lancashire Quality of Life Profile, a self-reported measure of subjective well-being [used with young people] (Huxley et al, 2001).

To complement these standardised measures, the Severity of Difficulties measure was designed for the study. This was a self-completion checklist which aimed to measure change in the severity of a range of difficulties on which social work professionals might reasonably be expected to have some impact. Young people and parents were each invited to complete a version of the checklist when interviewed at referral and again at follow-up. They were asked to indicate the presence and severity of a range of issues: behaviour within and outside the home, staying out late, concerns about peers, parent–child arguments, parent–child communication and drug and alcohol misuse.[1]

The qualitative interviews

At follow-up, in-depth interviews were conducted with a sub-sample of 50 families. Young people and parents were selected for the qualitative component of the study if, at referral, a social worker or support worker had assessed them as being at high risk of becoming looked after by the local authority. The first 50 cases to meet this criterion were included in the qualitative sample and in-depth interviews were undertaken with young people, parents and their workers too wherever possible. Those included in the qualitative sub-sample completed the same checklists as the other respondents at follow-up.

Data analysis

Quantitative analysis

Answers to pre-coded questions and self-completion checklists were analysed using the computer program SPSS-11. All associations between variables that are reported are statistically significant at $p = .01$ or less unless otherwise stated. As most of the variables were nominal, non-parametric tests were mainly used. Parametric tests were used where data for the dependent variable were normally distributed and were in the form of interval data. Details of the specific tests used in the analysis are given in footnotes.

---

[1] Potential difficulties were rated as "a major problem", "moderate problem" or "not a problem" at referral and at follow-up. Analysis using Cronbach's alpha test showed that reliability was good (.8839 for young person version and .7656 for parent). Principal components analysis revealed a "general severity" factor and correlation on this factor between the two versions was moderate (.499). Construct validity was also tested through comparison with the SDQ and found to be acceptable.

The fact that there were potentially three (mainstream service) or four (support team service) respondents per case helped us to deal with the problem of sample attrition to some extent. Since the same *factual* information on *events* (such as placement, stays with friends or relatives, formal exclusion from school or contact with the juvenile justice system) was sought from all respondents, there were up to four opportunities to find out whether a particular event had occurred. Composite variables were derived from the source variables on the four questionnaires, so that if any of the respondents indicated that, for example, placement had occurred, it was assumed that it had. Where responses appeared contradictory, the paper questionnaires for the entire interview set were scrutinised to establish what had taken place.

One of the difficulties of using quantitative methods to measure change is that, with a relatively small data set, a meaningful effect size is difficult to detect. Our recruitment difficulties resulted in a sample that was smaller than anticipated and, because of the particular problems in obtaining referrals from mainstream social work teams, less than one-third of our sample were using a mainstream social work service. This represented a potential limitation to the study. It was possible that sample size and the imbalance in the size of the groups might have a detrimental effect on statistical power, potentially making it difficult to detect differences between the two groups being compared.

The change scores for young people on the three principal standardised outcome measures were therefore analysed. Power calculations showed that the likelihood of detecting a difference in outcomes between the two groups (significant at $p=.05$), where the true difference was half a standard deviation from the mean, was 89 per cent for the FAD and 82 per cent for the SDQ (parent version). In other words, in terms of these measures statistical power was reasonably high. Statistical power was lower for Cantril's Ladder (part of the general well-being section of the Lancashire Quality of Life Profile) and for the child version of the SDQ, at 64 per cent for the former and 62 per cent for the latter.[2]

There was some indication of a significant variation in the duration of

---

[2] Results of power calculations: FAD 0.8874; SDQ (parent version) 0.8216; Cantril's Ladder 0.6360; SDQ (child version) 0.6176 (all one-tailed).

the follow–up period between the two groups being compared, with the mean follow-up period slightly longer for those using mainstream services (who were harder to trace at follow-up).[3] However, there was no significant correlation between the duration of follow-up and change on any of the standardised outcome measures used in the study.[4] Variation in the length of the follow-up period between the two groups did not, therefore, result in a systematic bias in respect of outcomes.

Where small sample sizes suggest that there are no effects of acceptable size, this can mean one of two things. Either there really is no appreciable difference between outcomes for the two groups being compared, or the design lacks sufficient statistical power due to the small size of the sample. Where the latter is true, then it may be wrongly concluded that an intervention has no effect, when actually it does. Also, it may be difficult for statistical methods to detect the kinds of modest changes in attitude or behaviour that social work typically achieves, as evaluation using such specific criteria produces only small groups for analysis and may not, therefore, produce statistically significant results (Sinclair, 2000).

Qualitative analysis

Methodological triangulation helps to address these difficulties, as it allows for a complementary analysis of change using qualitative methods. However, qualitative methods cannot answer precisely the same questions (such as, how likely is one intervention to produce change in comparison with another type of intervention?) as quantitative methods. However, these different methods can be used to answer different types of questions about effectiveness. For example, the problem with focusing *solely* on

---

[3] The T-Test (independent samples) showed that, for cases where young people were interviewed at both Time 1 and Time 2, there was no significant difference in the mean length of follow-up period for those using different types of service: support teams 7 months (SD=1.80) and mainstream service 7.69 months (SD=1.26), Levene's Test not significant p=.279. However, for parents the difference in mean follow-up period *was* significant: support teams 6.83 months, mainstream service 7.90 months, Levene's Test significant at p=.002. The range was 4.34–10.62 months for those in contact with support teams and 5.92–15.22 months for those using mainstream services.

[4] Pearson correlation showed that there was no significant association between duration of follow-up period and change on any of the standardised outcome measures used.

scale scores is that these cannot capture the complexities of a child's life, which may be better captured by in-depth interviews. Also, modest changes in attitude, behaviour or communication patterns, for example, may be experienced as significant by parents or young people, even if the small groups involved mean they are too small to be detected by tests of *statistical* significance. Qualitative analysis of a smaller number of cases may reveal how changes considered positive by service users arise. Intensive case analysis can be also be used to explore how different factors interact to produce particular outcomes.

In this study, in-depth interviews were tape-recorded and transcribed. Qualitative material both from the questionnaires and from the in-depth interviews was used to illustrate some of the issues uncovered in the quantitative analysis. Analysis of the in-depth interviews was principally used for individual case studies and to explore themes that emerged across cases. Qualitative data were also used to determine how, why and in what circumstances interventions appeared to be more, or less, successful in producing outcomes that young people and parents considered to be positive.

Using the computer program Atlas-Ti, qualitative data were first coded using both descriptive (e.g. "social work plans") and conceptual (e.g. "rationale") categories. Pen pictures of the circumstances and histories of each of the young people in the qualitative sample were also written, based on the data provided by all respondents in each case. One of the problems in analysing qualitative data in applied policy research lies in trying to grasp the complexity of each individual account while carrying out a cross-sectional analysis which can deliver useful insights across a range of subject areas. When data are first coded thematically and then analysed across cases, there is a danger that in the subsequent analysis these themes become detached from the context in which the fragments of text were situated. In order to avoid losing sight of a holistic apprecia-tion of each case while carrying out this cross-sectional analysis, data from particular respondents were always considered in the context of the pen picture describing the young person's circumstances and history and the views of the other respondents in that case. The aim was to build a cross-sectional analysis of the data based on a holistic interpretation of the interview transcripts.

In order to explore the question of how, why and in what circumstances positive outcomes occurred, cases where parents and young people both felt circumstances had improved and those where neither felt that circumstances had improved were selected from the qualitative sample for further analysis. All data (both quantitative and qualitative, collected at baseline and at follow-up) relating to each case were scrutinised to discover what were the ingredients in cases where outcomes were considered to be positive by family members or, alternatively, where they considered outcomes to be poor. Findings based on the statistical analysis, reported in Chapters 10 and 11, are therefore complemented by findings from the qualitative analysis in Chapters 12 and 13.

6 The support teams and the mainstream service

The eight local authorities which took part in the study included a major city and three large counties as well as four metropolitan districts with much smaller populations.

There was considerable variation between them in relation to the proportion of their budgets allocated to family support.

Four of the local authorities (Met East, City, Eastshire and Met West) devoted a high proportion of their resources for children's services to preventive services and were ranked by the Department of Health among the top quarter of English authorities in terms of their relative spend on family support. In contrast, Midshire, Borough, Northshire and Met North were among the lowest ranking English authorities in this respect (DH, 2002a).

In the two local authorities with no specialist support teams, Midshire and Borough, relative spending on family support services was particularly low.

City (pop. 700,000) is one of the largest metropolitan districts in England, comprising a large urban area surrounded by extensive suburban and rural areas, plus some smaller free-standing towns. Its previous manufacturing and engineering industrial base has been largely replaced in the past three decades by thriving financial, retail and service sectors. Although general prosperity has risen steadily in the past two decades, City has higher than average levels of deprivation, concentrated in particular areas.

Midshire (pop. 600,000) and **Eastshire** (pop. 550,000) are shire counties, both of which cover large geographic areas. Midshire has two main conurbations, several market towns and many smaller rural communities. Although there are some pockets of poverty, overall levels of deprivation are relatively low. This is also true of Eastshire, which comprises five large district councils and where overall unemployment levels are lower than the national average.

Northshire (pop.500,000) is less prosperous than the other two counties due to the decline of its traditional heavy industries in the past two decades. It is a mostly rural county with many of its towns and villages suffering high levels of urban and rural deprivation. Unemployment is well above the national average.

Met East (pop.200,000) is a metropolitan district largely comprised of a mix of small rural communities and older urban areas. In terms of overall levels of deprivation it is a middle-ranking metropolitan district, but there are sharp contrasts between areas. Unemployment has been a feature of this area for many years.

Met West (pop.200,000) comprises nine small towns and is another metropolitan district with a mix of urban and rural communities. It has a number of manufacturing industries but the service industry sector has grown in recent years. Levels of deprivation are average in comparison with similar authorities, but in some areas there are pockets of extreme deprivation.

Met North (pop.300,000) is a metropolitan district comprising a small city surrounded by numerous small towns and villages. Following a period of industrial decline, an expansion of the service sector has reduced levels of unemployment.

Borough (pop.250,000) is a metropolitan borough that retains some traditional heavy industries and also serves as a commuter dormitory town for an adjacent large city, with a mix of older housing and more recent urban development. There is a high concentration of deprivation in parts of the borough.

The support teams

Most of the teams were developed in tandem with the closure of children's homes, with resources transferred to the new community-based services.

Staffing

All but one of the teams was initially staffed by residential workers redeployed to the support teams and, at the time of the study, ex-residential workers continued to predominate among the staff teams. The majority of this group had had many years of experience working in residential care.

The remaining staff had backgrounds in youth work, nursery nursing, probation, family centres and education. Met North was an exception, as it had been developed from the merging of a former youth justice team with a former family support team, so most of its staff were former field social workers.

Apart from the Met North team, only a minority of staff held a professional social work qualification and most of these were team managers or deputies. Staff had a range of other qualifications including GNVQ certificates in social care, youth work, education or residential childcare and nursery nursing qualifications, but some had no qualifications of any kind.

Two of the teams included workers with a specialist role. In the Met North team, one worker specialised in adult mental health while the Northshire team had an education liaison officer. All of the teams employed a pool of sessional staff, who were normally paid an hourly rate. Their professional backgrounds included teaching, nursing, youth work and residential work and some were social work students. The role of sessional staff was primarily to befriend young people and help to engage them in age-appropriate leisure activities in their local communities. It was felt that many needed help in building their confidence and developing their social skills if they were to successfully engage in these positive peer-group activities. Sessional staff also aimed to challenge anti-social ideas and behaviour in a non-judgemental manner.

Caseloads

Staffing levels varied considerably in relation to the size of local populations. Eastshire had one small team based on a single site, which covered a large county. Northshire, which had a similar population, had a team that was three times larger and staff also had less travelling time to visit families as the county was smaller in size and the team was dispersed across three sites. Caseloads varied accordingly, ranging from five to six cases for most teams to 11 cases per support worker for the Eastshire team. Caseloads were considerably lower than for field social workers, whose average caseload was 17.

Aims and target groups

The six support teams had key features in common. Their principal objective was to prevent accommodation and to this end they all provided an intensive, short-term, family support service targeted at young people considered to be at risk of entry to the care system. In their statements of aims and objectives, the teams conceptualised placement in negative terms, as a "risk" to be avoided. Some offered a service only to those considered at high "risk" of entry while others also aimed to work with those considered at moderate "risk".

Although the prevention of admission to accommodation was the *raison d'etre* of these teams, some also had additional aims. Some aimed to facilitate rehabilitation after family breakdown, or to prevent foster placement breakdown and one also worked with children at risk of significant harm. The age groups served also varied. However, although only three teams worked exclusively with older children and adolescents, children aged 11 and over made up the bulk of the population worked with by the remaining teams.

Young people were normally assessed and then referred to the teams by social workers, although in Met West, the support workers were the case holders and once a case had been allocated to them no social workers were involved. In all the other teams, area social workers remained the case holders and, to a greater or lesser extent, remained involved with the family alongside the support worker.

Methods used by the support teams

All of the support teams offered a short-term, task-centred service and all aimed to work in partnership with parents and young people and to use a strengths-based approach. The teams felt that they were not in a position to tackle long-standing problems but instead aimed to work briefly with families in crisis to calm situations and renegotiate ground rules between young people and parents. The emphasis was principally on helping parents to develop more consistent and authoritative parenting skills and encouraging young people to change their behaviour. They also worked with young people on relationships, grief and loss, keeping safe, social skills and on building their self-esteem.

They used a range of structured materials including parenting programmes, offered individually or in groups, and often using workbooks and/or videos (using resources from the Trust for the Study of Adolescence, the Youth Justice Board, NCH and the Family Caring Trust as well as the Webster-Stratton Parenting Plus programme). Workbooks on anger management were also used, along with worries checklists and videos, for example, on life in stepfamilies and or self-harm.

It would be misleading to consider support team interventions in isolation from work by social workers since (except in Met West), they were often delivered in tandem with continuing social worker support. The extent of this support varied from case to case. In some cases social workers more or less withdrew from direct involvement with families for the duration of support team involvement, retaining only an overall case management role. In others, social workers worked alongside support workers, so that each delivered different aspects of the intervention.

After referral, initial meetings were normally held with parents and young people, at which written agreements were drawn up between support team workers and families. These agreements as to the goals and nature of the work were usually reviewed at four- to six-weekly intervals. The account of their work given by the Met West team is briefly summarised below as an illustration of the work that was typical of these specialist support teams. Although each team had its own particular character and emphasis, they had much in common so that, while the work of other teams may not have been identical to the description below, it was similar in many respects.

Intensive family support work by the Met West team

- Systemic assessment of family functioning (may use genograms).
- Problems identified, goals set, work planned, clear agreements drawn up.
- Work reviewed every 4–6 weeks.
- Identification of deficits in parenting skills and provision of support to parents in developing coping skills, taking responsibility and regaining control.
- Work with parents: emphasis on appropriate parenting including be-

haviour management through positive reinforcement, boundary-setting, developing routines.

- Work with young people: exploring views, identifying triggers to conflict and behaviours that are dangerous, being alert to any evidence of abuse.
- Use of sessional staff to befriend young people, build self-esteem and engage them in positive local activities.
- Assessing, repairing and enlarging support networks.
- Providing information and advice, e.g. on health or personal safety.
- Partnership work with parents.

Mainstream social work services in the comparison authorities

Borough

Borough's fieldwork teams were organised into four areas, each with an initial assessment team and two long-term teams. Staff at three family centres supported these teams, but their work focused on families with younger children so they were not a resource that could be drawn on in work with teenagers. There appeared to be few local resources to assist social workers in their family support work. Problems were compounded by high staff turnover, the resulting extensive use of agency staff and a local education authority that had been criticised by the Office for Standards in Education for failing to provide effective support to the most vulnerable children.

Midshire

Midshire had just three area teams. Within these areas, the assessment teams undertook initial work with families, normally for a period of up to one month and it was these teams, plus the hospital team, which referred cases to the study. Cases assessed as requiring longer-term support were then referred on to the family support team for ongoing work. This team worked with both child protection and family support cases. Although the authority had a number of family centres, their service was principally aimed at younger children, although a few did work with 11–12-year-olds.

Social workers working with older children and teenagers in this authority had a few other resources to draw on, however. Families were sometimes referred to the Family Workshop Service (provided by the Child and Adolescent Mental Health Service) for family therapy, or to a 12-week parenting course offered by an independent provider. There was also a youth mentoring scheme, jointly funded by the social services and education departments, and a youth outreach service. This was a small project that recruited sessional staff to work with young people, but waiting lists for this outreach service were long.

City

City was divided into five social work area teams, within each of which were a number of social work teams, amounting to a total of 27 children and families teams across the city. Each of the five areas had a Principal Caseworker for Adolescents, whose role was primarily to advise and assist social workers working with young people referred because they were deemed to be "beyond control", and to co-ordinate work on such cases. The principal caseworkers also recruited and managed a pool of sessional workers (who were separate from the sessional staff managed by the city's support teams). These were deployed to work alongside area social workers offering a mainstream social work service and were used in the same ways as sessional staff employed by support teams.

These Principal Caseworkers worked closely with children's team managers in initially dealing with "beyond control" cases through the three-stage Community Assessment Profiling scheme developed in City. This was aimed at any 10–17-year-olds referred by a parent or carer who was considered to be "at risk" of becoming looked after if community-based services were not provided.

Social workers in City were also able to draw on joint social services/ health service provision within a multi-agency system of child and Adolescent mental health services. The joint social work/mental health service Therapeutic Team offered assessment and therapeutic work for children who have been abused, or display sexually harmful behaviour or mental health problems such as self-harm or eating disorders. Area social workers could consult or co-work with this team or simply refer young people to it.

Within the area social work teams, the Principal Caseworkers for Adolescents acted as gatekeepers for referrals to the support teams, but in our sample there appeared to be no difference between those referred to the support teams and those who were not in terms of the nature and severity of child and family problems. However, there was some indication that those considered to be at more immediate risk of family breakdown were referred to the more intensive service offered by the support teams.[1]

Of all the authorities in the study, City had the highest proportion of its children's services budget allocated to family support. With its Principal Caseworkers for Adolescents, sessional staff, Community Assessment profiling scheme and inter-agency Therapeutic Team, social workers working with young people in the comparison group in City appeared to have a more extensive range of resources to support them in their work than social workers in Midshire or Borough.

Theories and methods

Most teams did not draw on an explicit theoretical base, although the Met West team was an exception to this, as it had produced a document outlining its approach which indicated that their work drew on family systems theory, attachment theory and social learning theory. The Met East team said their work was informed by family systems theory too and that they also used cognitive-behavioural methods. Although the other teams did not indicate that they were using any particular theoretical models, the work on anger management that was common to all teams clearly drew on cognitive-behavioural theory and much of the structured work on parenting skills appeared to be informed by social learning theory. The teams also spoke in more general terms of undertaking general "family work", "direct work" with young people or having a "therapeutic approach", as well as providing practical and emotional support.

At follow-up, both support workers and social workers were asked whether they had drawn on any specific theories or methods in their work with this family. Less mention was made of theories than of methods, but

---

[1] Details of the comparisons between the two groups within City are given at the end of Chapter 8.

just a few mentioned drawing on attachment theory or family systems theory and one support worker mentioned concepts drawn from psycho-dynamic approaches. A few social workers mentioned using task-centred methods and support workers from most of the support teams said they used Solution Focused Brief Therapy.

This approach, which was mentioned more than any other, has its roots in Strategic Family Therapy and has often been used by services which have the aim of preventing family breakdown (Lethem, 2002). It was developed in the early 1980s mainly by de Shazer and his colleagues at the Milwaukee Brief Family Therapy Centre (Parton and O'Byrne, 2000). Employing the notion of "problem-free talk", it focuses on finding excep-tions to reported problems and on negotiating concrete strategies to bring about change. It therefore 'concentrates on the how, when, what and where of solutions' and rarely asks 'why' questions (Lethem, 2002, p. 191). The approach encourages practitioners to adopt a collaborative therapeutic style, which focuses on developing family strengths. Apart from this, a small number of support workers reported using behaviour modification techniques and a few social workers said they had used counselling techniques or crisis intervention. Support workers and social workers were often eclectic, drawing on more than one of the above approaches, and some said they were unsure as to what theories informed their work.

7 Circumstances, histories and needs

The young people and families who approached social services for support had remarkably high levels of need. Although all were in crisis at the point of referral, for many the problems were long standing. This chapter describes their characteristics and histories, while the chapter which follows outlines the particular difficulties which young people and families presented at referral.

Characteristics of the young people and families

The vast majority (88%) of the young people in the sample were age 12–15 years. Just over half were male (55.5%) and just under half were female (44.5%).

Table 7.1
Age of young people in the sample

Age	%	Number
11	8	17
12	20	42
13	21	44
14	23	48
15	24	50
16	4	8
Total	**100**	**209**

The majority of young people who took part in the study were white (80%). Just four per cent defined themselves as being of mixed ethnic origin and only one per cent defined themselves as black. None of the young people indicated that they were of Asian origin. In total, just 10 young people reported that they were from minority ethnic groups. However, data on ethnic origin were missing for 15 per cent of the sample.

Family context at referral

Less than one-fifth of the young people were living with both birth parents and nearly half were living with a lone parent, as shown in Table 7.2. In comparison with the wider population of children in England and Wales, they were twice as likely to be living with a lone parent and two-and-a-half times as likely to be living in a stepfamily (National Statistics, 2003). Of the 13 per cent living in other circumstances, five per cent were with adoptive parents, four per cent with grandparents and just over two per cent with other relatives at referral. One young person was living with only a step-parent and two were temporarily living away from home.

Where young people were living with only a single birth parent, either in a lone parent family or a stepfamily, the vast majority (90%) were with their mothers. Families were far more fragmented than for children in the wider population, where 65 per cent live with both birth parents (National Statistics, 2003). Instead, family composition was similar to that for two

Table 7.2
Family composition (n = 209)

Family type	%	Number
Single parent	46	95
Parent + step-parent	25	53
Both birth parents	16	34
Other	13	27

Table 7.3
Family composition compared to families of looked after children

Family type	This sample %	Residential sample %[a] (n = 176)	Foster care sample %[b] n = 285
Single parent	46	37	38
Parent + step-parent	25	35	20
Both birth parents	16	16	13
Other	13	12	28

(a) Sinclair and Gibbs, 1998 (b) Sinclair *et al*, 2000

recent samples of looked after children, one in residential and one in foster care (Sinclair and Gibbs, 1998; Sinclair *et al*, 2000).

Young people with disabilities, health problems and emotional or behavioural difficulties

We asked parents and workers whether young people had physical or sensory impairments, learning disabilities, mental health problems or emotional and behavioural difficulties. These matters can be difficult to define and people do not always agree on definitions. We accepted that young people experienced one of these difficulties if either a parent or a worker reported that they did, but we are aware that this may slightly inflate the figures in each category.

Information on whether hyperactivity was a problem was not specifically requested, but a substantial minority of respondents reported Attention Deficit Hyperactivity Disorder (ADHD) so it is recorded here. As we did not ask everyone this question, the figure given may perhaps be an underestimate. This seems likely, since the standardised measure of emotional and behavioural difficulties used in this study, the SDQ, indicated that hyperactivity was a serious problem for 71 per cent of the sample.

The proportion of young people reported to have an impairment, health problem, mental health problem, emotional or behavioural difficulty is

Table 7.4
Young people with each type of difficulty (n = 209)

	%	Number
Physical impairment	3	7
Learning disability	15	32
Sensory impairment	3	6
Emotional and behavioural difficulties (with a statement of special educational needs)	14	30
Emotional and behavioural difficulties (but no statement of special educational needs)	19	40
Mental health problems	14	30
Serious health problems	5	11
ADHD	11	22
None of the above	*62*	*130*

shown in Table 7.4. It should be noted that many had multiple difficulties and therefore appear more than once in this table.

One-third of the young people were considered by parents or professionals to have emotional and behavioural difficulties (EBD) and 14 per cent had a statement of special educational needs specifically for this reason. Research has shown that whether young people are said to have EBD can sometimes be a function of the attitudes and practices of their mainstream schools rather than an accurate assessment of their real difficulties, but that nevertheless children said to have EBD often have significant mental health difficulties (Cole *et al*, 2002). Where mental health difficulties were specifically mentioned and details were supplied, these usually referred either to depression or self-harm.

The young people with learning disabilities had particularly high levels of need. Half of them were reported also to have emotional or behavioural difficulties, four of them were said to have mental health problems and three had a sensory impairment. The total proportion of young people who suffered from one or more difficulty is very high, amounting to 38 per cent, as shown in Table 7.5.

Overall, 19 per cent of the sample had one or more physical or sensory impairments or a learning disability. The Office for Population Censuses and Surveys (OPCS) definition of disability is wider than this,

Table 7.5
Young people with one or more disability or health problem (n = 79)

	%	Number
Physical and/or learning and/or sensory impairment	19	40
Emotional and behavioural difficulties (but none of the above)	8	16
Total with one or more disability and/or emotional or behavioural difficulties	*27*	*56*
Mental health problems (only)	8	17
Serious health problems (only)	3	6
Total with one or more disability/mental health/health problem	*38*	*79*

encompassing children with emotional or behavioural difficulties too (Bone and Meltzer, 1989). If a fairly tight definition of emotional and behavioural difficulties is employed (embracing only those who had a statement of special educational needs specifically for this reason), and this group is included along with the others already defined as disabled, the proportion reported as disabled rises to 27 per cent. This is just slightly higher than the estimated figure of 25 per cent for looked after children (Gordon et al, 2000).[1]

Even if only a narrow definition of disability is employed, encompassing only those with physical, learning or sensory impairments, the proportion reported as disabled is far higher in this sample than among either children in need (13%) or children in the community (3.2%) (Gordon et al, 2000; DH, 2002b). However, some caution is needed in making sense of these comparisons due to the problems of definition raised earlier. Also, bearing in mind our earlier note of caution regarding our figure of 11 per cent reported to have ADHD, it is nevertheless worth noting that in the general population of 11–15-year-olds the prevalence of hyperkinetic disorders is under two per cent (Meltzer et al, 2000).

Special educational needs

As might be expected from the number with impairments or emotional or behavioural difficulties, a substantial minority had been assessed as having special educational needs under the Education Act 1981. Over one-fifth (22 per cent) had a statement of special educational needs and a further three per cent were undergoing assessment for this purpose at the time of the referral. This proportion is the same as for the 13–18-year-olds in residential or foster care in a recent study of children living away from home (Berridge et al, 2002).

The OPCS definition of disability allowed for recognition of the extent to which emotional and behavioural difficulties may co-exist alongside

---

[1] This estimate was derived from a re-analysis of the OPCS data referred to above, which was reclassified by means of cluster analysis in order to make it consistent with more recent models of disability.

other impairments (Gordon *et al*, 2000). Among the young people in this study, special needs were in most cases associated with difficulties that were behavioural or emotional. Two-thirds (30) of those with a statement of special educational needs had emotional or behavioural difficulties and most of this group had other difficulties too. Nearly half of them (14) also had learning disabilities, five were reported also to have mental health problems and five were reported to have ADHD. Very few young people had been assessed as having special educational needs solely due to a physical disability, sensory impairment or learning disability or mental health problem, without concern about accompanying emotional or behavioural difficulties.

Duration of the young people's difficulties

Parents were asked how long ago they had first become concerned about their children. Less than a quarter (23%) replied that they had first become concerned only in the last year. They indicated that over two-fifths of the young people had caused them concern from the age of nine years or younger, as shown in Table 7.6.

For nearly one-fifth of the young people, difficulties were said to have emerged when they were under five years old and it was clear that these parents were principally referring to concerns about the young people's behaviour. We considered that this might be a particularly difficult group to help. A variety of longitudinal studies have indicated that the origins of persistent youth aggression and violence are to be found in early childhood (Scott, 1998). Where children display behaviour problems at an early

Table 7.6
Age of young person when parent was first concerned (n – 200)

Age group (years)	%	Number
0–4	17	35
5–9	23	47
10–12	34	67
13–16	26	51
All ages	100	200

age, usually before the age of five, they are more likely to persist in anti-social behaviour into adulthood. This persistence is considered to be related to parent–child relationships, at least to some extent (Rutter *et al*, 1998).

Consistent with the findings of studies of anti-social behaviour, in this sample, boys' behavioural problems were more likely to be of early onset. Nearly a quarter of the boys (24%) were said to have first caused concern when under five years old compared to 10 per cent of the girls. In contrast, parents were more likely to first become concerned about girls during adolescence, as this was the case in relation to 34 per cent of the girls compared to 18 per cent of the boys.[2]

Past contact with social services

Few of the young people were new entrants to the system, as other studies of social work with teenagers have also found (Sinclair *et al*, 1995; Triseliotis *et al*, 1995). Nearly three-quarters had been in contact with social services at some time in the past, indicating that problems were not new for most of them. Over half (56%) had been known for a year or more prior to this referral, and a third had been known for more than three years.

Reasons for past contact with social services

In over one third (37%) of cases, workers reported that parents had requested the accommodation of this child on a previous occasion. Workers' reports indicated that child behaviour was the most common reason for past social services contact, although this had also been due to relationship breakdown or abuse.

For a sizeable minority there was evidence that abuse or neglect had occurred at an earlier stage in their lives. Workers reported that 36 per cent (76) of the young people had been the subject of past concern about abuse and/or neglect. For 32 per cent there had been past concern about abuse and for 12 per cent concern about neglect (and for 9 per cent concerns had been about both abuse and neglect).

---

[2] Chi-square test, significant at p = .012.

Table 7.7
Reasons for past contact with social services (n = 209)

Reason	%*	Number
Child behaviour	55	114
Relationship breakdown	39	81
Parent unable to care	16	33
Neglect	12	25
Abuse (all)	32	67
• *physical abuse*	*16*	*33*
• *sexual abuse*	*7*	*15*
• *emotional abuse*	*9*	*19*

*Percentages do not add up to 100 as the items are not mutually exclusive.

One-tenth (21) of the young people had been placed on the Child Protection Register at some time in the past and a further seven per cent had been the subject of a child protection case conference (but not registered) at some time prior to the current referral. So for half (35) of those for whom there had been past concerns about abuse or neglect, these must have been relatively serious.

Care history

One-quarter (53) of the young people had been looked after at some time in the past. Indeed, around one-tenth (20) of the young people in the study had been looked after during the previous six months.

Information on whether young people had been previously looked after was drawn from questionnaires completed by parents, young people, social workers and support workers. Comparison of these information sources revealed that in nearly half (24) of these cases one or both workers were unaware that young people had previously been looked after. Either agency record keeping was poor or staff were not making use of agency records.

Around one-third (18) of those who had been looked after prior to this referral were known to have been looked after just once, but nearly a quarter of them had been looked after on more than one occasion and, indeed, for one young person this had occurred five times. This picture is incomplete as data on times looked after, and also on age first looked after, were available only on just over half of those who had been looked after. A quarter were reported to have first been looked after before the age of 10 years, but for over half this had happened relatively recently, at age 11 or over.

Data on the total length of time they had been looked after during the course of their lives were available for only half of these young people, but it was clear from this that many had been looked after for considerable periods of time. At least 21 per cent of those previously placed were known to have been looked for 1–12 weeks, 15 per cent for 3–12 months, and six per cent for more than a year.

Parents' difficulties

The parenting of adolescents can be a difficult task, as adolescence brings with it the emotional changes that accompany puberty and the strengthening of peer group influences, which for some may be negative. Yet for parents of adolescents the parenting role is poorly defined and they have few models available to them regarding the appropriate exercise of authority (Coleman, 1997). Parents who have additional difficulties of their own are likely to find this task even harder and may be particularly in need of support. To understand the other stresses that might make the parenting task harder to accomplish, we asked parents about other difficulties in their lives in relation to their health, mental health, relationships with partners and material problems, such as financial and/or housing problems. We also asked workers for their assessment of the parents' strengths and difficulties in their role as parents.

Health and mental health difficulties

Many parents suffered from health problems. Over a quarter reported serious health problems, 13 per cent reported mental health problems and 10 per cent indicated that they had a physical disability. Some parents had more than one of these difficulties so that, overall, over one-third (36%) indicated that they had serious health or mental health problems and/or a physical disability. One in ten parents said they had problems with alcohol, but only a few (3%) reported a drug problem.

The vast majority of parents (81%) reported that they often felt depressed. Most of these were mothers, since three-quarters of those young people living either with one birth parent or in a step-family were living only with their mothers. Workers, perhaps using a tighter definition of depression, considered that only 13 per cent were depressed. However, the General Health Questionnaire (GHQ-12) indicated that mental well-being was poor for the majority of the parents (Goldberg *et al*, 1997). The GHQ is a standardised measure designed for use as a screening instrument to detect psychiatric disturbance in community settings. It is normally used to detect breaks in normal functioning rather than lifelong traits and focuses principally on detecting symptoms of depression and anxiety (Goldberg and Williams, 1988).

Even though a relatively high threshold score was used for detecting psychological difficulty on this measure, it was evident that nearly three-quarters (72 per cent) of the parents in the study were experiencing high levels of psychological distress.[3] This is far higher than the proportion that would be expected in the wider community, since an international study evaluating the GHQ found that the mean prevalence of mental disorder in the general population was 24 per cent (Goldberg *et al*, 1997). As we have seen, social workers and support workers between them considered that only 13 per cent of parents were suffering from depression. When their assessment is compared to the GHQ scores for this sample, it appears that they seriously underestimated the levels of psychological distress that parents were experiencing.

Just over a third of all parents said they had begun feeling depressed only in the last year but just under a quarter reported suffering from depression for three or more years. Chronic social difficulties such as poor housing conditions and "daily hassles" may predispose individuals to a greater risk of depression. As with risk factors for emotional and behavioural problems in children, it is the accumulation of difficulties

---

[3] Since a substantial minority of parents in this study suffered from poor health and/or a disability, the cut-off score used to indicate anxiety or depression was increased from three to four in order to control for the influence of physical illness, as recommended by Goldberg and Williams (1988).

rather than a single stress factor that creates the highest risk of psychological distress (Goldberg and Huxley, 1992).[4]

Relationships with partners and others

Relationships with past and current partners were also very stressful for many of the parents. Many (43%) reported experiencing domestic violence either recently or at some stage in the past. This is far higher than estimates for the prevalence of domestic violence in the wider community. Although it is difficult to assess the prevalence of domestic violence due to victims' reluctance to report it, a number of self-report studies have indicated that it is experienced at some time by around one-quarter of the population, almost all of whom are women (Cleaver *et al*, 1999). This suggests that for children whose difficulties brought them to the attention of social services during adolescence, domestic violence past or present was an element of the family stress that over two-fifths of them had experienced. Some young people's accounts illustrated the continuing distress and anxiety they experienced as a result of domestic violence that they were aware of, or witnessed, even several years in the past.

Nearly half (49 per cent) of parents reported that they currently had many arguments with their partners and one-third of the young people also reported conflict between parents (or parents and step-parents). Parents also indicated that for 22 per cent of them conflict with partners had been a problem just in the past year, but for 27 per cent it had occurred over a longer period. Workers reported that nearly one in ten parents had recently separated from their partners at the time of referral. Not surprisingly, parental difficulties were a source of stress to the young people, as two-thirds of them reported that they had often felt worried about their parents.

---

[4] Scores on this measure of parents' mental distress were not strongly associated with the severity of current emotional and behavioural problems for the young people. Although statistically significant, Pearson coefficients were weak for correlations between parents' GHQ scores and young people's SDQ total difficulties scores (.235), the SDQ conduct problems score (.221) and emotional problems score (.244). Thus, although the mental well-being of parents was to some extent correlated with young people's emotional and behavioural difficulties, this association was relatively weak.

Friends were the most common source of support, mentioned by 40 per cent of parents, followed by their own parents (33 per cent), siblings (25 per cent) and other relatives (21 per cent). A substantial minority of parents (25 per cent) were socially isolated, however, reporting that they knew no one they could turn to for support. Parents of teenagers who have no strong networks of relatives and friends are likely to find it harder than parents of younger children to find support from other parents at a similar stage in their lives, as they no longer have the opportunity of meeting others at playgroups, nurseries or at the school gates. Other studies have suggested that neurotic symptoms may be a cause, rather than an effect, of a lack of a social network (Goldberg and Huxley, 1992). The high proportion of parents scoring above the "case detection" threshold on the GHQ may therefore help to explain, at least to some extent, the lack of social support for some of these parents.

Material problems

There was evidence of more concrete problems too. Housing problems were mentioned by 18 per cent of the parents, with overcrowding being the most common (13%), followed by eviction (4%). Conflict with neighbours was also mentioned in a few cases.

Over two-fifths of parents (42%) mentioned that they had 'serious money worries' largely due to low income (24%), debt (8%) or both (8%). Wages were the principal source of family income for only a third (34%). Two-thirds (65%) were clearly living on low incomes (income support, unemployment or other state benefits or claiming family credit to supplement low wages). Single parents were twice as likely to report financial problems (two-thirds of them did so) compared to those living with partners.[5] Social workers and support staff appeared to be unaware of the stress caused by financial problems for many families. They may have viewed financial problems as the norm among the families that they worked with, or families may not have shared these concerns with them.

---

[5] Chi-square test, significant at p = .016.

Parenting strengths and difficulties

As we have seen, many parents had considerable difficulties and these strains may well have had an impact on their style of parenting. Numerous studies have found that certain aspects of parenting style are closely associated with long-term anti-social behaviour (West and Farrington, 1973; Rutter *et al*, 1998; Scott, 1998). We therefore asked workers about those aspects of parenting style known to be associated with better or worse behaviour in children.[6] We asked them for their assessment of whether parents made their expectations clear to the young people, were warm, encouraging and consistent in their responses towards them, were able to set clear boundaries or were harsh towards them – 'most of the time', 'only some times' or 'hardly ever' – and these items were scored accordingly.

Workers considered that difficulty in setting (and presumably enforcing) boundaries was the most common, as this appeared to be an issue for nearly three-quarters of the parents. Possibly linked to this, around two-thirds of parents were considered to be generally inconsistent in their responses to their children. Only 56 per cent were thought to display warmth towards their child most of the time and nearly one-fifth

Table 7.8
Worker assessment of parenting strengths and difficulties (n = 178)

	Most of the time %	*Only sometimes/ hardly ever* %
Makes expectations clear	52	48
Consistent in responses	34	66
Warm towards young person	56	44
Encouraging when young person does something well	48	52
Sets clear boundaries	28	72
Harsh towards young person	19	81

Note: the percentages add up to 100 across the rows.

---

[6] The risk and protective factors associated with certain aspects of parenting style were outlined at the beginning of Chapter 3.

were considered to be harsh most of the time. There was a significant association between high scores for parenting difficulties and worker concerns about physical or sexual abuse and emotional abuse at the time of referral.[7]

There was also a significant association between high scores for parenting difficulties and worker assessments that parents were suffering from depression. There is extensive research evidence which indicates that parenting skills may be affected by mental illness, domestic violence and problem drug or alcohol use. Parents who suffer from depression or misuse drugs or alcohol may display apathy and listlessness, which may make them inconsistent and ineffective in their parenting. The experience of domestic violence can have a negative impact on parents' ability to look after their children too (Cleaver et al, 1999).

Witnessing domestic violence can also have an adverse psychological impact on children (Cleaver et al, 1999). A number of studies have found that children who witness domestic violence have significantly more emotional and behavioural problems than those who do not, and those who also experience physical abuse show the highest levels of emotional and behavioural disturbance (Humphreys and Mullender, undated). Serious behavioural problems have been found to be 17 times higher for boys and 10 times higher for girls who have witnessed the abuse of their mother, and some may themselves behave aggressively (Wolfe et al, 1985, cited in Cleaver et al, 1999).

Domestic violence has been found to be a correlate in a substantial minority of cases of child abuse. A study of nearly 2,000 child protection referrals found that domestic violence was an issue in the family in 27 per cent of cases (Gibbons et al, 1995), while another study found that 59 per cent of mothers whose children were on the Child Protection Register were themselves the subject of domestic violence (Farmer and Owen, 1995).

It is also known that child perceptions of inter-parental conflict are associated with an increase in negative parent–child interactions and in problems in child adjustment. This effect is particularly strong with regard

---

[7] Mann Whitney U test, significant at p = .006 for physical or sexual abuse and p = .038 for emotional abuse.

to mother–son relationships. Children do not have to be directly involved in this conflict for it to affect them in these ways, as already noted (Buchanan and Ten Brinke, 1998). The young people were well aware that parents were experiencing difficulties, as two-thirds of them reported feeling worried or upset about their parents. One quarter reported feeling this only in the last year, but 42 per cent had been worried about their parents for longer than this.

Contact with other agencies at referral

As might be anticipated, given the high levels of difficulty, the majority of the young people were already receiving support from other agencies when the referral was made, as shown in Table 7.9.

In total, 87 per cent were receiving, or had recently received, some form of professional support apart from their contacts with social workers and support workers. The agency most likely to be in contact with these young people was the education service. The seriousness of the emotional and behavioural problems of many of the young people is reflected in the fact that 30 per cent had recently seen an educational psychologist and 35 per cent had seen a psychiatrist or psychologist.

Parents were less likely to be in contact with other agencies than young people but, as might be expected given the high levels of psychological distress, the health service was the agency most likely to be in contact with them. Ten per cent had been in recent contact with a psychiatrist or

Table 7.9
Support to young people from other agencies in last 6 months (n = 209)

Type of professional/agency	%
Education welfare officer	61
Educational psychologist	30
Psychiatrist or psychologist	35
Youth offending team	13
Young carers group	3
Youth worker	9
Drug or alcohol project	3
No professional support	13

psychologist, six per cent with a community psychiatric nurse and eight per cent with another health professional.

Comparing young people using specialist and mainstream services

There were few significant differences between young people using support teams or mainstream services. However, there was some evidence to suggest that young people using the specialist service were more likely to have chronic difficulties. The young people using this service were twice as likely to have been known to social services for more than three years (44%) in comparison with those receiving a mainstream service (20%). Past concerns about abuse were also reported more often in relation to those using the specialist support team service.

As for contact with other agencies, the young people referred to the support teams were more than twice as likely to have had recent contact with a child psychiatrist or psychologist (44 per cent) than those referred to the mainstream service (17 per cent). They were also almost twice as likely (35 per cent) to have been in recent contact with an educational psychologist than those referred to the mainstream service (19 per cent). Taken together, young people's histories of past abuse, length of contact with social services and contact with mental health and educational psychology services all suggest that those referred to the support teams may have had more severe, and long-standing, levels of difficulty at referral.

In contrast, a greater proportion of parents using the mainstream service had high scores for psychological distress, as measured by the General Health Questionnaire, than those using the specialist service.[8]

Summary points

- Social workers were sometimes unaware that children had been looked after in the past or that parents had significant psychological problems, such as depression and anxiety, or were under stress due to financial problems.

---

[8] Independent samples T-Test significant at p = .004.

- Very few of the young people were living with both birth parents at referral. Families were far more fragmented than in the wider population. Patterns of family composition were similar to the pattern for looked after children.
- Levels of need were high and many had long-standing and serious difficulties.
- Many (38%) had a high level of need due to emotional/behavioural difficulties (14%), disability/impairment (19%) or health/mental health problems (11%) or more than one of these, and 22 per cent had a statement of special educational needs. Although comparisons are difficult due to problems of definition, the proportion reported to have a disability of some kind appeared to be far higher in this sample than among the total population of children in need or those in the wider community.
- Nearly three-quarters had been the subject of past referrals to social services and a quarter had been looked after at least once in the past.
- There had been previous concern about abuse or neglect in respect of over one-third of the sample and one in ten had been placed on the Child Protection Register at some time in the past.
- Domestic violence was reported by 43 per cent of families. This was a source of continuing distress for many young people, even if it had occurred several years earlier.
- Nearly three-quarters of parents were found to have high levels of mental distress (measured by the GHQ) and the majority reported feeling depressed; 43 per cent reported past or present domestic violence and 49 per cent reported current conflicts with partners.
- There were few differences between those using the specialist service and those using the mainstream service, but the former group were more likely to have been known to social services long term and to have been the subject of past concern about abuse. Mean scores for psychological distress (on the GHQ scale) were higher for parents using the mainstream service.
- Young people referred to support teams were more than twice as likely to have had recent contact with a child psychiatrist or psychologist, and almost twice as likely to have been in recent contact with an educational psychologist than those referred to the mainstream service. Their

recent pattern of service use and the longer duration of their contact with social services suggest that the support teams group may have had more entrenched difficulties.

8 Young people's difficulties at referral

The young people had multiple difficulties at the point of referral, which were often severe. In most cases the young people's behaviour within the home was seen as the key issue, but emotional problems, behaviour outside the home and parent–child relationship problems were frequently mentioned too.

Family perspectives

Recent problems

Young people and parents were each asked to complete a Severity of Difficulties checklist to indicate whether a list of potential difficulties constituted 'a major problem', 'a moderate problem' or 'not a problem at all' in the past few months.

There were marked differences between parents and young people in their ratings of the problem severity, with a far higher proportion of parents considering that the difficulties mentioned constituted 'a major problem' than did young people. However, when parent and child views were compared on a case-by-case basis, there was a fairly strong correlation between their ratings of problem severity.[1] It was also clear that, for each problem specified, between two-thirds and three-quarters of the young people and parents agreed as to the nature of their difficulties, even if they did not always agree on their severity.

Self-harm and violence

Parents were also concerned about the young people's violence to themselves and to others. They reported that over one-third of the young people had attempted to harm themselves: nearly 20 per cent (40) had self-harmed in the past year and a further 15 per cent had done so prior to this. This represents a very high incidence of self-harm, since the rate of self-harm

---

[1] Pearson correlation .485, significant at p<.001.

Table 8.1

Difficulties rated as 'a major problem' in the past six months (n = 209)

	Parents (%)	Young people (%)
Young persons' behaviour at home	85	37
Parents upset about behaviour outside home	64	29
Parents' concern about young person's friends	51	26
Stays out late	36	17
Parent/child arguments	78	34
Child/parent 'doesn't listen'	63	22
Child/parent 'can't talk things over'	54	32
School problems	59	34
Drug problems	12	3
Alcohol problems	10	4
Offending	22	12

among 11–15-year-olds in the general population who have no mental disorder is negligible (1.2%). The rate in this study is closer to the rate for 11–15-year-olds with depression (18.8%) and higher than the rate for those with conduct disorders (12.6%), anxiety disorders (9.4%) and hyperkinetic disorders (8.5%) (Meltzer, 2001). The survey from which these comparisons are drawn provides some clues to why so many of these young people may self-harm, since this is more common among adolescents in families with a high degree of family discord or where parents have high GIIQ scores. As we saw in the previous chapter, both of these were common among our sample.

Over half of the parents (55%) reported that their child had been violent to them in the past six months, and 29 per cent considered this to be 'a major problem'. Even more young people (69%) were reported to have been violent to others in this period, and for nearly half of these the violence was rated as 'a major problem'. Girls were just as likely to display aggressive behaviour as boys, both to their families and to others. The likelihood of violent behaviour increased with age. Nearly half of the 12-year-olds, over half of the 14–15-year-olds and nearly three-quarters of the 13-year-olds were violent to parents. Even more were violent to others: around three-quarters of the 11–14-year-olds and nearly two-thirds of the 15-year-olds were said to be violent to others.

Multiple difficulties

It was clear that it was an accumulation of stresses that had brought the family to crisis point, rather than a single stressor, since most parents reported multiple difficulties in respect of their children. These included the above difficulties as well as school exclusion, running away, self-harm, and violence to parents or to others.

Table 8.2
Number of difficulties reported by parents at referral (n = 203)

Number of problems	%	Number of Young people
1–5	7	15
6–10	51	104
11–15	42	84

Duration of young people's problems

For a sizeable minority, behavioural problems and problems at school had emerged three or more years earlier. Self-harming behaviour, on the other hand, had in most cases begun more recently. This is not surprising since internalising behaviour of this kind is more likely to emerge during adolescence than in earlier childhood (Coleman and Hendry, 1999).

Table 8.3
When young people's problems emerged (n = 200)

	In last year	1–3 years	3+ years	Total
Behavioural problems	29%	23%	42%	94%
School problems	24%	26%	32%	82%
Self-harm	19%	10%	4%	33%

Sources of support for young people

Over one-tenth (11%) of the young people appeared to be quite isolated, as they said they felt there was no one they could turn to for help or advice. Difficulties in relationships between young people and parents were also clear from the fact that only just over a quarter (26%) of the young people saw their parents as a source of help or advice, although grandparents (19%), siblings (14%) and other relatives (15%) were also seen as a source of support. They were more likely to turn to friends (42%) than anyone else, which is not surprising as the peer group is an important source of support and influence for teenagers.

Professional perspectives

Social workers and support workers were concerned about a range of behavioural and emotional problems, but were almost unanimous in their opinion that the young people's behaviour was problematic (98%).[2] They also reported concerns about truancy (66%), petty theft from families (51%), offending (33%) and drug or alcohol problems (23%).

One-fifth of the young people were said to be engaging in sexual behaviour that put themselves or others at risk. This was reported far more frequently in relation to girls, who accounted for three-quarters of all such reports. Professionals were concerned about sexual behaviour in respect of 31 per cent of girls compared to just nine per cent of boys.[3] They also reported that nearly half (48%) of the young people were violent to parents and 43 per cent were violent to others. Violent behaviour outside the home was closely associated with violent behaviour within it, as 76 per cent of those reported to be violent to parents were also violent to others.[4]

Alongside these behavioural difficulties, relationship problems between birth parents and children were noted by workers in respect of virtually all the families (98%) and problems in relationships with step-parents were also common (46%). Social workers and support workers also considered that nearly half (48%) of the young people experienced rejection by a parent. Previous research has indicated that the potential effects of parental rejection include aggression, hostility, emotional

---

[2] Problems were noted if mentioned by either the social worker or support worker (or both).

[3] Chi-square test, significant at p<.001.

[4] Chi-square test, significant at p = .03.

unresponsiveness, delinquency and, not surprisingly, low self-esteem (Rohner, 1986).

Emotional difficulties were also reported by professionals. Workers were concerned about mental health problems in respect of one-quarter and self-harm/suicide attempts by nearly one-fifth (19%). Loss was a major issue, as 20 per cent had experienced a recent bereavement and 28 per cent had experienced recent separation from a parent. Emotional problems often went hand in hand with behavioural problems, since virtually all these young people were also reported to have behavioural problems. For example, 38 per cent of those thought to have drug or alcohol problems were also reported to suffer emotional abuse.[5]

Accounts of behavioural and relationship difficulties

Difficult behaviour

Parents spoke of their difficulty in dealing with the young people's behaviour, describing their children as defiant, challenging parental authority and refusing to do as they were told. Numerous parents said that they felt unable to cope with their children any more and that they desperately needed help. Some found it hard to cope because they were depressed or lacked confidence, feeling consumed with anxiety about their children's behaviour but at a loss as to how to change it. In particular, the parents of five young people with Attention Deficit Hyperactivity Disorder (ADHD) were clearly at their wits end.[6] One was being treated for depression and two said they felt suicidal, such was their despair about their children:

I was having serious thoughts of suicide, both for myself and harming him. I decided if I took my own life I couldn't leave him behind as he isn't capable of looking after himself. No one else for that matter is capable of looking after him. (mother of 14-year-old boy)

---

[5] Chi-square test, significant at p = .032.

[6] As mentioned in Chapter 3, we do not know if all of these young people had a clinical diagnosis of ADHD. Young people are here classified as having ADHD if a parent or worker mentioned that they had this condition.

The influence of peers was often thought to be an important factor. In many cases parents felt that undesirable peers were leading their children astray. Some parents were concerned at them staying out late or overnight against their wishes, and many described them as 'out of control' or 'uncontrollable'. From their accounts, it seemed that many were struggling to set boundaries to the young people's behaviour but were unsuccessful in enforcing them. Some expressed a sense of helplessness and despair about their ability to set limits to their children's behaviour:

From now on I could see he was going to do what he wanted, not what I or his mother wanted. (father of boy, 12 years)

I can't win. I can't ground her, she'll break out and wear me down. She won't let up. (mother of girl, 13 years)

If his dad was here he'd be different. I give in a lot for peace and quiet. I feel I can't control him. (mother of boy, 14 years)

Young people's own accounts indicated that many of them seemed to accept that their behaviour was problematic. In total, nearly half mentioned having behavioural problems either at home or both at home and at school and some mentioned that their behaviour at home, their 'attitude' or temper had occasioned the current referral. Several also mentioned staying out late or overnight as a source of conflict with parents. A number of them referred to being 'angry' or 'in a mood', or admitted to stealing from their families or lying. A few mentioned offending or using drugs.

Some of the young people blamed themselves for the difficulties they were experiencing, either describing themselves as 'bad' or saying that they felt they needed help with their behaviour. One 12-year-old girl explained that she had been 'bad' for the past three years, and that her behaviour had deteriorated recently:

I hit my mum and shout at my mum, but afterwards when I'm good I can't remember it. My mum has to tell me.

In a few cases, parents and young people ascribed their child's behaviour problems to loss of some kind. The loss of a father through bereavement was thought, by parents and workers, to account for the development of angry, aggressive behaviour in two boys. More commonly, young people experienced loss as a consequence of parental separation. One 15-year-old girl, living with relatives, described her unhappiness since her father had died and her mother had left home and said that she did not want to be separated from her brother and sister. The loss of contact with a father who had left the home was thought to have led to another young person's anger and aggressive behaviour. The parent of yet another explained:

> *She was having behavioural problems through being confused emotionally after the separation of myself and her father.* (mother of girl, 15 years)

Several of the young people gave some account of why they felt their behaviour was poor. Some said they were 'misbehaving' because they were unhappy, or that they felt 'angry inside'. Sometimes they linked problems in their current behaviour to past difficulties, including parental separation and abuse:

> *I covered up my upset with anger. I smashed things up and punched friends. It's been going on for quite a lot of years. I know why I get angry – because of my past.* (boy, 13 years, who previously experienced abuse)

> *Mum made me choose between her and my brother and I got messed. I would come in drunk, go out early in the morning and come back at 10.30 pm.* (girl, 13 years)

> *My stepfather caused it because he was battering me and winding me up. He left ages ago but it still has an effect.* (boy, 14 years)

Violent behaviour

Parents described an astonishing catalogue of violent behaviour by the young people, directed both towards members of their families and towards others. Parents' accounts of their children's violence within the family indicated that it was most often directed towards their mothers. In a number of cases siblings were physically attacked; less frequently, attacks on fathers or stepfathers were reported and in two cases, attacks on grandparents. Some young people directed their violence solely at one family member, but in a number of cases they appeared to lash out at everyone around them. Most of the incidents described involved quite serious assaults on family members:

She'll come up behind me and kick me and she chucks things at me. (mother of girl, 14 years)

He has hit me a few times, kicked me in the stomach and made me bleed. (mother of boy, 14 years)

His violent behaviour towards me . . . biting, kicking and pushing me around. (mother of boy, 12 years)

The main thing was he came home one night in a foul mood and went upstairs and tried to strangle his younger brother. (grandparent of boy, 12 years)

Some parents admitted that the violence could be two-way, occurring during major arguments:

We actually fight and she punches and kicks me. She's actually told me to get out of the house now. (mother of girl, 13 years)

(His stepfather) is now smaller than him and is confrontational with him, which has led to fights and bloodshed between them. (mother of boy, 11 years)

Violence to others was mostly directed at other children, usually at school, but parents also reported assaults on adults. Attacks on teachers were mentioned in several cases, including an incident where a 12-year-old boy broke a teacher's nose, and one parent referred to complaints from neighbours that her 11-year-old daughter was 'torturing people'. In many cases, violent behaviour was accompanied by general destructiveness. Nearly one in ten parents mentioned their children 'smashing up the house', 'kicking in the door', 'smashing up his room' or generally 'smashing things up'.

Apart from those who were physically violent, many of the young people were verbally aggressive. A number of parents referred to 'temper tantrums', aggression or general bullying behaviour within the family.

Two also mentioned mood swings, with one parent likening her son to Jekyll and Hyde. In a few cases the aggression appeared to be linked to young people's drug or alcohol abuse:

> *Drinking, drug abuse, violent temper, he's on a short fuse all the time and extremely volatile. My daughters are frightened of him . . . It's like a living bomb, a miniature volcano.* (mother of boy, 15 years)

Many young people also referred to problems with their temper or to having 'temper tantrums'. A few described their violence or generally aggressive behaviour to siblings as being rooted in their conflicts with parents:

> *When my mum used to shout at me I used to go to my brother and beat him up.* (boy, 12 years)

Others linked it to their experience of abuse:

> *I hate it that mum tells everyone that I batter her – she hits me.* (girl, 14 years)

In a few cases, it was clear that there was a link between domestic violence and the child's own violence:

> *There was violence from my partner which she saw and that's when she started being different, when I kicked him out two years ago.* (mother of girl, 14 years)

A few young people also juxtaposed their descriptions of their own difficult behaviour, sometimes including violence, with accounts of witnessing domestic violence:

> *I physically hit my sister and brother (play fight) for no reason. I was getting into trouble with the police and stealing from my mum. Mum argues with my dad. My dad was hitting my mum with a plate and cut her head open and I had to go and get help.* (boy, 12 years)

Family relationships
Some parents graphically described the breakdown in relationships with their children. Several pointed to difficulties in communicating with their children, complaining that they simply could not talk to them because

their child would not listen or arguments would develop. As the parent of one boy, about whom there were current child protection concerns, explained:

We couldn't reach him, he wouldn't listen or respond to us – just one syllable answers, didn't want to interact at all. (mother of boy, 14 years)

Some parents expressed despair at this breakdown in relationships and some felt that these parent–child relationship difficulties had a far-reaching impact on the rest of the family. They felt that the child caused arguments between them and their partners and in some cases actively sought to break up their relationships with partners.

Many of the young people also mentioned conflict with parents, sometimes accompanied by serious conflict with siblings. Most of them referred to 'arguing' or 'not getting on' with parents and, occasionally, step-parents. Few explained why they felt this was happening, although a number set this conflict in the context of other difficulties. Behavioural problems at school or truancy, sometimes provoked by bullying, were mentioned by several young people as one of the reasons for their arguments with parents. Behaviour at home and 'attitude' were also linked to descriptions of arguments and sometimes multiple difficulties were associated with parent–child conflict.

Family accounts of emotional problems

Some parents gave graphic accounts of their children's attempts at self-harm or suicide. In around half of these accounts there were complaints about their child's behaviour too, which was most often described as aggressive or out of control. In a few cases, self-harm by young people, such as cutting themselves, was accompanied by suicide threats. Two had been diagnosed as suffering from depression and one appeared to be anorexic. A few young people had not actually self-harmed but were described as 'being on self-destruct', for example, a 12-year-old boy repeatedly 'playing chicken' in the road, on buses and on railway lines. Eight other parents described their children's (sometimes multiple) suicide attempts, which in most cases took the form of overdoses. It was unclear from most parents' accounts why the young people were self-harming or suicidal, although mention was made of sexual abuse, bullying and alcohol abuse in a few cases. One young person felt that her self-harming and other problems were directly linked to past abuse, explaining the reasons for her referral as:

> *Because me and mum weren't getting along. Being in trouble with the police, cutting my arms, my behaviour, running away. I was sexually abused for years.* (girl, 13 years)

A few explained that they were unhappy as a result of past parental separation, particularly when this had resulted in their separation from siblings:

> *I go to my dad's and when I come home I don't talk to my mum because I feel bad about leaving my brother and sister. I feel upset with my mum.* (girl, 12 years)

There was some uncertainty among both parents and workers as to whether certain emotional or behavioural difficulties were caused by mental health problems or had some kind of organic component, or alternatively whether the young people were simply badly behaved, as the following comments illustrate:

> *Basically, the social worker said she needed to go to my doctor so she could assess whether he was mentally ill or just plain naughty.* (parent of boy, 13 years)

> *With her ADHD it's difficult and she's very hard to parent. She's not like an ordinary teenager and you don't know what's adolescence and what's ADHD, it's hard to determine between the two.* (parent of girl, 14 years)

> *His parents wonder if he's schizophrenic whereas other professionals have focused on the behavioural and emotional problems. I have to say I'm a bit at my wit's end about it.* (social worker of boy, 12 years)

Abuse and neglect

Professionals were concerned about abuse or neglect in relation to over half of the young people, although just six per cent (12) were the subject

Table 8.4
Professional concerns about abuse or neglect at referral

Nature of problem	%	Number
Neglect	17	36
Physical abuse	11	22
Sexual abuse	3	7
Emotional abuse	34	71
Total abuse and/or neglect	54	112

of a child protection enquiry and four per cent were on the Child Protection Register when the study began.

There was a clear association between current and past difficulties in this respect. For 46 per cent of those young people about whom there was current concern about abuse or neglect, there had been similar concern in the past. For those for whom the current concerns related specifically to physical or sexual abuse, 58 per cent had experienced abuse or neglect in the past.

In six cases, parents or young people said the referral had been triggered by an incident of physical abuse during a row between a parent and a young person. Some parents justified this in terms of the young person's abusive and violent behaviour towards them. They spoke of lashing out after years of coping with difficult behaviour. For example, the mother of one 12-year-old boy described the following incident:

> *His step-dad lost his temper with him; he got a mark from him and went to school with it. Teachers saw it and called social services, but there was his behaviour at home and school . . . going into moods, snarling, screaming. He lights fires, we have to hide all the lighters. He pinches, you name it, he does it. It's been like this for over seven years.*

Another mother described an incident with her 15-year-old daughter, who had been looked after in the past:

> *She came home drunk, she was abusive to us, my husband loses his temper so he slaps her one . . . She is swearing, throwing things around the room, pulling pictures down off the wall. She hits me with a baton*

so my husband phones the police...We asked for her to be accommodated, we didn't want her back.

Her daughter's vivid account of the same incident linked it to her parents' marital problems and indicated that her difficulties were long term:

My parents are aggressive to me, but they think I'm aggressive to them too. I'm right cheeky. It's gone on for several years now, it's always about the same thing but I lose my temper. Dad says I'm a tart, a slag, that I've got no friends. He always brings it up. This time mum and dad had been having problems, on the verge of splitting up, and I'd started drinking more. I'd come home drunk, dad started on me, we had a massive row. It all got out of hand, all the street was out looking. My dad hit me and I ended up in hospital.

In these situations, there was an explosive mix of difficult and sometimes violent child behaviour, parental violence, and, in some cases, parental rejection. As one parent explained, because of her 11-year-old son's physical aggression towards her, 'I was worried what I might do'. Professionals had had past concerns about the possible abuse of this child and he had been looked after in the past. A few parents and young people mentioned the continuing repercussions of past abuse, both physical and sexual, as the source of young people's difficulties.

The abuse of adolescents is not always recognised as a serious problem. This may be because adolescents may respond to it differently than younger children. Research on abused adolescents in the USA has shown that, while they are more physically durable than younger children, they tend to display the effects of abuse in other ways, through self-harm, depression, running away or offending (Rees and Stein, 1997).

School problems

A remarkably high proportion of the young people appeared to be to some extent, or completely, detached from the school system. One-fifth had not attended mainstream school at all during the six months prior to referral and 14 per cent appeared to be completely detached from school, having received no form of education at all in the preceding six months.

The four-fifths who *had* attended school during the past six months had not necessarily done so continuously, as rates of truancy and school exclusion were high.

Three-quarters of the young people displayed behavioural problems at school, including disruptiveness, refusal to go to classes, rudeness to teachers and aggression to other pupils. Young people and parents reported that 42 per cent had truanted in the month prior to referral and 60 per cent had done so in the past year. Parents described how truancy was often accompanied by problems at school, offending or substance abuse.

Rates of exclusion from school were also extremely high. Parents and young people reported that 42 per cent had been temporarily excluded during the past year and that the majority of these (35%) had, in fact, been temporarily excluded just in the past month. However, rates of temporary exclusion may be affected by local policy and practice as well as by the nature of young peoples' behaviour, so they cannot be seen as a straightforward indicator of difficulty. Permanent exclusion was also an issue. A total of 10 per cent (21) had been permanently excluded from school in the past year, five of them just in the past month.

Around the time of referral, then, there was evidence that a remarkably high proportion of the young people were, to a greater or lesser extent, detached from school. In the past month, over two-thirds (67 per cent) of the young people had truanted and/or been either temporarily or permanently excluded from school.

Home and school problems often appeared to reinforce each other.

Table 8.5
Educational provision during the past six months (n = 209)*

Educational provision	%	Number
Mainsteam school	80	168
Pupil referral unit	7	15
Home tutor	2	4
No provision	14	29

*Seven young people appear in this table more than once because they had more than one type of provision.

In some cases, trouble at school, or non-attendance, 'ratcheted up' parent–child conflicts. As earlier research has found (Biehal *et al*, 2000), when young people were out of school due to truancy or expulsion, problems at home could be reinforced:

> *I was excluded from school, bored, in bad moods. I was getting angry because I wasn't at school and started taking it out on mum and dad.* (boy, 11 years)

Offending

Over half of the parents (55%) reported their child's involvement in offending to have been a problem in the past six months and 49 per cent of young people also reported this. Surprisingly, professionals appeared to be unaware of the extent of young people's involvement in offending since, in comparison with parents, they reported only half as many young people to have recently been in trouble with the police.

Only half of those recently involved in offending (22% of the total sample) had been involved in the criminal justice system in the past six months. All of these had received a reprimand during the past six months. Compared to other children above the age of criminal responsibility, this is higher than the rate of 9.5 per cent for looked after children, or 3.3 per cent for all children (DfES, 2004b). However, these figures include children higher up the criminal justice tariff, who received not only reprimands but also final warnings or convictions for offences, whereas none of the young people in this study had received a final warning or been convicted in the six months prior to referral.

Running away

Running away was a major issue for this group of young people and was a clear indicator of their unhappiness at home or at school. Seventy-one per cent (149) had run away in the past year and over a quarter of parents (29%) reported that running away had been a major problem in the past six months.

Just two-thirds of the reported runaways indicated how many times they had run away in the past year. Of these, nearly one-quarter (23%) had run away only once but over one-third (36%) reported that they had run away three or more times in the last six months. Thirteen per cent had run away more than three times during this period, a proportion similar to that found among the wider population of young runaways, of whom 12 per cent have reported running away more than three times, (Safe on the Streets Research Team, 1999). In 12 cases, parents or young people mentioned running away or being thrown out as a reason for referral.

Although most runaways were missing for only short periods, some seemed quite determined to stay away. One parent reported that her 14-year-old daughter had been missing for five weeks while another girl of the same age had spent some time sleeping rough and had also taken several overdoses. Yet another 14-year-old, about whom there were current concerns regarding abuse, was truanting and was reportedly involved with drugs, alcohol and 'bad company'. He was staying away for days at a time and, according to his mother, had said that 'he didn't want to be here. Anywhere else would be better, even dossing.' Some explicitly linked running away to problems in their relationships with parents:

I kept falling out with mum, kept going away to get away from it all, so I was never at home. (boy, 15 years)

I'd been on the streets for one week . . . I wanted help, I couldn't face another night out. I couldn't stay at home, my mum can't cope. She says I have a bad attitude. (girl, 14 years)

Two mentioned threats of violence that had led them to run away and others described these threats as a response to their own behaviour:

I ran away from home. My mum's boyfriend threatened to beat me up. I was back-chatting to my mum and hanging around with older people. (girl, 13 years)

A number of studies have shown that running away may be an attempt to escape abuse, and given the high level of professional concern about abuse in respect of the young people in this study, this may have been a motivating factor for some of those who ran away (Stiffman, 1989; Cohen *et al*, 1991; Widom and Ames, 1994; Safe on the Streets Research Team, 1999). This highlights the importance of taking running away seriously and carefully assessing the difficulties that may prompt young people to run away (Biehal and Wade, 2000).

Drug and alcohol misuse

Young people and parents were asked whether the young person had a problem with drug or alcohol use. This question is fraught with problems of definition – the extent of substance use that has to occur before it is considered 'a problem' will vary from person to person. It is also more than likely that this issue will be under-reported. Young people may be reluctant to admit to substance misuse, or may consider their usage of drugs and alcohol to be normal, and parents may not be aware of it. Just over one-fifth of the young people in this study were known to have problems with drug or alcohol misuse.

There was a strong association between recent involvement in offending and both drug and alcohol misuse. These were both significantly associated with truancy too, although not with any form of exclusion from school. Sexual behaviour 'putting self or others at risk', as reported by workers, was also closely associated with alcohol and drug misuse. In all cases where drug or alcohol misuse was reported, parents were also concerned about the people with whom their children were associating.

Substance misuse appeared to be more closely linked to the young people's peer group and to other behavioural problems outside the family home rather than to problems within the family, as no associations were found with parental depression, marital conflict, domestic violence or parental alcohol misuse. Neither was there any association with young people's past experience of abuse or neglect.

Table 8.6
Reported substance misuse by young people (n = 44)

Nature of substance use	%	Number
Alcohol	13	28
Drugs	17	35
Both drugs and alcohol	*9*	*19*
Total substance misuse	21	44

Young people's strengths and difficulties

In order to obtain an objective measure of the young people's emotional and behavioural difficulties, they and their parents were asked to complete the Strengths and Difficulties Questionnaire (SDQ) (Goodman, 1997). A comparison of scores on this measure to the scores anticipated for a community sample, confirmed our findings from other measures that levels of need were extremely high, as shown in Table 8.7. Even if young people's considerably more positive views of themselves are taken rather than their parents', the proportion with a high level of need is still substantially higher than would be anticipated among children in the community as a whole.

Table 8.7

Comparison of SDQ Total Difficulties scores with community sample

	Low need %	*Some need* %	*High need* %
Community sample	80	10	10
Parent ratings	9	15	76
Young person ratings	26	24	42

Sub-scales of the SDQ indicated the proportion of young people experiencing specific difficulties, including conduct disorder, hyperactivity, emotional problems and peer problems as well as the proportion displaying pro-social behaviour, as shown in Table 8.8.

Only 10 per cent of children would be expected to have high levels of need in any of these areas (Goodman, 1997), so it is clear that the proportion of young people in the sample with specific emotional and behavioural difficulties was far higher than would be likely among children in the wider community. The proportions with high scores for conduct problems or hyperactivity were particularly high. Parents also indicated that the proportion of young people with high scores for emotional problems and peer problems and low scores for pro-social behaviour was also considerably higher than among children in the community. Scores for conduct problems, hyperactivity and problems with

Table 8.8
SDQ sub-scale scores*

Sub-scale	Parent rating			Young person rating		
	Low need	Some need	High need	Low need	Some need	High need
Conduct problems	7	13	80	18	14	68
Hyperactivity	17	12	71	32	20	48
Emotional symptoms	59	15	26	76	12	12
Peer problems	40	29	31	58	27	15
Pro-social	50	10	40	66	16	18

*Where percentages do not add up to 100 this is due to rounding.

pro-social behaviour were also higher than those found in a recent study of 50 looked after children, although the looked after children were twice as likely to have high scores for emotional difficulties and peer problems (Mount *et al*, 2004).

Domestic violence clearly had a major impact on the young people. Those young people whose parents had reported experiencing domestic violence had higher average scores on the SDQ emotional problems sub-scale than the other young people.[7] Young people reported by parents to have witnessed this domestic violence scored highly on the conduct problems sub-scale too.[8] Young people's violence to their parents was also closely associated with their emotional problems. Young people reported to display violence to their parents also scored highly on the emotional problems sub-scale.[9] However, current or past experience of abuse or neglect was not significantly associated with higher scores for emotional or conduct problems.

We saw in the previous chapter that nearly one-fifth of parents had been concerned about their children since they were under five years old. These young people scored significantly higher on the SDQ hyperactivity and peer problems sub-scales than those whose difficulties apparently

---

[7] Kruskal-Wallis test significant at p = .009.
[8] Kruskal-Wallis test significant at p = .048
[9] Kruskal-Wallis test significant at p<.001.

emerged later and they were clearly a group with a long history of considerable difficulties.[10]

Gender

There were some gender differences in respect of the difficulties reported. Analysis of both versions of the SDQ revealed that boys had higher scores for hyperactivity than girls. Analysis of the child questionnaires indicated that girls had higher scores for emotional problems and also for pro-social behaviour.[11] However, girls were no more likely to self-harm than boys were. They were, however, more likely than boys to have a problem with alcohol misuse, although there was no gender difference in the pattern of drug misuse.[12] Alcohol problems were reported for twice as many girls (19%) as boys (9%). We have also seen earlier that concerns about sexual behaviour were more than three times as common in relation to girls.

Parental reports on the age when difficulties started suggested that onset was earlier for boys. Boys also accounted for around three-quarters of those temporarily excluded from school (72%) and those with a statement of special educational needs (76%). As might be expected from national patterns of offending, boys were also more likely to be involved in offending (43%) than were girls (24%).[13]

Hopes for and expectations of the service

The young people's and parents' hopes and expectations for the help that social services might provide were remarkably similar. Parents wanted help from workers in controlling their children's behaviour or expressed a wish for back-up in setting boundaries and enforcing them. They wanted social services to:

Help me put in place discipline. My children don't listen to me. (mother of boy, 14 years)

---

[10] One-way anova: p = .014 for hyperactivity; p = .004 for peer problems.

[11] One-way anova. Hyperactivity: child version, p = .036; parent version p = .002. Pro-social and emotional problems p<.001.

[12] Chi-square test significant at p = .024.

[13] Chi-square test significant at p = .009.

> *Help me to get her to understand that there has to be discipline in her life and that when I tell her not to do things, it's for her own good.* (girl, 12 years)

Some parents simply wanted 'support' in coping with their child, but others hoped for more specific advice, to give them greater confidence in their parenting:

> *I want help to identify when I need to take action about her behaviour and when I need to stand back, as at the moment I react to everything.* (mother of girl, 12 years)

> *How to deal with his aggression. How to defuse a situation when he gets out of hand.* (mother of boy, 14 years)

> *I need help when he goes into one of his rages or when he gets so low that I know he is going to harm himself.* (mother of 15-year-old boy with ADHD)

It was striking that, when asked what help they hope for from social services, the most common response from young people was also for help with their own behaviour. A number of them were clearly motivated to accept social work help and wanted workers to:

> *Calm me down – stop me being angry.* (boy, 14 years)

> *Help me with my behaviour – telling me different ways to react.* (girl, 12 years)

> *Help me to understand and change my aggressive behaviour, anger and bad language.* (boy, 13 years)

Both young people and parents expressed a wish for some kind of family mediation. Several of the young people mentioned that they wanted all the arguments at home to stop, to 'stop us arguing and fighting', 'calm us both down' or 'help to make family life happier'. Most felt that their own 'attitude' was part of the problem and wanted help to change that, but a few felt that it was principally a parent who needed to change.

A number of parents also said that they hoped that workers would offer support, understanding and guidance to their children, and in some cases they specifically asked for counselling for the child, for example, 'to sort out what is going on inside his head.' Some anticipated that support workers would be able to offer their children a positive relationship, someone they could talk to. They hoped the young people might open up to someone outside the family and begin to work on their difficulties:

> *To help her get to the bottom of her problems that she couldn't deal with me.* (mother of girl, 14 years)

A few parents anticipated that through this relationship workers might help to build up their children's confidence and self-esteem. Similarly, some young people expressed a wish for someone who would listen to them and understand them to whom they could talk about their problems and who would help them to change:

> *I wanted them to help me and to see what was wrong with me.* (girl, 12 years)

> *Help me stop taking overdoses.* (girl, 15 years)

Education was recognised as a major area of difficulty and both young people and parents hoped for assistance with school problems. At least some of the young people accepted that they had to go to school and felt they needed help to make this happen. This meant help in finding a school for them to go to because they had been excluded, or help in stopping their truancy, or stopping bullying or moving to a school where they would be happier.

The overwhelming focus, however, was on a desire by both young people and parents for advice regarding child behaviour problems and their consequences, often accompanied by a wish for help in rebuilding parent–child relationships.

Comparing the groups using specialist and mainstream services

There were no significant differences between the group referred to specialist support teams and the comparison group using the mainstream service in terms of age, gender, disability, family composition or whether the child had a statement of special educational needs, as we saw in the previous chapter. Neither were there any significant differences between them in relation to truancy, school exclusion, offending, running away, the number and severity of problems reported at referral, nor in the ages at which parents considered the child's difficulties to have started. There was also no difference in whether young people had ever been accommodated in the past or, specifically, during the six months prior to this referral. This was important for the purpose of comparison, since studies in the USA have found that those previously placed were at higher risk of further placement.

However, the young people using specialist teams were more than twice as likely to have been known to social services for more than three years (44%) as those receiving a mainstream service (20%), an indicator that their difficulties were more likely to have been long term.[14] Past concerns about abuse (though not neglect) were more likely in relation to those in contact with specialist teams, as these concerns had been raised in the past in respect of 40 per cent of those in the experimental group but only 17 per cent of those in the control group.[15] Chronic difficulties therefore appeared to be more common among those referred to support teams, and this might potentially have an effect on outcomes for this group.

In addition, young people's mean scores for total difficulty on the SDQ (young person questionnaire only) were significantly higher for the group using specialist teams.[16] On their own assessment, this group's emotional and behavioural difficulties appeared to be more severe. However, there was no significant difference between groups on the *parents'* SDQ ratings. As we saw in the previous chapter, there was also some difference between parents in the two groups. Mean scores for mental distress, as measured by the General Health Questionnaire, were significantly higher for parents using the mainstream service.

---

[14] Type of service by whether there had been contact with social services for less than three years or for three years or more was tested using the chi-square test: significant at $p = .009$.

[15] Chi-square tests: duration of problem by type of service significant at $p = .001$; past abuse by type of service significant at $p = .002$.

[16] One-way anova significant at $p = .032$.

Scores on the two other standardised outcome measures used in the study and on the Severity of Difficulties measure were also compared. Across the sample as a whole, no significant differences in scores were found between the two groups in terms of family functioning (using the Family Assessment Device) or young people's ratings of their well-being (using Cantril's Ladder from the Lancashire Quality of Life Profile). Scores for young people using either specialist or mainstream services are shown in Appendix 1.

Taken together, the differences in young people's scores for emotional and behavioural difficulties, in their histories of past contact with social services and past abuse, their recent use of mental health services and contact with psychologists suggest that, as a group, the difficulties of young people using support teams were both more long-standing and more severe. However, the picture is somewhat mixed, as measures of the number and severity of problems at referral, family functioning, young people's sense of well-being (quality of life) and parents' mental well-being did not indicate greater difficulty for this group.

Although *past* concerns about abuse were more likely to be reported in relation to the group using the specialist teams, there was no difference between them in terms of workers' *current* concerns about abuse or neglect. However, those currently on the Child Protection Register were significantly more likely to be in the group using mainstream teams than those using the specialist service.[17] All but one of the five young people using the mainstream service who were registered came from a single authority (Midshire) and it is possible that this result may be influenced by local policy and practice on registration. Alternatively, it may be that thresholds for receiving a service are particularly high in this authority, since a quarter of our sample in this authority were on the Child Protection Register.

Families in both groups were, however, similar in their hopes for and expectations of the service that social workers and support teams would provide. They wanted advice on parenting strategies, help to change

---

[17] Chi-square test significant at p = .049.

undesirable behaviours, help in understanding young people's problems and support for both young people and parents.

Summary points

- Multiple difficulties were reported by parents and young people at referral and reports of violence were common. This included violence by young people towards parents, other family members or others outside the home and, as we saw in the previous chapter, in 43 per cent of the families there was known to be a history of domestic violence.
- Social workers and support workers also reported concern about abuse or neglect in relation to over half of the young people, with concerns about emotional abuse particularly common, although physical abuse was reported in relation to over one in ten.
- The majority of the young people had high levels of need, which were shown by an objective measure of behavioural and emotional difficulties (the SDQ) to be far more extensive among this group than in the wider community. For example, parents' ratings on the SDQ indicated that 76 per cent had high levels of need, whereas scores at this level would be anticipated among only 10 per cent of children in the community. SDQ scores were particularly high in relation to conduct problems and hyperactivity.
- Problems within the home went hand in hand with problems outside it, as three-quarters of the sample displayed behaviour problems at school. Rates of exclusion from school were high and truancy was a serious problem. Only 80 per cent attended mainstream school and 14 per cent had no school provision at all.
- Offending was reported by one-fifth of parents, but social workers and support workers were not always aware of this.
- Both social workers and support workers were therefore working with a group of young people with serious and multiple difficulties whose parents, as we saw in the previous chapter, had serious problems of their own.
- There was some indication that, as a group, those young people in contact with support teams were more likely to have severe emotional and behavioural problems than those using mainstream services. They

were also more likely to have long-term difficulties. In other key respects, however, the two groups were similar.

9 The interventions

Thresholds for receiving help from social services were extremely high, as the severity of difficulties for the young people who did receive either a support team or a mainstream social work service demonstrates. In most cases, it was only when families reached crisis point that social services intervened. This chapter first considers the strategies deployed by social services to manage the demand made on family support services.

The work of the support teams is then compared to that of the mainstream social work service. The methods used by the support teams and the theoretical base underpinning their work have already been outlined in Chapter 6. In this chapter, the focus is on comparing the nature, duration and intensity of the interventions by specialist and mainstream services. The chapter concludes with a discussion of competing social work aims and strategies for working with troubled and troublesome young people.

Managing demand

A number of parents described how they had approached social services for help in the past, to no avail:

> *And I'm like in tears on the phone . . . [the social worker] basically didn't want to know. And this is what I'm like saying to social services 'Please could somebody help me here, I've got an abusive violent child, I've got two little ones,' but nobody wanted to do anything.* (lone mother of boy, 13 years)

> *I was having a lot of trouble with her and I also suffer from depression . . . I'd hit her and then I ended up taking an overdose and my doctor wrote to them and then they thought they would get involved . . . I had a meeting with social services, we went to the meeting and I had a letter back saying they didn't want to know.* (mother of girl, 14 years)

> *They were not interested when we wanted help. Then they would call*

when one of our little ones had fallen off his bike. (mother of boy, 12 years)

I ring them up, they don't take me seriously. I feel you have to physically damage your children before they do anything. (mother of boy, 13 years)

When we've rung and asked for help they've said there's no one available. When we adopted the children we were told support would be available. (adoptive father of boy, 13 years)

It was particularly difficult for area social work teams to offer family support work. Many of the area teams in the study were seriously under-staffed, to some extent due to the national social worker shortage. In these circumstances, the majority of social workers' time was taken up by work on child protection or with looked after children, leaving little scope for preventive work. Several social workers and team managers spoke of the gatekeeping strategies employed to manage demand. Unless there were serious child protection concerns, many families referred initially received only a letter or phone call rather than a visit, on the assumption that if they were in serious need of a service they would make contact again. One team manager spoke of holding new referrals in his in-tray for a number of weeks and then closing them without assessment if the family made no further contact.

Area social workers and team managers were very concerned about the amount of unallocated preventive work, often involving young people at serious risk although not necessarily in crisis at that point in time. Some social workers appeared to be quite honest with families about the financial reasons for their inability to offer a service, as parents in two authorities explained:

I think the facilities that they say they offer should be improved because it is always the thing that they have run out of funding. They can't afford to do this and they can't afford to send nobody out and I'm sick of hearing it, I've heard it all my life. (mother of boy, 13 years)

Instead of saying 'I am sorry, there is nothing we can do, we haven't got no money' [social workers] should actually listen to us, as in support us. (father of girl, 12 years, with severe mental health problems)

Another strategy for managing demand appeared to be the downplaying of parents' concerns. A few parents complained that they had not had their concerns taken seriously on this or on previous occasions. Social workers, and occasionally support workers, had portrayed behaviour that parents considered serious as being little different from normal adolescent behaviour. In some cases, this may have been entirely justified if workers considered that parents were unduly critical of their children and that the problem lay principally with the parent rather than the child. On the other hand, we have seen that the majority of the young people were displaying some serious behavioural and emotional problems, so this response may well have been a form of "counselling out", with a view to reducing the demand for a service which was in short supply.

One reason for this "normalising" of the young people's behaviour may have been that both social workers and support workers were so used to working with families with high levels of need that some became inured to the severity of their difficulties even though parents, and often young people, were expressing considerable distress. Some workers came to see young people's problems as normal for the population they worked with, and therefore not requiring intervention, as these comments indicate:

In this case it's about troubles with behaviour, stealing, staying out late, drinking, boyfriends, school exclusion. They are pretty run-of-the-mill stuff, aren't they? (social worker of girl, 14 years)

My daughter had been sexually abused, she had taken an overdose. I needed that help but I didn't get it . . . They are very patronising and say there are children much worse off than my child. (mother of girl, 15 years)

They seemed to think a 15-year-old staying out and experimenting with drugs was normal behaviour, they actually said that. (mother of girl, 15 years)

Evidence from this study is supported by a government inspection report on one of the authorities from which our comparison group was drawn, which was published during the course of the fieldwork. This Joint Review report commented that access to social work services was inconsistent and that thresholds for receiving a service were very high. Children's cases often reached crisis point before help was offered and only a small proportion of initial referrals were transferred on for longer-term work. This inspection recommended that more resources were needed to divert older children from the care system.

The gatekeeping strategies employed by authorities in this study meant that, in effect, agency needs were prioritised over young people's needs. Such strategies were also likely to be effective (for the agency) as a short-term means of reducing rates of accommodation, through a privileging of service outcomes over outcomes for young people. Levels of resourcing for children's services, together with the effects of the national social worker shortage, clearly have a profound impact not only on the level of family support services available but also on workforce psychology. In the struggle to manage demand, managers and workers develop strategies that in themselves serve as a further barrier for families seeking much-needed help from hard-pressed services.

While rationing and demand management are inevitable in the provision of any publicly funded service, it is clear that there are particular pressures on social services to manage the demand for family support services. In the context of the performance targets for social services, discussed in Chapter 2, and of wider public pressure to manage the risks associated with abuse, there may be a perverse incentive for managers and social workers to prioritise child protection services and services for looked after children at the expense of family support services.

Duration and intensity of interventions

Support workers typically worked with families for a shorter period of time than did social workers, as shown in Table 9.1.

One-third of support team cases were closed within three months and over three-quarters (77%) within six months, whereas just 17 per cent of social workers had closed cases within three months and just over a third (37%) within six months (irrespective of whether a support team was also working with the family). Social workers worked with families about

Table 9.1
Duration of contact with families

	Social workers % (n = 71)	Support workers % (n = 126)
Under 6 weeks	11	6
6 weeks to under 3 months	6	28
3 months to under 6 months	20	43
6 months and over	63	24
Mean (weeks)	*36*	*19*

Table 9.2
Face-to-face contacts with families

Type of worker	*Mean number of contacts*	*Mean number of hours*
Support workers (n = 13)	18.6	33
Social workers (n = 93)	10.1	11

twice as long as support teams, for an average of nine months in comparison with an average of just under five months for support teams.

The total duration of contact with families was similar for social workers across all authorities. However, there was more variation between support teams. For example, whereas Met East support workers were involved with families for just over 14 weeks on average, their colleagues in City were involved for just over 25 weeks.[1]

Although support workers typically stayed in touch with families for a much shorter period of time, they had on average a *greater number of contacts* and *more hours* of contact with them than social workers, as shown in Table 9.2.[2] On average, support workers had nearly twice as many face-to-face contacts with families and spent three times as many hours with them, compared to social workers. However, the number of

---

[1] Kruskal Wallis test, significant at p = .027.

[2] Independent samples T-test, significant at p = .014. As we saw in Chapter 1, in most cases follow-up time was in the range 6–7 months and variations in follow-up time did not result in any systematic bias (see Table 1.6).

contacts by both types of worker varied considerably between local authorities.

Social workers offering only a mainstream social work service had less direct contact with families (a mean of 8.5 hours) than they did with families who received the specialist service (a mean of 12.5 hours of face-to-face contact). Overall, the intensity of contact with social services staff was greater for families receiving the specialist service (who saw both social workers and support workers), who had on average over 45 hours of contact with social services over the six-month period compared to less than nine hours for those receiving the mainstream service.[3]

The nature of the interventions

At follow-up, workers were asked to tick a list of possible areas of work that they had undertaken with families (and could indicate any other interventions not included in the list if necessary). Although both social workers and support workers worked on the same issues, there were differences in the balance between different types of work undertaken. Where support teams were involved, families were twice as likely to receive interventions that offered strategies to young people, parents, or both, in respect of changing the young person's behaviour and addressing their emotional problems. Workers delivering the specialist service were also roughly twice as likely to offer direct work on improving family relationships, including working on reframing parent–child communication and mediating between them.

The specialist service also appeared to offer a greater emphasis on exploring underlying problems within families, although this was somewhat surprising as most teams said that they were principally concerned with a focus on change in the here-and-now. They were also more likely to offer support to improve parental care. However, there were no significant differences in the provision of other interventions to improve parenting capacity. Neither were there any significant differences between the two types of service in the provision of practical, financial or other material help.

---

[3] One-way anova, p = <.001.

While social workers offering a mainstream service did undertake direct work with young people and parents, support workers typically engaged in *more* direct work both with young people and parents. Social workers' case management role involved the co-ordination of services from other professionals within or outside social services. However, apart from some social workers in City who were able to draw on a pool of sessional staff, in the absence of a specialist family support team they generally had fewer resources available to them to allow for the provision of very much direct work by others and, as we have already seen, in most cases they themselves had fewer opportunities for face-to-face contact with families referred for family support. This was due to the prioritisation of other types of work.

Interventions by the support workers

With their greater opportunities for direct work, support workers were able to develop their specialist skills in working with older children and teenagers. This helped them to engage successfully with many of those referred to them. Since their contact was more intensive, this also helped them to rapidly build relationships, as they could spend time listening to young people and demonstrating their understanding and concern. Contact time was needed to build trust, which was often a prerequisite to engaging young people and so working with them successfully. Social workers, on the other hand, rarely had the time to build relationships with young people due to other demands on them. The support teams' participative approach centred on building strengths rather than focusing on deficits, and this too may have helped workers to engage both young people and parents.

In most cases, support workers focused both on helping parents to develop more effective parenting strategies and on helping young people to manage their own behaviour. Although the intention was usually to focus on the present situation and how it might be changed, there was sometimes some exploration of underlying causes of problems as well.

> *We used the parenting group to reinforce her parenting, support her parenting and support her in setting some boundaries, and allowing her to talk to him about the reasons for his angry outlook as well . . . In his past there's quite a lot of issues, so it was to give him the chance to explore those to see if they were causing his behaviour and also we*

talked about how he could manage his anger. (support worker of boy, 13 years, previously abused by his father and currently involved in offending)

(The support worker) was brilliant. With Emma it was about her boundaries, what she should be looking for in the home, what she should be looking for out of the home. With me it was about things like, when she does start, help her step back, things like that. It was really helpful . . . A lot of good things she told us, like confronting her, and because we were predicting what she was going to do, she wouldn't do it . . . If we do have a grievance with her, instead of using 'you' we've got to use 'I' statements. Like when she's late in, instead of saying 'You are late, you're supposed to be home' I've got to say 'I'm not very happy and I'm worried because you're not home.' And that seems to work as well. (mother of girl, 13 years, violent to her parents and to others)

Although workers paid a lot of attention to helping young people change their behaviour, they were obviously aware that the development of behavioural problems was often linked to their experience of emotional or other kinds of abuse, or severe conflict between their parents, or inconsistent parenting. The two-pronged focus on parenting and on young people's behaviour was therefore likely to be helpful. However, workers sometimes felt it was a little unfair to expect young people to change in cases where the underlying problems were clearly rooted in a parent's negative attitude towards them. Nevertheless, in the context of such difficult practice dilemmas, they were usually pragmatic about what they felt needed to be done in the child's best interests, as one explained:

I mean, the social worker is very much coming from the point of view that the mother has got to change before we can do any work with this child, but that isn't to me realistic. Yes, I wanted to avoid the trap, I did not want to put pressure on him to come up to his mum's expectations to get mum off his back, but at the same time I knew that this is a real, ongoing, deeply entrenched thing, so we had to move a little way towards it. (support worker, explaining his reasons for working on behavioural problems with 11-year-old)

While the focus was principally on enhancing parenting skills and changing the young people's behaviour, workers were also concerned to build the young people's self-esteem and develop their social skills, sometimes through involving them in groups or encouraging them to take part in youth clubs and local sports or other leisure activities. The intensive work undertaken by support workers was usually multi-faceted, addressing difficulties in different domains of the young people's lives: in their families, at school, in their peer groups. The following case example illustrates the wide-ranging nature of the work typically undertaken by support workers.

Heather, age 11, lived with her mother, who suffered from depression and had recently separated from Heather's stepfather. The social worker felt her mother was emotionally abusive, neglectful and unable to demonstrate affection, due to her own institutionalisation during a lengthy episode in care as a child. Heather was deeply unhappy at home, did not like her stepfather and had run away repeatedly, explaining: 'I was scared coming home all the time.' She stole from her family, was violent, was sniffing gas and had made several recent attempts to hang herself. Her support worker described the wide-ranging nature of her intervention.

With mum, I've tried to talk to her about strategies that are likely to work and strategies that aren't and tried to help her improve her understanding of why Heather behaves the way she does and talking to her about the way she copies mum's coping strategies. Mum will go on and on and then throw her hands up and say "I'm going to take all my tablets" as a means of controlling Heather. I've tried to say to mum "you need to be clear with her what you want". What she tended to do was not give her any guidance, not give her any boundaries and then when she overstepped them, you know, go up like a bottle of pop. I see a lot of the difficulties coming from the past. I didn't do many in-depth discussions but I've tried to encourage her to look at them, to think about it.

I did some work (with Heather) around the dangers of gas. We have got some cards, you know, all about gas and dope and that sort of stuff. I tried to introduce her to youth clubs and things that wouldn't cost a lot of money, that her mum would continue doing after the service was withdrawn . . . She has been introduced to a counsellor . . . She has done the anger management course and that had a double purpose as well. It is done in a group so it is with other young people, to try to improve co-operation and that kind of thing between young people.

She had several episodes of weekend respite with her paternal grandma . . . I have tried to engage with mum's partner but that's not been very successful because he just comes and goes. I've tried to help her link up with her birth father but that's proving difficult because his new wife doesn't know anything about her so it's not possible, which is a shame.

Heather was positive about the help she received:

We watch TV and then I talk to her about how school's been, how the past has been, if I had had any bad feelings or anything, iron the anger out . . . I tell her everything and then I don't have the problem again. It's just like, when I release them, I don't have them again, the problems. Feels like . . . a clean part of my heart's been put in, instead of the bad side of it.

The role of social workers

In most cases, the social workers of young people referred to the support teams remained responsible for case management and co-ordination. They often liaised with other agencies to obtain services for the family and sometimes worked more closely with other agencies on the young person's behalf, particularly with schools. They were also responsible for dealing with any child protection concerns that arose. In some cases, they would work with a parent while the support worker worked with the young person, or vice versa, or they would visit the family from time to time to discuss how the work with the support team was going. In most cases, however, responsibility for direct work with the family was handed over to the support team for the duration of their involvement. Most social workers had little time to work directly with families, but could commission this work from support teams, as this support worker explained:

What you do is, you work with families, you work with them to empower them to sort out their problems . . . If the social workers haven't got the

> *time to do it then at least somebody's doing it . . . I haven't got case-holder responsibility, so that means I can concentrate on the work that needs doing.*

For those young people receiving the mainstream service, the extent of social worker intervention was also variable. In some cases, social workers focused predominantly on obtaining services for the family from other agencies, such as family therapy or adolescent mental health services or, for example, battling with an education authority to provide schooling for a child permanently excluded from school. Some also tried to involve young people in local leisure activities, such as youth clubs or sports activities. A few social workers went further than this and worked directly with parents on parenting and communication, took young people out to talk to them about their difficulties, or mediated between parents and young people and addressed problems in communication between them. However, a more limited role was more common. As we have seen earlier, social workers offering a mainstream social work service generally had fewer direct contact hours with families than those who commissioned the specialist service. A greater proportion of their time was spent on the co-ordination of resources and liaison with other agencies. Details of differences between support workers and social workers in the balance of the work undertaken are given in Appendix 2.

Earlier research has shown that an informal, participative approach by workers is generally welcomed by older children and teenagers and may be more successful in engaging them (for example, Biehal *et al*, 2000). Shortly after referral, young people were asked to indicate how far they felt that workers understood them and involved them in decision-making. At this early stage in the work, young people were generally more positive

Table 9.3
Young people's views of workers (n = 106)

	Social worker %	Support worker %
Understands how she/he sees things	58	88
Involves her/him in decisions	80	92

about the support workers' working style and less positive about their social workers' approach to them, as shown in Table 9.3.

The use of sessional workers

In around one-quarter of the cases, a sessional worker also worked with the family, in most cases with the young person. Young people in touch with support teams were twice as likely to see sessional workers, as 31 per cent did so, compared to 14 per cent of those using mainstream services only. Sessional workers were mainly used to befriend young people and, through this, to give them an opportunity to discuss their difficulties and to involve them in positive activities. As one social worker explained:

> *He's a very quiet person, he hasn't got any friends or anything, he hasn't had any relationships with any sort of grown-up, so the reason* [for having a sessional worker] *was for him to have somebody he could form a relationship with, to explore activities in the local area.* (social worker of 14-year-old boy, living with a relative while parent was in prison)

Support from other agencies

Between referral and follow-up, young people were in contact with a variety of other agencies as well as with social work staff. In comparison with the six-month period prior to referral, there had been little change in the proportion in contact with child psychiatrists or psychologists, but the number in contact with education welfare officers, educational psychologists and youth workers had decreased.

Help, or alternatively a lack of support, from schools and education authorities, could have a major impact on young people. Nearly one-quarter (24 per cent) of them reported that they had received help from school staff and many were particularly appreciative of this. However, some education authorities could be less than helpful, and this often exacerbated family stress. This was particularly the case where young people had been permanently excluded for lengthy periods of time with inadequate, or no, alternative provision for their education.

Table 9.4

Professional contact with young people between referral and follow-up

Type of professional	Young people receiving service	
	%	Number
Education welfare officer	47	91
Educational psychologist	9	18
Child psychiatrist/psychologist	34	67
Youth offending team	16	31
Family centre	10	20
Drug/alcohol project	7	13
Young carers group	4	7
Youth worker	3	6

Comparing service use by the two groups

Between referral and follow-up, young people receiving the specialist service were significantly more likely to receive services from other agencies too, in comparison with those receiving the mainstream service, as shown in Table 9.5.[1] They were also likely to receive services from *more* agencies.[2]

Those referred to support teams were therefore likely to be in contact with a greater number of other agencies, and were more likely to have contact with agencies dealing with mental health, school or substance

Table 9.5

Agency involvement by follow-up by service type (n = 195)

Type of professional	Mainstream social work	Specialist support team
	% (n)	% (n)
Education welfare officer	26 (15)	56 (76)
Psychiatrist/psychologist	16 (9)	42 (58)
Drug/alcohol project	0 (0)	10 (13)

[1] Chi-square test – education welfare p<.001; psychiatrist/psychologist p = <.001; drug/alcohol project p = .015.

[2] Chi-square test: p = .007.

Table 9.6
Number of agencies involved between referral and follow-up (n = 195)

Nature of service	No other agencies %	1–2 agencies %	3 or more agencies %
Mainstream social work (n = 58)	33	57	10
Specialist support team (n = 137)	17	56	27

misuse problems. They received services that were both more intensive (on the part of social services) and more extensive (in terms of other agency involvement). Those with the highest levels of need may attract a wider range of services but this may also be an indication that this group might be the most difficult to help, which could have implications for the outcomes that might be achieved in work with them.

The multi-agency context in which both the specialist support team service and the mainstream social worker service took place also has other important implications for attempts to measure the outcomes of these services, as it is difficult to disentangle the relative effects of specific types of service being offered at the same time. For example, a social worker may have a considerable, but indirect, impact on outcomes for a family through assessing them and then referring them to a family therapy service or mental health practitioner, or by lobbying the child's school or education authority to improve the support offered to the child. At the same time, they may or may not undertake direct therapeutic work with families themselves, or may commission their local support team to undertake this. Equally, while support teams normally undertook direct work with families, they too tried to link them to other resources or intervened with other agencies, such as schools.

The multi-agency environment in which children's services are delivered, and the complex ways in which services may interact to produce a particular effect, make it difficult to tease out the relative impact of each separate service. It follows that, in teasing out the relative effectiveness of a support team or a mainstream social work service in this context of concurrent interventions by other agencies, caution is needed to avoid making over-certain claims about causal links between any single intervention and the outcomes with which it is associated.

The nature of work with young people

Support workers who, for the most part held vocational rather than professional qualifications, often used structured programmes and resources, while professionally qualified social workers acted as case managers and had a largely administrative role. Of course this pattern varied, with some social workers engaging more directly in work with families, but the general pattern was for them to oversee work undertaken by others. Taken together with the extensive use of sessional staff, this represents evidence of a degree of de-professionalisation in work with young people. This is part of a more widespread trend towards de-professionalisation in public sector services, as evidenced by the use of learning mentors in schools and the shift towards increasing use of unqualified sessional workers and volunteers to carry out face-to-face work in youth justice (Pitts, 2001). De-professionalisation results in a cheaper, more flexible workforce, making it easier for overstretched services to respond to demand.

Professionally qualified social workers were assessing families and then passing on much of the work with them to support teams largely composed of staff without professional qualifications, to carry out task-focused work (often using structured programmes, worksheets and similar resources). These staff had considerable skills and experience, in most cases developed over many years of looking after children in residential care. However, the shrinkage of the children's residential sector will mean that in future years such a pool of staff with long experience in work with young people will no longer be available and more attention will be needed to ensuring that staff are suitably qualified.

The goals of the largely task-focused work undertaken by support teams were, principally, helping parents to develop skills that were more effective in managing young people's behaviour, a reduction in problematic behaviour by young people and parents, and a reduction in parent–child conflict. Of course, such goals were agreed with families at the start of the work and, as we saw earlier, this was the kind of help that they wanted. Parents and young people were therefore helped to change their behaviours, and as we shall see in the chapters that follow, many felt that this was helpful. There was little time, however, to address broader questions of motivation and need, underlying issues that might have longer-term consequences both for young people's well-being and their behaviour. In work on anger management, for example, people are not asked to consider why they feel a loss of control or reflect on the roots of their impulsive behaviour, but are instead taught to "manage" their anger, to work out what actions to take if they feel aggressive (Howe, 1996). This may indeed be very helpful, but underlying conflicts may continue to manifest themselves in other ways.

Given the tight timescales and demands of other work, social workers and support workers were obliged to focus largely on changing behavioural performance rather than consider in depth such issues as poor attachment, emotional abuse, rejection, or the continuing effects on young people's emotional health of domestic violence or other parental problems. Non-professional staff were not trained for work of this kind and in any case it would have been difficult for them to undertake it in the context of providing a short-term service. As for social workers, they had little opportunity to do it, given the demands of their case management role and the prioritisation of other areas of work. Where they did not have local support teams or sessional staff to assist them, as in two of the comparison authorities, little face-to-face work could be undertaken with families.

This concentration on changing surface actions and behavioural performance, with little time to focus in any depth on the messy, complex problems that might underlie them, has been identified as a more widespread phenomenon within social work, not confined to preventive work with young people (Howe, 1996). This is not to say that underlying problems were ignored, as both support workers and social workers clearly recognised their impact and some indicated that they had addressed these issues. However, this was not a central strand in their work.

The task-oriented practice which has become increasingly common in contemporary social work, with its focus on the development of concrete skills and performance-related changes in child and family functioning, allows staff without a professional grounding in psychologically- and sociologically-based social work theories to undertake work with families. These strategies allow for the de-professionalisation of work with young people, which may help to reduce service costs and facilitate the provision of help to families who might not otherwise receive a service. It has been argued elsewhere, however, that the shift in focus from a concentration on the actor to a concentration on the act, requires workers to perform as technicians following a handbook rather than as skilled, autonomous professionals (Howe, 1994). The "here and now" focus on what people do rather than why they do it, in the context of brief, time-limited interventions, means that each time a case is re-opened, a fresh set of negotiations leads to a fresh set of goals for the behaviour of service users, which may be unrelated to past events and past interventions (Howe, 1996).

To sum up, families' expectations of the service that they wanted, described in the previous chapter, appear to have been met by the service that was provided to them. They had wanted advice on parenting strategies, help to change undesirable behaviours, help in understanding young people's problems and support for both young people and parents. On the whole, this appears to be what they got. Their views on whether they found this service helpful are discussed in the next chapter.

Summary points

- Thresholds for receiving a service were very high. Many parents spoke of their difficulties in obtaining help before the situation reached crisis point. This problem appeared to be particularly severe in areas which did not have a support team service.
- Social workers were very concerned about their inability to allocate preventive work due to resource shortages, including staff shortages.
- Parents felt that some social services staff failed to take their concerns seriously.
- Support workers worked with families for around half as long as social workers (on average less than five months, compared to just over nine months).
- During the six-month follow-up period, support workers had nearly twice as many face-to-face contacts with families as social workers and spent three times as many hours with them.
- Support workers were able to undertake more direct work with families than social workers, which gave them greater opportunities for building relationships with young people and engaging them in the work.

Their principal focus was on helping young people to change their behaviour and helping parents to improve their parenting strategies.

- Young people using the support team service were more likely to be in contact with psychiatrists, psychologists, education welfare staff and drug/alcohol counselling agencies, than those using the mainstream service. They were also typically in contact with a greater number of agencies overall.

- There was some evidence of deprofessionalisation in interventions with young people and their families. Most direct work was undertaken by unqualified staff, who often used a variety of structured programmes and resources.

- The focus was principally on changing behavioural performance by both young people and parents, with relatively little attention to questions of motivation and need.

10 Outcomes for the young people

A key question for this study is whether, given the differences in the nature of their work, the support teams were *more* likely to be successful in helping young people and families resolve their difficulties than the mainstream social work service. Six months after referral, we compared the outcomes for the young people receiving the two types of service in relation to the number and severity of the difficulties reported at this point, their emotional and behavioural difficulties, their perceptions of well-being, general family functioning and their parents' psychological state.

This chapter also explores whether any particular characteristics of either the young people or the types of service had any effect on outcomes. Finally, it reports on whether families were satisfied with these changes and whether they thought that the services they received were effective in helping them.

Comparing levels of need in the two groups

Comparisons of effectiveness are only meaningful if the groups of young people using each type of service are equivalent in key respects. If they are not, then any differences in outcomes might arguably be due to differences in the characteristics and circumstances of the young people rather than differences between the two types of service. This study attempted to identify young people using the mainstream service who were similar to those using support team services, as outlined in Chapter 5. Inevitably, though, there were some differences between them despite these efforts. These have been discussed in the preceding chapters and are summarised in Table 10.1.

Table 10.1
Similarities and differences between the groups at referral (n = 209)

Differences	*Support team service*	*Mainstream service*
Chronic difficulties (>3 years)	44%	20%
Past abuse	40%	17%
Recent contact with child psychiatrist/ psychologist	44%	17%
Recent contact with educational psychologist	35%	19%
SDQ score for emotional/behavioural difficulties (on young people's rating, but not parents' rating)	Worse	Better
Score for parents' mental well-being (on GHQ)	Better	Worse

No difference between groups

Child characteristics, family composition, school exclusion, truancy, offending, running away, drug and alcohol misuse, number and severity of difficulties reported, past placement in care and initial scores for family functioning and child quality of life.

Changes in the number and severity of problems

The vast majority of the young people had multiple difficulties at referral and there were no differences in this respect between those receiving the two types of service. At follow-up, there was a substantial decrease in the number of problems reported, as shown in Table 10.2.

Table 10.2
Change in number of problems reported by parents (n = 209)

Number of problems	*At referral % (n = 203)*	*At follow-up % (n = 134)*
1–5	7	34
6–10	51	37
11–15	42	29

Table 10.3
Parents' view of changes in child behaviour

	Better %	*Same* %	*Worse* %	*Number**
Young person's behaviour at home	58	40	2	*135*
Behaviour outside the home	37	53	10	*132*
Parents' concern about friends	35	48	16	*122*
Stays out late	58	24	18	*101*
Parent/child arguments	47	47	6	*132*
Child 'doesn't listen'	39	50	11	*131*
Child/parent 'can't talk things over'	45	43	12	*127*
Alcohol problems	38	32	30	*66*
Drug problems	35	28	37	*60*
Violence to parent	63	24	13	*83*
Violence to others	44	36	20	*101*

*The number given is the number of young people for whom data on this measure were available both at referral and at follow-up.

The average number of problems reported fell from 9.73 to 7.62.[1] Over half (55%) reported one to five fewer problems at follow-up and 16 per cent reported six to eleven fewer. However, while there was a marked reduction overall in the number of problems, there was no significant difference in the extent of change between those receiving specialist or mainstream services.

Ratings of the severity of specific problems at referral and at follow-up (as being either major, moderate or not a problem) were also compared. There was improvement for many of the young people in relation to most of the issues that families had reported at referral, as shown in Table 10.3.[2]

Positive change appeared more likely to take place in behaviour within the home than outside it. In particular, there was a considerable decrease

---

[1] T-test significant at $p<.001$.

[2] Scores were compared using the paired samples t-test. *Better* = issues rated as a moderate or major problem at referral which were subsequently given a lower rating. *Worse* = issues rated as no problem or a moderate problem at referral which were subsequently given a higher rating. *Same* = issues rated as a moderate or major problem at referral where the rating did not change.

in young people's violence towards parents. Nearly half of the parents and young people who had previously had difficulty in resolving their problems now reported that they were better able to talk things over and over half of those who had previously complained of arguments now considered this to be a less serious problem. Staying out late, often a source of parent–child conflict, had also become less of a problem to 58 per cent of those parents who had previously complained about it. Six months after their contact with social services began, many families seemed to be finding it easier to negotiate with one another to resolve conflicts.

Where young people had been rated by themselves or by parents as having a "major" problem with alcohol at referral, they were significantly more likely to show general improvement (on both the parent and young person versions of the Severity of Difficulties measure). Presumably for the 38 per cent whose alcohol problems were reported to have improved, a decrease in alcohol use was accompanied by a general reduction in difficulties at home, although it is unclear which influenced which. There was also a greater degree of positive change among those young people whose behaviour in the home parents had rated as a moderate problem, in comparison with those whose behaviour they had considered to be a major problem. In other words, general improvement on this measure appeared more likely among those whose behaviour had been considered somewhat less problematic at referral.

Problems in behaviour outside the home also appeared to have improved, but to a lesser extent. Nevertheless, over one third of parents who had previously reported problems in behaviour outside the home, peer-related difficulties and violence to others felt that matters had improved by follow-up. For those with problems of drug or alcohol misuse, improvement was reported in over one-third of cases. However, positive change in any of the above problems was not significantly associated with whether young people received the specialist support team service or the mainstream service.

At referral, running away was reported to be a major issue for many of the young people, but by follow-up there had been a substantial decline in this behaviour. Most of the young people who had run away during the six months prior to referral had ceased to do so, as shown in Table 10.4.

Table 10.4
Changes in running away between referral and follow-up (n = 195)

Change	Running away	%	Number
Improved	At referral but not at follow-up	51	59
Same	At referral and again by follow-up	20	39
Worse	At follow-up but not at referral	2	5
	Did not run away at all	27	52

Since running away is often an indicator of parent–child conflict or abuse, this finding adds substance to the emerging picture of positive change in family relationships for many of the young people (Safe on the Streets Research Team, 1999).

Some improvement was also reported in respect of young people's problems at school. At referral, 60 per cent of the young people were reported to have recently truanted (42 per cent in the month just prior to referral), whereas at follow-up, just 34 per cent were reported to have truanted in the past six months. However, there was little change in rates of temporary exclusion, as 35 per cent had been temporarily excluded in the month prior to referral (and 42 per cent in the preceding year), while at follow-up 34 per cent were reported to have been temporarily excluded in the preceding six months. Furthermore, permanent exclusion had become a greater problem, as 14 per cent were reported to have been permanently excluded at follow-up, compared to 10 per cent in the year prior to referral.

There was also little improvement in offending behaviour, as shown in Table 10.5. Just over one fifth of the young people (22%) had been reprimanded during the six months prior to referral, and more than half

Table 10.5
Involvement in offending between referral and follow-up (n = 195)

Change	Reprimanded or charged	%	Number
Improved	At referral but not at follow-up	9	18
	At referral and again by follow-up	13	26
Same	No reprimand or charge at either time	54	105
Worse	At follow-up but not at referral	24	46

of these had been either reprimanded or charged by the time of the follow-up interview. Furthermore, nearly a quarter who had not been in the juvenile justice system in the six months prior to referral had been reprimanded or charged in the subsequent six months. In total, 14 per cent were charged between referral and follow-up and 34 per cent (72) were reprimanded and/or charged.

Neither did there appear to be any substantial improvement in patterns of self-harm. At referral, parents had reported that 20 per cent of the young people had attempted to harm themselves in the past year. There appeared to be only a slight reduction in self-harm by follow-up, as 18 per cent were said to have harmed themselves in the preceding six months, although for six per cent this was rated by parents as a "mild" problem.

Overall, then, there appeared to be a greater degree of change in behaviour at home and in patterns of parent–child communication and negotiation, that is, in precisely those areas where social work interventions might potentially have an impact. Behaviour at school and in the community showed less improvement. It seems unlikely that social work intervention might change patterns of school exclusion since this is a product of the interaction between child and school. Although social work staff may intervene both with children and with schools, ultimately exclusion is determined by local education policy and practice. Similarly, youth offending teams might be expected to have a greater impact on patterns of offending than either mainstream social workers or the support teams.

Abuse and neglect

Between referral and follow-up, the number of young people involved in formal child protection processes doubled, so that in total one-fifth were either the subject of child protection enquiries or placed on the Child Protection Register. During the six-month study period, an additional 22 young people became the subject of new child protection enquiries or registrations. The total proportion involved in the formal child protection process during the study is shown in Table 10.6.

This increase in formal enquiries and registration as time progressed suggests that family support interventions may serve a case-finding

Table 10.6
Involvement in the formal child protection process

	At referral % (n) (n = 207)	At follow up % (n) (n = 179)	At any time % (n) (n = 209)
New enquiry	6% (12)	8% (14)	12% (26)
Newly registered	4% (8)	4% (8)	8% (16)
Total young people	10% (20)	12% (22)	20% (42)

function. A similar phenomenon was found in a large US study of family preservation services, where there was a significantly larger increase in the percentage of cases of child abuse in the group receiving intensive services, in comparison to the control group (Schuerman *et al*, 1994). This study concluded that more intensive contact with families brought with it greater surveillance, so that more abuse was detected. It is likely to be the case here, too, that contact with social services in itself made it more likely that possible abuse or neglect would be identified. At follow-up, as at referral, there was no difference between the groups in respect of the proportion of child protection enquiries or registration. The case-finding effect of contact with social work services was presumably similar for both groups.

Changes on measures of outcome for young people and families

Six months after referral, scores on all of the outcome measures showed considerable improvement overall but there were no statistically significant differences in the extent of change between the two groups on any of the measures used. Details of the change scores on our measures of the severity of the young people's difficulties, their emotional and behavioural difficulties, their perceptions of well-being and in general family functioning and parents' psychological health are given in Appendix 2. In comparing the differences in scores on these measures between referral and follow-up, we took young people's initial scores into account.[1]

---

[1] For all the outcome measures compared, differences in mean scores between referral and follow-up were tested using a one-way anova, with the initial score as covariate to adjust for differences in initial state.

Change in the severity of difficulties

Given that many families reported positive changes in relation to the specific difficulties they had complained of at referral, it is not surprising that total scores on the Severity of Difficulties measure had decreased by follow-up. The mean score for young people fell from 10.42 at referral to 7.41 at follow-up, while the change was even greater on the parent version, which fell from a mean of 17.21 to 12.53.[2] Many parents and young people clearly felt that, in overall terms, difficulties were less severe at follow-up than they had been at referral. However, there was no difference in the degree of change between those using specialist and mainstream services.

Changes in emotional and behavioural difficulties (the SDQ)

Scores on our measure of emotional and behavioural difficulties, the SDQ, showed a striking degree of improvement overall.

Table 10.7
SDQ Total Difficulties scores at referral and at follow-up*

| *Source* | *Low need* | *Some need* | *High need* |
(number at follow-up)	%	%	%
Goodman community sample	*80*	*10*	*10*
Parent ratings *(n = 134)*	25 *(9)*	20 *(15)*	55 *(76)*
Young person ratings *(n = 105)*	42 *(26)*	29 *(24)*	28 *(42)*

* % at referral is given in brackets.

A substantial minority of young people whose scores had indicated particularly high levels of difficulty showed positive change by follow-up.[3] This is remarkable, as one would not expect change in the

---

[2] T-tests significant at p<.001 for both. On the young person's version of this measure, sample attrition was 50% overall, but there was little difference in attrition between those with low scores at referral (56%) and those with high scores (50%). On the parent version attrition was 38% both overall and for those with low scores, but was only 24% for those with high scores. Therefore the difference in means noted above was *not* due to the fact that only the less difficult children were contacted at follow-up.

[3] T-tests showed that parent scores decreased significantly from a mean of 23.68 at referral to 20.50 at follow-up. For young people, scores decreased from a mean of 18.89 to 16.65, significant at p<.001 for both. This and subsequent t-tests comparing scores at T1 and T2 are for paired samples.

deep-rooted traits measured by the SDQ to be associated with a short-term social work intervention. Although those with very high scores for difficulty at referral may have shown some natural improvement over time, this is unlikely to account for the full extent of change that occurred across the sample and it is therefore possible that the services provided did indeed have a beneficial impact.

Young people reported to suffer from ADHD had considerably worse scores on the SDQ at referral (on parent rating) than those not reported to have ADHD. Positive change appeared to be harder to achieve with this group since, although there was some improvement in their mean SDQ scores by follow-up, there was significantly less change than for other young people.

However, there was no significant difference in the degree to which emotional and behavioural difficulties improved between young people receiving each type of service. Furthermore, overall levels of need for the sample remained high, in comparison with scores for a community sample (Goodman, 1997).

Changes in general family functioning (the FAD)

General family functioning, as measured by the FAD, also showed significant improvement overall. For many families, positive change therefore occurred on those dimensions measured by the FAD, namely family problem-solving, communication, behaviour control, affective involvement and responsiveness, and general functioning. However, again there was no significant difference in the degree of change between the groups receiving each type of service.[4]

Changes in young people's perceptions of their well-being

The change in scores on Cantril's Ladder, our measure of young people's perception of their own well-being, suggested a considerable improvement in the majority of cases. For nearly three-quarters (71%) of the young people, there was some improvement in their scores on this measure and for over half (53%) this improvement was considerable (an increase of 10

---

[4] T-test showed statistically significant improvement in overall family mean scores: reduced from a mean of 2.38 to 2.23, significant at p = .001.

or more points).[5] However, for a minority (13%), scores were much worse at follow-up (decreased by 10 points or more). Yet again, there were no significant differences regarding changes on this measure between young people receiving a specialist or a mainstream service.

Changes in parents' psychological state

At referral, high levels of psychological distress were found for 72 per cent of the parents, as measured by the General Health Questionnaire (GHQ-12). By follow-up, mental well-being had improved substantially, as only 38 per cent now scored above the threshold.[6] Although initial scores had indicated slightly higher levels of mental distress among those in the comparison group, this difference had disappeared by follow-up. Yet again, there were no significant differences in the degree of change between parents receiving each type of service.

Predictors of change

The nature of the service

Since the degree of change on our measures of child and family functioning was similar for those receiving both types of service, there was no indication that receiving a service from a support term was more likely to lead to positive outcomes than receiving a mainstream social work service. The degree of change over time could not be predicted from the type of service families received. We examined this more closely, considering whether any particular *features* of the service might be associated with improvement on our outcome measures.

We saw earlier that young people receiving the specialist support team service were likely to have both a greater *number* of face-to-face contacts with social services staff and more *hours* of contact than those receiving the mainstream service, even though the support teams worked with families for a much shorter period of time overall than social workers. However, neither the extent of face-to-face contact by workers nor the

---

[5] T-test shows mean score rose from 53.81 at T1 to 66.59 at T2, a mean overall change of 12.78 points, significant at p <.001.

[6] The t-test showed a mean score at referral of 6.96, while at follow-up it was 3.85, p<.001.

total duration of the intervention were associated with change on our outcome measures. There have been similar findings in the USA, where the largest randomised experimental study of family preservation services found that the duration and intensity of contact with workers was not associated either with subsequent child maltreatment or with rates of placement (Schuerman *et al*, 1994).

The only exception to this pattern was for young people who reported that they did *not* feel that their situation had improved since referral. For this group, the total duration of contact with social workers was longer (a mean of 21.57 weeks) than for those who rated their current circumstances more positively (mean total duration of contact 13.65 weeks).[7] This is likely to be due to the fact that cases open for a longer period of time are normally those that are most difficult to resolve. Equally, for those who improved, the duration and intensity of contact is likely to be influenced by the interaction between the range, nature and severity of problems, by how rapidly workers manage to engage young people and parents in working to change them and by the pressure of other work. In other words, factors relating to the families themselves and system factors are both likely to be important in determining the amount of worker contact.

We also examined whether specific elements of the interventions, such as help with young people's behaviour, work on parenting strategies, mediation, help with substance abuse (and others outlined in Appendix 2), were associated with change on our five outcome measures, but this was not the case. This is not surprising, since it is not only the type of intervention *per se* (for example, help with parenting strategies) but the skill with which it is delivered and its integration with other aspects of the service that is likely to lead to change. These processes may be captured more easily through the analysis of case studies in Chapter 13 than through statistical analysis.

---

[7] Significant at $p = .037$.

Characteristics of the young people and families

We therefore explored whether other factors, such as child and family characteristics or history, might predict change in relation to our key measures of child and family functioning, the SDQ and the FAD. In order to do this, we took account of the initial scores, which in the case of both these measures was strongly correlated with improvement ($p<.001$ in both cases). In other words, young people who scored "worse" at referral showed a greater degree of change for the better. After adjusting for the initial scores in this way, we found that there was no variation in the scores on either of these measures in relation to the age or the sex of the young people and little variation in relation to the specific nature of child difficulties at referral.

We also considered whether areas of difference between the two groups at referral, namely recent contact with a psychiatrist, child psychologist or educational psychologist and the presence of chronic problems, were associated with the degree of change at follow-up. However, none of these proved to be associated with changes in either child or family functioning.

For all of our outcome measures, the key predictor of the extent of change that occurred was the severity of difficulties at referral. Those whose scores indicated the most severe difficulties at referral improved to the greatest extent.[8] For those in a state of extreme crisis at referral, there is little scope for matters to get even worse and, in any case, after any crisis there is likely to be some (relative) improvement so that scores for difficulty are likely to move closer to the average for any particular group of people, a phenomenon known as regression to the mean.

Comparing specialist and mainstream services

We have seen that, although there was considerable improvement across the sample as a whole, there were no significant differences between the groups receiving specialist or mainstream services. No significant differences between the two groups were detected in relation to the decrease in the number of problems reported, the proportion for whom specific

---

[8] Linear regression showed that for all measures except the SDQ, scores at referral were the only significant predictors of change.

problems improved and changes in scores on our measures of emotional and behavioural difficulties, child perceptions of well-being, family functioning, the severity of child difficulties and parental mental health. Since the specialist teams offered a more intensive service, we might have expected better outcomes in comparison with mainstream services, but this was not the case.

There are various possible explanations for this rather disappointing result. First, the young people receiving the specialist service may have been in greater difficulty, but in ways that we were not able to take into account. Second, the services provided by the mainstream teams may have been adequate for the problem. Third, the difficulties presented by some young people may have been too severe to allow for more than a temporary improvement.

We saw earlier that, although the nature and severity of specific problems was similar for young people receiving both types of service, for the sample as a whole those with high scores for total difficulty (on the child-completed version of the SDQ) were more likely to be found in the group receiving the specialist service. Further analysis showed that these young people with high scores for emotional and behavioural difficulties at referral were also more likely to have high scores for problems in family functioning and to have given lower ratings for well-being.[9]

Also, as we saw in Chapter 8, young people in contact with specialist support teams were more than twice as likely to be known to social services long term. Several studies of interventions with children have found that positive outcomes are harder to achieve with families with multiple, longer-term problems (Cleaver and Freeman, 1995; Biehal *et al*, 2000; Thoburn *et al*, 2000). Similarly, a study of social work with families found that longer-standing social problems and poor coping abilities were associated with poor outcomes for parents at 12-month follow-up, whereas short-term acute crises were associated with prompt restitution (Goldberg and Huxley, 1992).

---

[9] Correlations significant at p = .017 (FAD) and p = .010 (Cantril's Ladder). There was a weak but significant correlation between initial SDQ child scores and both the FAD (.250, p = .001) and Cantril's Ladder (−.250, p = .001).

These differences suggest that the young people receiving the specialist service were indeed in greater difficulty, despite our efforts to ensure the equivalence of the two groups of young people. However, the differences in difficulty that we detected between them were not sufficiently great to account for the lack of difference in the extent of improvement (although it is possible that with more sensitive measures or larger numbers, we may have detected some difference in outcomes).

It was also clear that in City, from which half of our comparison sample was drawn, at least some of those receiving the mainstream service could receive substantial support. This possibility could have reduced the apparent effects of the specialist intervention. It remains likely, however, that the specialist teams provided support to some young people who, in other authorities, would have received no support whatsoever.

It is possible therefore that if there *were* some difference in the effectiveness of the two types of service, we have not been able to detect it, either because the specialist teams were working with a group of young people whose difficulties were more likely to be chronic and severe, or because around half of those in the comparison group were receiving an enhanced service. Alternatively, of course, it may equally be true that neither service was more effective than the other in producing change.

We should not, perhaps, be surprised at the absence of any detectable difference in outcomes between the two groups. As we saw in Chapter 4, numerous large-scale studies of intensive family preservation services in the USA also failed to find any major differences in outcomes between intensive and mainstream services. As in this study, none of the US studies have succeeded in resolving the question of whether this lack of observed differences in effectiveness is due to the absence of any real difference, the poor targeting of services or problems in study design.

Motivation and change

Qualitative analysis of case study material (discussed in Chapter 13) suggested that there was a relationship between child and family motivation to work on addressing their difficulties and positive outcomes, and other studies have indicated a similar relationship (Buchanan, 1999; Biehal *et al*, 2000). This link between motivation and positive change was therefore explored through statistical analysis. In order to establish whether or not they were motivated, both parents and young people were asked shortly after referral whether or not they wanted to try to work with support workers and social workers to deal with their difficulties.

Almost all parents using the specialist service (97%) and nearly three-quarters of the young people referred to it appeared to be motivated to work with support workers. Slightly fewer were keen to work with social workers as 89 per cent of parents and 64 per cent of young people indicated some motivation. For both, motivation was associated with perceptions that each worker understood how they felt, involved them in making decisions and made their plans clear to them. Those who were motivated also indicated that they were optimistic about workers' ability to help them.[10] These associations suggest that motivation and worker skills in engaging service users were closely related to one another. Certainly, young people who were motivated were likely to be easier to engage in a working relationship, but equally, if workers were skilful in engaging young people, they might become motivated even if they had not been so initially.

Motivation was also associated with whether problems were long term. Both young people and parents were significantly less likely to indicate motivation if they had been known to social services for three or more years.[11] Having chronic difficulties, which as we have seen were more common among those using the specialist teams, therefore made families less motivated and hence they were likely to be harder to engage. Despite this, young people receiving the specialist service were significantly more likely to indicate that they were motivated to work towards change (65%), in comparison with those receiving the mainstream service (40%). The pattern was similar for parents, and also for cases where both parents and young people were (jointly) motivated. It is therefore possible that support workers, through their more intensive contact with families (particularly

---

[10] Chi-square tests: most associations significant at $p = .01$, some significant at $p = .05$.

[11] Chi-square test showed that 57% of young people who indicated motivation and 61% of parents who were motivated had been known to social services for three years or less, significant at $p = .024$ (young people) and $p = .047$ (parents).

in the early stages of the work), were able to engage them more successfully and engender greater motivation for change.

Across the sample as a whole, positive changes in family functioning, measured by the FAD, were more likely if the young person was motivated or if both the young person and parent were motivated.[12] In other words, those who were motivated were likely to make good use of either type of social work service. Since, as we will see in Chapter 13, the principal focus of interventions proved to be on changes in family interaction, it is not surprising that our measure of family functioning reflects this change once motivation is taken into account, rather than the other measures used.

Unlike the studies cited earlier, there was no association between duration of problems and the degree of change. However, the effect of having chronic difficulties may have operated indirectly through its association with motivation, which *was* directly associated with outcomes. The fact that those who were motivated tended to improve upon receiving a service, irrespective of the nature of that service, perhaps swamps any possible differences in outcome between specialist and mainstream services.[13]

Young people's and parents' views of outcomes

At follow-up, young people and parents were invited to comment on whether they felt the young person's situation had improved since referral. The majority of the young people and around half of the parents reported a positive change in circumstances, as shown in Table 10.8.

Overall ratings of satisfaction with outcomes were associated with improvement on other measures of change. Where young people reported that their situation had improved, there were improved scores on the child well-being scale, the parent's version of the SDQ and the child's version of the Severity of Difficulties measure. Similarly, parents' ratings of

---

[12] Controlling for FAD score at referral, significant at $p = .022$ for 'young person motivated' and $p = .004$ for 'both young person and parent motivated'.

[13] This effect is not due to differential sample attrition,since those receiving each type of service were equally likely to be interviewed at follow-up, as were those who did or did not show motivation.

Table 10.8
Young people's and parents' views of outcomes at follow-up

	Young people % *(n = 98)*	*Parents %* *(n = 122)*
Situation has improved	79	51
Situation has stayed the same	15	28
Situation has got worse	6	21

improvement were associated with improved scores on the parent versions of the SDQ and the Severity of Difficulties measure and also on the GHQ.[14] However, there were no significant differences in views of their current circumstances between those referred to specialist support teams and those who received only mainstream social work services.

Young people and parents did not always agree as to whether their situation had changed for the better. While the majority agreed as to whether matters had either improved or not (59%), in over one-third of cases young people felt life had improved but their parents did not, as shown in Table 10.9.

Table 10.9
Agreement between young people and parents on outcomes (n = 88)

	Per cent	*Number*
Agree situation has improved	44	39
Agree situation has not improved	15	13
Parent 'improved'/child 'not improved'	7	6
Child 'improved'/parent 'not improved'	34	30
Total	**100**	**88**

Around three-quarters of parents indicated that circumstances had improved where there had been improvement in child behaviour in the home, in child violence to parents or in staying out late. Two-thirds of those parents who indicated that the situation was "better" at follow-up reported a reduction in parent–child arguments and an improvement in

---

[14] T-test, significant at p = .001 for all tests.

their ability to talk things over with one another. Over half reported general satisfaction where there was improvement in respect of their child's peer group, behaviour outside the home or violence to others.[15]

However, 35 per cent of all the young people nevertheless reported that in the last month they had felt that they would like to leave home and live with someone else. Surprisingly, even among those who felt life had improved, nearly one in three (29%) reported that in the past month they had felt that they would like to live elsewhere.[16] Matters may have improved somewhat but clearly some were experiencing continuing difficulties.

Family views on the effectiveness of professional help

Young people and parents were also asked whether social workers and support workers had helped them in any way in the past six months. Their assessments of the degree to which workers had helped are shown in Table 10.10 and Table 10.11.

Table 10.10
Parents' views of professional help (n = 140)*

How far professional helped	Social workers % (n = 85)	Support workers % (n = 81)
Helped improve situation considerably	24	43
Helped a little	26	30
Had no effect on situation	51	27

*Percentages do not add up to 100 due to rounding.

Both young people and parents were more likely to report that workers from the specialist teams had helped "considerably" than that social workers had done so. It is difficult to know how these perceptions were formed. They may be directly related to the comparative skills and efforts of the workers or they may be influenced by the degree to which each

[15] Chi-square tests: p = .001 for all items except 'staying out late', 'peer group' (both = .024) and 'violence to other' (p = .002).
[16] Chi-square test significant at p = .035.

Table 10.11
Young people's views of professional help (n = 106)

How far professional helped	Social workers % (n = 51)	Support workers % (n = 55)
Helped a lot	39	56
Helped a little	39	33
No help at all	22	11

worker had succeeded in forming a positive relationship with them. As we saw in Chapter 9, support workers are more likely to undertake direct work with families which may, in itself, be helpful, but which also involves the building of relationships with them. Also, in their role as case managers, social workers may have helped indirectly, by referring the family to a specialist support team.

Among those using the specialist service who reported that their situation had improved, the vast majority considered that the support workers had helped to bring about this change. Appraisals of help from social workers were also positive, although to a lesser degree, as shown in Table 10.12.

Table 10.12
Appraisals of social services staff by families satisfied with outcomes

	Parents % (n = 85)	Young people % (n = 53)
Social worker helped	68	78
Support worker helped	86	90

Many of the parents and young people who reported improved outcomes therefore felt that this improvement was directly related to the interventions of support workers and/or social workers.

When asked who else had been helpful, they indicated that schools and family members had been the principal sources of help. Schools were clearly an important source of support to some families, as over a quarter of the young people and nearly one-fifth of parents felt they had been

Table 10.13
Others who helped in last six months

People who helped	Parents % (n = 140)	Young people % (n = 106)
Partner	12	–
Family	19	32
Friends	–	5
School	18	26
Child psychologist	2	–
Health professional	4	–

helpful. Headteachers, teachers and learning mentors were all mentioned as sources of support in recent months.

However, neither the specific sources of help (from any agency) nor the number of sources of help were associated with change on the five outcome measures.[17] As with the specific elements of social work interventions, it is less likely to be solely the types of help or number of sources of help that predict change but the nature and quality of each intervention and the way in which it interacts with other factors. In other words, it is *how* particular interventions combine to produce change, in the context of support (or a lack of it) from relatives and friends, that is likely to be important.

Conclusion

The picture we are left with shows positive change overall for many of those referred to both types of service, rather than a clear distinction between the two in terms of effectiveness. Since many of the young people receiving both types of service had considerable difficulties and long-term underlying family problems, punctuated by periodic crises, it is unlikely that brief interventions by either type of service will definitively resolve these difficulties. However, they may defuse tensions, help to resolve crises and bring about positive changes in child behaviour within the home and in parent–child relationships. These changes may or may

---

[17] There were no statistically significant associations in this respect.

not persist over the longer term and it is likely that many of the young people with chronic difficulties, in particular, will need further help from social services from time to time.

Summary points

- Six months after referral, many of the young people and families experienced positive change in a variety of aspects of their lives. The mean number of difficulties reported fell and there was also a marked decrease in the severity of a range of specific difficulties that had troubled families at referral.
- The greatest change occurred in behaviour within the home and in patterns of parent–child communication and negotiation. Behaviour in the community showed less improvement.
- Scores on measures of emotional and behavioural difficulties, family functioning, severity of difficulties, well-being and parental mental health improved for many young people and families and there was a decrease in truancy and running away, although not in school exclusion or offending.
- Despite this promising result there was no difference in the extent of change between those receiving the specialist and the mainstream service. The specialist group were, on a number of measures, more difficult, but the extent of these difficulties was not sufficient to explain the lack of difference in apparent effectiveness.
- Some of those in the mainstream services group may have received a high standard of service, thus further diminishing the extent of difference likely to be found.
- Another important point relates to motivation, as those who were motivated tended to show improvement irrespective of the nature of the service. A proportion of people in both groups appeared likely to make use of any good social work service that is offered as a catalyst for change, particularly if they are motivated to change.
- Seventy-nine per cent of the young people and 51 per cent of parents felt that matters had improved by follow-up. However, in over one-third of cases young people felt their situation had improved, but their parents did not.

- Families were more likely to consider that support workers had contributed "considerably" more to the improvement in their situation than social workers. Young people were generally more positive than parents in their appraisals of the help given by both support workers and social workers.
- Some families also indicated that schools and other family members were important sources of support. Both of these were more likely to be viewed as helpful by young people than by parents.

11 Preventing placement: patterns, policies and resources

All of the young people recruited to this study were considered to be at some risk of placement at referral. This chapter examines whether specialist teams were any more successful in preventing placement than mainstream services. It also considers the circumstances in which placement occurred and workers' attitudes to placement.

Patterns of placement

Only a quarter of the young people entered care placements within six months, despite the fact that all of them had been considered to be at risk of placement at referral. The majority were accommodated only short-term, most often in a crisis, as one element of family support provision. Only eight per cent were expected to remain in the care system long-term.

There was some ambiguity about what actually constituted "placement". Not all of the young people placed with foster carers were accommodated under Section 20 of the Children Act 1989 as, in five of the authorities, a few placements were instead funded under the provision for

Table 11.1
Placement between referral and follow-up (n = 196)*

Placement	%	Number
Short-term placement as family support	15	29
Long-term placement anticipated	8	15
Other placement	2	5
Occasional respite care	1	2
Not looked after	74	145

* One person accommodated at referral but lost to the study by follow-up is included. The "other" types of placement included young people involved in the juvenile justice system placed in secure units or remand foster placements.

family support in Section 17 of the Act. Apart from this administrative distinction, to all intents and purposes their circumstances were no different to those of young people placed short term with ordinary foster carers so they are included with those "placed short term". Most placements tended to be short, as shown in Table 11.2:

Table 11.2
Time accommodated by follow-up (n = 39)

Time period	%	Number
Less than 1 week	33	13
1 to 4 weeks	13	5
More than 4 weeks to 3 months	18	7
More than 3 months to 6 months	28	11
More than 6 months	8	3

Nearly half of those accommodated were placed for four weeks or less, and these constituted 9 per cent of the total sample. Just 11 per cent of the total sample (21 young people) were accommodated for more than one month. Most of those placed were looked after in foster placements, although placement details were not available for all of the young people.

Table 11.3
Placement type (n = 41)

Placement	%	Number
Foster care	68	28
Children's home	27	11
Secure unit	5	2

Predictors of placement

Previous placement, which can be taken as a proxy measure of persistent child and family difficulties, was the strongest predictor of placement on this occasion.[1] Nearly half (47%) of those placed had been in care at some time in the past. This pattern is consistent with the findings of a number of US studies of family preservation services (Nelson *et al*, 1988; Fraser *et al*, 1991; Schwartz *et al*, 1991; Yuan and Struckman-Johnson, 1991). There were no significant differences between those using the specialist support teams and those using the mainstream service regarding their histories of past placement.

We then tested whether other factors were also associated with the likelihood of placement, such as emotional and behavioural difficulties, family functioning, child's quality of life, parent's mental health, severity of difficulties and a range of specific issues such as child characteristics, current child protection concerns, past histories of abuse or neglect, duration of contact with social services and involvement in offending. Multi-variate analysis showed that most of these factors were not associated with placement. Behavioural problems were cited in many cases as one of the factors that had ultimately precipitated placement in care, but no distinctions regarding the severity of behaviour problems were apparent between those who entered care and those who did not, due to the fact that complaints about extremely difficult behaviour were a feature of the vast majority of referrals.

There was, however, some evidence that young people's own view that their current problems were severe, as indicated by their scores on the Severity of Difficulties measure, were also associated with placement on this occasion.[2] Taken together, these findings suggest that, where young people had a history of chronic family difficulties (as indicated by their past placement in care) and a particularly bleak view of their current

---

[1] Chi-square test significant at p<.001. Of those previously placed in care, 46% entered care on this occasion and 18% did not.

[2] Logistic regression, with current placement as the dependent variable, showed that severity of problems on the child version of the Severity of Difficulties Scale (p = .019) and past placement were both significant predictors of placement (past placement significant at p = .001; severity of Child Difficulties significant at p = .035).

circumstances, placement on this occasion was more likely.

We also examined whether living in a particular local authority affected the likelihood of entry to care. It is well known that nationally, placement rates vary across local authorities. Consistent with this, we found significant variations between local authorities in the proportion of young people who entered care placements, with young people in Borough the most likely to be placed, followed by those in Midshire, while those in Eastshire were the least likely to be placed, followed by those in City. Although the local variation in placement suggests that there is likely to be some relationship between system factors related to local authorities and placement rates, we were not able to discern a strong local authority effect in this study, perhaps due to our small sample sizes in the individual authorities. However, there was stronger evidence that young people in the two authorities without support teams were significantly more likely to be accommodated than those which did offer this specialist service.[3] To summarise, the principal factors which appeared to influence the likelihood of placement (either short or long term) were:

- previous placement (which may be an indicator of chronic family problems);
- young people's perceptions that their difficulties were especially severe at referral;
- living in a local authority which did not have a support team.

Placement that was anticipated to be *long term* was associated with high scores for severity of difficulties when rated by young people and with poor family functioning (as measured by the FAD). Multivariate analysis showed that these factors were predictive of long-term placement irrespective of whether the child had been previously placed.[4] Scores on these

---

[3] Logistic regression: once scores on the Severity of Difficulties Scale, past placement and length of contact with social services were taken into account, local authorities had little additional effect on the likelihood of current placement, although the results were suggestive (past placement $p = .002$, length of contact with social services $p = .032$, Borough $p = .030$, Midshire $p = .021$, but other variables were not significant).

[4] Logistic regression: Child Difficulties scale $p = .001$; FAD scale $p = .001$ (chi-square 19.67, df = 2, $p<.001$). They remained significant when past placement was added to the equation: Child Difficulties $p = .002$; FAD $p = .001$; past placement $p = .007$ (chi-square 27.56, df = 3, $p<.001$).

157

two measures showed no significant difference at referral between those using specialist or mainstream services, so neither group was more likely to enter long-term care.

The nature of family structure was not associated with short-term placement. However, young people's family circumstances *were* associated with the likelihood of placement in care being long term. Those living with neither parent were more likely to enter long-term placements, even if they were living with relatives at referral. This group (who were living with adoptive parents, grandparents or other relatives) were five times more likely to be placed in what was anticipated to be long-term care than those living with both birth parents, with a lone parent, or in a stepfamily. However, poor family functioning, young people's views that their difficulties were severe and past placement were much stronger predictors of long-term placement than family structure.[5] To summarise, long-term placement appeared to be more likely where:

- young people rated their difficulties as especially severe at referral;
- young people rated family functioning as especially poor at referral;
- young people were living with neither birth parent at referral (although this factor was less influential than the other two).

Placement patterns for those using specialist or mainstream services

As we have seen, variations in placement rates between authorities suggested that placement might be less likely for young people in authorities which had specialist support teams. On the whole, a smaller proportion of young people tended to be accommodated in authorities which had specialist support teams in comparison with authorities that offered only a mainstream service. City was a clear exception to this and within-authority differences there in placement patterns for those using specialist and mainstream services will be dealt with separately. Since over half of

---

[5] Chi-square test showed that 26% of those living with neither parent were placed long term, compared to only 5% of those liiving with one or both parents (p<.001). When tested through multi-variate analysis (logistic regression), this factor was no longer significant as its effect was overwhelmed by the effects of FAD scores, Severity of Difficulties scores and past placement.

those using mainstream services came from City, the particular pattern observed there meant that there was no significant difference in *overall* placement patterns when users of support teams and of mainstream services were compared. We therefore compared placement patterns in matched groups of authorities offering the different types of service and then compared the two types of service within City itself.

When placement patterns in the two shire counties, Eastshire and Midshire, were compared, it became clear that a lower proportion of young people were placed in Eastshire, which had a support team. These counties were similar in terms of socio-economic indicators of deprivation, yet only six per cent of those referred to the Eastshire specialist support team were accommodated compared to 38 per cent of those referred to social workers in Midshire, which did not have a specialist team. With its support team and large pool of sessional staff, Eastshire had far more resources available for working with young people and their families in their home environment.

Similarly Met East and Northshire, both of which had specialist teams, were comparable in terms of socio-economic indicators to Borough, which had only a mainstream service. Two-thirds (66 per cent) of the young people from Borough were accommodated compared to only 19 per cent of those in Met East and 35 per cent of those in Northshire. Furthermore, half of all those referred in Borough were expected to remain looked after long term, compared to only seven per cent of those from Met East and 11 per cent from Northshire.

In City, where within-authority comparisons could be made between the two types of service, the picture was quite different. Overall placement rates were low, as only 15 per cent of the sample in this authority were accommodated and all of these placements were short term. The pattern, however, was quite the reverse of that found across the other authorities, since those receiving the specialist service were *more* likely to be placed (29%) than those using the mainstream service (7%).[6] There are two possible explanations for this.

First, as mentioned earlier, those referred to the support teams in City were five times more likely to have been looked after at some time in the

---

[6] Chi-square test significant at p = .03.

past and, as we have seen, those with a history of past placement are more likely to experience subsequent placement. It therefore appears that the two groups of young people in this authority were not strictly comparable, as those more likely to be placed were referred to the support teams. It is possible that this pattern may be similar in other authorities, with support teams working with those at the highest risk of placement.

Second, teenagers using mainstream services in this authority were likely to receive a more comprehensive community-based service than those in the other two authorities where mainstream services were studied, as described in Chapter 6. This may help to explain why placement was less common for those using the mainstream service in City than in Borough or Midshire, in which hard-pressed social workers appeared to have few resources for family support work other than their own (limited) time.

When City was excluded from the analysis for the above reasons, those using mainstream services were found to be twice as likely to enter care placements (50%) compared to those using the specialist support teams (25%). They were also nearly five times more likely to be placed in long-term care (29%) than those using specialist teams (6%).[7]

Table 11.4
Placement (any duration) by type of service (n = 142)

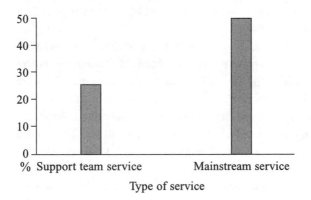

Type of service

---

[7] Chi-square test of placement by service type (excluding City) significant at p=.008. Chi-square test of actual/planned duration of placement significant at p = .004.

Table 11.5

Long-term placement anticipated by type of service (n = 142)

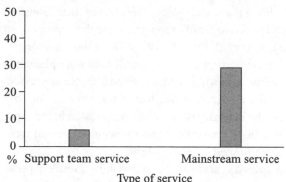

As we saw in Chapter 8, there was some indication that emotional and behavioural difficulties were more severe among young people using the specialist services, so the severity of these problems cannot explain why those using the mainstream service were more likely to be placed.

Families using the mainstream service in Midshire and Borough were generally more likely to have a bleak view of their current situation. The young people rated family functioning, the severity of their problems at referral and quality of life significantly worse in comparison with those using the specialist services in other authorities. Equally, as we saw in Chapter 7, parents' scores for psychological distress were significantly worse for those using the mainstream service.[8] This suggests that thresholds for receiving a service were higher in those authorities offering only a mainstream service, as already suggested in Chapter 9. If these families did not receive a service until they felt both desperate and depressed about their circumstances, this may help to explain why a higher proportion of those young people who *did* eventually receive a service entered care.

---

[8] Mann-Whitney U test: child version of FAD significant at p = .026; child version of Child Difficulties scale significant at p = .021; GHQ significant at p = .004; Cantril's Ladder significant at p = .017 (City was excluded from this analysis).

The influence of local policy and resources

As we saw in Chapter 6, the two authorities without support teams, Midshire and Borough, had a particularly low proportion of their resources for children's services allocated to family support, although the proportion for Northshire was the lowest of all the authorities. These three authorities also had a relatively high proportion of young people who were placed, in comparison with most of the authorities which offered a specialist service. However, nearly half of those placed in Northshire were in care for only one or two days whereas the majority of those accommodated in the other two authorities remained in placement for two weeks or more and were also more likely to remain looked after long-term.

The provision of dedicated resources for undertaking family support work, in most cases through the establishment of specialist support teams, meant that support workers, sessional workers (or, in City, specialist Principal Caseworkers for Adolescents plus sessional staff) were available to work with teenagers and their families. Where resources were not ring-fenced in this way, hard-pressed social workers offering a mainstream service struggled to balance their work with teenagers in crisis against the competing demands of other work. Adolescents are typically accorded lower priority on field social workers' caseloads than younger children or those in the child protection system (Sinclair *et al*, 1995).

The availability of residential and foster placements is also likely to have an impact on placement rates. Although, on the whole, having specialist support teams appeared to be associated both with lower placement rates for local authorities and less extensive use of long-term care, this was likely to be due to their location within a particular policy and resource context as well as to the quality of their work. If resources are diverted from residential services to outreach work, as had occurred when most of the teams were set up, then fewer young people are likely to receive a residential service. The availability of foster placements for older children and teenagers is also likely to be influential. As one social worker explained:

No teenager is at risk of placement here because there aren't any beds for them.

The in-depth interviews carried out with workers and parents also suggested that local policy, in terms of the vehement exhortations to workers to avoid placement, was also influential. In situations where workers felt that accommodation was not in the young person's best interests, these policy directives could provide helpful back- up, especially if reinforced by resources, as several of them commented:

> *Obviously the local authority's policy and the government policy on not accommodating children was very helpful because we needed to keep this young person with her family.*

> *If you have got a parent ranting and raving in reception about 'you must take this child now' there's got to be a clear policy from management. You are not allowed to say OK.*

The impact of local policy and resources is illustrated by the accounts of workers in different authorities. A social worker in Borough, which had no specialist team, explained that two things had hindered her attempts to return home a young person who had been accommodated. First, neither the young person nor her mother would engage in any discussion of alternatives to care and second, there was 'a major issue with local authority funding and resources and policy and procedures affecting outreach work with young people'.

In contrast, a specialist support worker in Met West described how the support team had dealt with a crisis regarding one young person:

> *At the time of the initial referral, things were so bad at home, she was saying she didn't want to be there and mum was refusing to keep her so she was accommodated, I think, three nights over the weekend and on the Monday we held a panel and that was the first thing, the first job if you like, to take her home, to reintroduce her home with a support package . . . She was just given an emergency weekend placement because mum was told that we don't accommodate children, we work on relationships and to keep the child at home, unless of course we have to . . .*

We have seen that young people living in authorities which did not have support teams were twice as likely to be accommodated as those in authorities which did have a support team service. They were also five times as likely to placed long-term. It is clear that the allocation of resources to support work with young people and families, the level of placement resources for teenagers and the local policy context had a strong influence on placement patterns (although this does not mean that the *quality* of the work undertaken may not also have had an influence on whether placement occurred). These system factors appear to account for much of the variation in placement rates between those authorities offering a specialist support service or a mainstream service, whereas differences in the level of children's needs appeared to be less influential.

Summary points

- Although one-quarter entered care, most of these placements were of short duration. Only 11 per cent were placed for more than four weeks and only 8 per cent of placements were expected to be long-term.
- The principal factors which influenced the likelihood of placement were:
  - previous placement (which may be an indicator of chronic family problems);
  - young people's views that their difficulties were especially severe at referral;
  - local policy and resources, which affect thresholds for the provision of both family support services and placements in care.
- long-term placement was more likely where:
  - young people rated their difficulties as especially severe at referral;
  - young people rated family functioning as especially poor at referral;
  - young people were living with neither birth parent at referral.
- in authorities without support teams, 50 per cent of the young people referred to the mainstream service were accommodated compared to 25 per cent of those using a support team service.
- those using the mainstream service were nearly five times more likely to be placed in (anticipated) long-term placements than those referred to support teams.

12 The use and avoidance of placement

The focus of the previous chapter was on placement rates, which are *service outcomes*. This chapter now considers the experience of placement away from home for individual young people, and in doing so it focuses on *child outcomes*.

We have already seen that the most likely explanation for placement appears to lie in some interaction between system factors, such as policies and the local availability both of placement resources and of resources for family support work with young people and parents, and factors related to the child and family (whether child difficulties were long term, whether young people considered them to be severe at referral and whether parents were experiencing high levels of psychological distress). Analysis of individual case histories can shed some light on this complex inter-relationship between child, family and system factors.

This chapter also considers other moves away from home, which served as an alternative to placement for many young people. These informal arrangements involved stays with friends or relatives rather than in formal care placements, but such informal arrangements also raise issues that deserve no less attention than the question of placement in care.

Short-term placement for emergencies or "cooling-off"

Many of the placements made were emergency admissions that took place shortly after referral, a pattern that is common for teenagers who are accommodated (Sinclair *et al*, 1995; Packman and Hall, 1998). The young people were briefly accommodated in an emergency situation, either because they had been thrown out by parents or carers or, in a few instances, because they themselves refused to return home.

In most cases, parents requested only short-term accommodation, a "cooling off" period of a few nights when relationships had broken down temporarily. Many parents described the state of sheer desperation they had reached when they had requested placement, although some insisted they had wanted only a brief respite from their children. For example, one mother explained:

> *When I phoned them I told them what I wanted, I know they wouldn't do it, but what I really wanted them to do was to say 'Right, things have got so volatile we will come and remove him from the home'. Even if it was just for a couple of hours, because I couldn't protect the other children from him.*

Workers often explained that accommodation had been provided short term to relieve pressure and avoid longer-term family breakdown, as a strategy for family support. Occasionally, concern for the young person's safety was a factor in short-term accommodation, as in the case of a young person with severe ADHD who was removed for one night because, under extreme stress, her mother feared she might harm her daughter.

There was often more to short-term accommodation than simply a brief separation to defuse tension. Although it might be unplanned, it was often used as an opportunity for workers to help families rebuild relationships. In some cases placements lasted weeks rather than days to allow for a fuller assessment to be made of young people's behaviour and circumstances or for therapeutic work to be undertaken. Sometimes the young people themselves felt the need for a cooling off period, such as the 12-year-old boy whose family was threatened with eviction from a hostel for the homeless due to his behaviour, who said he wanted time away from his mother 'to calm us both down'. Family stress was exacerbated by living in the hostel, together with the fact that he was permanently excluded from school with no alternative educational provision and so had nowhere else to go during the day. His behaviour improved during six weeks in another environment and he returned to his family once they were settled in new accommodation.

A key ingredient in the rapid rehabilitation of these young people with their families was quite simply the fact that their parents were willing to have them back. Sometimes parents were clearly committed to these young people and simply needed some respite from dealing with their extremely difficult behaviour. In other cases, they were reluctant to have them home but the combination of a steadfast refusal by workers to allow them to remain in placement and the provision of support and advice to parents persuaded them to accept the young person back. This required workers to be successful in engaging parents in working on their parenting and on family relationships, and where this did not happen, rehabilitation was less likely to take place. In general, a failure to engage parents in working on family difficulties was linked to less positive outcomes for young people, an issue which will be explored further in the chapter which follows.

Young people also had to agree to return home. Two young people who were accommodated short term moved on to stay with friends instead of returning to their families, in one case because a boy's father refused to accept him home but in the other because the young person herself refused to return. The period of accommodation had been short, but it seemed probable that family breakdown would be long term.

Where family breakdown occurred, the availability of staff to undertake immediate work to reunify parents and children was also an important factor in rehabilitation. In Northshire, for example, the support team worked closely with staff in a small children's home used solely for emergency overnight or weekend accommodation. Staff appointed to this home were called residential/community workers, blurring the boundaries between community support to families and the care system. They would work with families where crises occurred out of normal working hours to avoid accommodation but then, if this was not possible, they would care for young people overnight. Two workers from the support team were also linked to this resource and would pick up the work with the young people and parents early the next morning with a view to reuniting them as quickly as possible.

Longer-term placement

As we saw earlier, young people living with neither of their parents at referral were the most likely to enter long-term care. In at least half of the cases where long-term placement was anticipated, parents or carers (including two adoptive parents) had simply refused to allow the young people home. Some of them had already earlier had episodes away from home with other relatives or in short-term accommodation, but attempts at rehabilitation had failed and parents or carers said they were no longer prepared to put up with their behaviour.

Some workers observed that a lack of resources for work with families could make successful rehabilitation harder to achieve. The other main reason for long-term placement was the severity of young people's difficulties. Long-term placement was planned for a 12-year-old girl with mental health problems whose behaviour was considered extremely dangerous, while a 13-year-old who experienced abuse and neglect was placed long term for his own safety. The mother of another child graphically described the severe problems that had led to her long-term placement:

She went berserk, punching and violent behaviour to everyone. She tried to hang herself. I had to get the police because she was running away – when she came back she was taking drugs. She disclosed that she had been sexually abused by her father and her behaviour deteriorated then. She has overdosed and ended in casualty. She has voices in her head, the devil talks to her.

The likelihood of longer-term placement therefore appeared to be influenced by factors relating to the family, to the young person and to local resources for family support.

The reluctance to accommodate

Social workers and support workers were extremely reluctant to accommodate young people and often viewed placement as something to be used only as a last resort, as other recent studies have also found (Sinclair *et al*, 1995; Triseliotis *et al*, 1995; Packman and Hall, 1998). There were several reasons for this. First, they felt that placement was rarely the best way to meet young people's needs and that parents should be encouraged to accept responsibility for their children. Although some parents insisted that they could no longer be expected to cope with their children's behaviour and that social services should take over, workers made it clear to parents that their children were their responsibility. As Packman and Hall have pointed out, these situations raise the wider issue of parental responsibility and the role of the state.

Workers, as well as parents, felt that young people should be discouraged from thinking that life in care would be free from any restrictions, as a number of them appeared to do. A parent commented:

(The support worker) *just explained the downfalls if she did go into care, it is not all good, and that the best place for her was at home with her family.*

Workers were also concerned about the potentially harmful psychological effects of placement, as one explained in respect of a girl who had not been placed:

She didn't come into the care system. She's still at home, so she doesn't feel the rejection. Mum still has the self-esteem.

In general, many workers displayed a degree of scepticism as to the value of accommodation for teenagers and few appeared to view the care system as a positive resource that might be beneficial to some young people, in some circumstances. They were particularly concerned to avoid placing young people in residential settings, fearing that they would be "contaminated" by the behaviour of others. As a social worker commented with regard to a 15-year-old boy:

The staff were very caring and they did do work with him, but the kind of people he was mixing with . . . He wasn't a bad, bad child, he was just having a bad time, and there were some kids there who were, you know, into drugs and things, and he wasn't, so it was exposing him to a lot.

This pessimism about residential care was perhaps misplaced, in some instances at least. In several cases, young people's behaviour was said (by parents) to have improved after a period in residential care and one young person placed long term reflected: 'Things are better since I left the family home and moved to the care unit.'

While social workers' reluctance to accommodate young people was usually grounded in genuine concerns as to whether placement would be beneficial, it was also heavily influenced by local policies on avoiding accommodation. These could be helpful, as they made it easier for workers to resist families' demands for accommodation when they felt strongly that this was not the best course of action. This was not always communicated in a positive manner, though, as in at least two cases (in the same authority) parents claimed that they had been threatened with prosecution for child abandonment if they refused to accept their child back after an emergency placement had been made.

The pressure to avoid accommodation could also mean that practice was sometimes resource driven rather than needs led, although social workers were often aware of this and were not happy with it. A number of parents and workers commented on the way that decisions about placement were apparently determined as much by local resources as by any practice concerns. For example, one social worker, describing her battle to arrange a placement, illustrated the tension between professional judgement and the constraints imposed by financial restrictions:

> *At the time he was accommodated there was this huge cut in social services here and no child was being accommodated; yet it just screamed out that there was going to be a complete breakdown. He needed to be away from the family home and mum was very nearly sectioned.*

Two parents' comments reveal that some social workers were quite candid about resource constraints:

> *Their attitude was 'Sorry, we haven't got no beds, especially for teenagers, we haven't got no foster families'.*

> *And I said, 'When will I hear about respite?' And they says, 'Well whoever it was told you we could give you respite shouldn't have, because we can't, we haven't got the availability'.*

Bureaucratic delay could also be used as a means of rationing scarce resources as the following case illustrates.

Anthony, age 12, had run away from his mother to escape abuse and had gone to live with his father. He developed depression and severe behavioural problems but was told that he did not need help as he was no longer living with the abuser. His mental health deteriorated further and his behaviour became very violent, to the extent that his social worker described him as dangerous. A multi-agency assessment concluded that he needed to be placed in a therapeutic community. However, lengthy bureaucratic delays, which did not appear to have occurred entirely by chance, meant that this decision was not implemented. The boy's father was eventually told that, as no resources were available to fund this expensive placement, the family would be offered regular respite foster care instead.

Where local policy and practice was grounded in the assumption that accommodation should be avoided wherever possible, this could nevertheless be perceived as helpful by parents if it was accompanied by an offer of an alternative form of support. In many cases, when families were in crisis, skilled and intensive work by support workers helped to defuse the situation. One parent, recalling her request for accommodation some months earlier, reflected:

She was running away, she was trashing our home, she was just totally out of control and I phoned them up to say 'Get her put in a home'. Well (the support team) came in and basically, the reason they came in was to keep him in the home, to see if there was any way to resolve it in the home. They were really helpful.

Another explained how she had made this request in sheer desperation:

'Take him away, take him away!' Well actually, that's not what I really wanted, I wanted everything to be better but seriously, I didn't think . . . The family unit was just breaking up because of his behaviour, but I did wonder whether we would have to have . . . we needed . . . some respite. I felt we needed some respite but we didn't get that. I'm glad, because looking back, we got through it.

However, the tendency among social workers to avoid care at all costs could sometimes engender a somewhat blinkered attitude, resulting in a failure to consider fully some children's needs. This was apparent in relation to two children who had suffered severe and long-term rejection and had regularly been re-referred to social services by parents complaining about their difficult behaviour. At each referral, it seemed that the principal consideration had been to find the best means of resolving the current crisis and maintaining the children at home, even though this may not necessarily have been in their best long-term interests. In one case, a child was repeatedly returned to a situation where he suffered severe emotional abuse. These two cases illustrate these dilemmas.

Tom, age 12, had been thrown out by his mother and had been moved by social services to his father and stepmother in another local authority, although he was reluctant to go to them. His social worker reported that he suffered from rejection and had problems in his relationships with both parents and with his stepmother, who was harsh towards him. He truanted, had been temporarily excluded from school, had become involved in offending and was sometimes violent.

Throughout his life he had been shuttled backwards and forwards between his parents 'like a yo-yo', as his social worker put it, but each time the situation had broken down. When social services had returned him to his father on this occasion, a support worker initially worked with him on his behaviour and attempted to look at family dynamics with his father and stepmother, but they were reluctant to address this issue. He was returned to his mother after his father 'beat him up', but she said she was unable to have him at present because of her work so he was placed in foster care with his brothers, who were already there. He settled well and said he was happy there.

Gary, 12, who lived with his mother and her partner, described himself as 'naughty' and 'angry inside'. His behaviour was causing problems at home and at school. His mother complained that his bad behaviour had commenced when he was five weeks old, at which point she had 'realised' that 'he just did not like me'. She was quite candid in saying that 'Basically, I do not like him'. She had first approached social services when he was six years old and since then both social services and mental health services had tried to help over the years. She felt she understood why she felt so negative about him, but that she could not change this. As she explained:

The sad thing is, I treat him the way my mum treated me but I don't the other two, so it's not fair, I know that but I can't help it. 'Cos it happened to me and I know you're supposed to change and not do the same . . . I was honest with them, I told them I hated him, I said 'I absolutely hate him'. With me and him there's just something there that doesn't click, you know. As soon as I see his face when he comes home from school I get annoyed.

His support worker commented that at referral:

The family was in crisis, it was at the point of breakdown. Not that he was doing a lot. The issue was around mum's feelings to him rather than his actual behaviour.

The support worker referred the family for family therapy and a mothers' support group, but the mother refused to take up these services, so he worked with her one-to-one on her relationship with her son and at the same time worked with him on his behaviour. At follow-up, the child felt that his mother was now 'nicer' to him, which he ascribed to the work of the support worker. Conflict may also have been reduced because his mother was now preoccupied with her new baby and he was now spending more time with his father, so his mother saw less of him. However, his mother felt that nothing had changed at all and said that she continued to hate him.

The preoccupation with avoiding accommodation at all costs appeared to have led to short-term thinking rather than a considered review of how these young people's needs might best be met in the longer term and proper planning for their future. Such an approach may simply delay placement without any real resolution of serious family problems. The small sub-group of children whose parents show not only low warmth and high criticism but also a continuing rejection of them may in some cases benefit from long-term care (Thoburn *et al*, 2000). Such cases are, of course, complex and difficult to deal with.

These scenarios are evidence of a phenomenon that Stevenson has characterised as 'bumping along the bottom', whereby social workers become used to a level of persistent emotional abuse in certain families and tolerate the *status quo* until an incident occurs, such as physical or sexual abuse, which prompts a reassessment of the situation (Stevenson, 1996, p. 16). She argues that the challenge is to judge when, and how far, imaginative work can help to improve children's quality of life at home and when a judgement is needed that removal from home may be in their best interests. Neither option is likely to involve a short-term response. Stevenson suggests that support to such children at home is likely to involve long-term work, which is currently out of favour.

Our evidence suggests that the preoccupation with avoiding care at all costs may lead to a failure to move beyond short-term crisis resolution to a consideration of the longer-term needs of children, particularly for those experiencing extreme rejection.

Similarly, researchers in the USA have observed that a fixation with avoiding placement can result in episodic intervention instead of continuing support (Maluccio and Whittaker, 1997; Whittaker and Maluccio, 2002). They argue against an undue emphasis on whether or not the child is placed, whereby placement is conflated with failure, and for a broader focus on the welfare of the child. Others have argued that since placement prevention is not always in a child's best interests, the focus of policy should instead be on removing risks to children and achieving continuity of care, either within the home or out of it (Littell and Schuerman, 1999).

To sum up, this reluctance to accommodate could be helpful in some instances, as long as an adequate alternative service was offered to families in crisis. Unnecessary disruption could be avoided and work could be done to resolve family problems in the very environment in which they had arisen. Nevertheless, even where a good community-based service is offered, there are always likely to be some crisis admissions of teenagers to care placements. If staff are immediately available to work intensively with families, in many cases young people can be rapidly returned home where this work can continue.

However, emergency admissions to care might be less common if planned short-term admission as part of a family support intervention was considered more often. As we have seen, this could help to defuse conflict, provide respite from family stress for both young people and parents and provide a platform for further work. Some teenagers may benefit from a short placement, accompanied by intensive work, before stabilising at home. It may be, therefore, more helpful to view short-term placements for teenagers as a therapeutic intervention that would be available as one of a broad range of services for families under stress, as others have suggested in relation to younger children (Aldgate and Bradley, 1999). For some families in extreme difficulty, regular planned respite care for a period of time may be helpful, through arrangements for support care which offer regular overnight breaks to relieve family stress as part of a package of family support services.

Informal stays away from home with friends and relatives

Although relatively few young people were accommodated, a far higher proportion stayed in informal placements, in most cases with friends or relatives. The majority of the young people moved away for a while and only 42 per cent lived continuously with the same parent or carer during the six months following referral.

Table 12.1
Accommodation and informal moves away from home (n = 196)

Placement status	Per cent	Number
Accommodation only*	16	31
Both accommodation and informal placement	10	20
Informal placement only	32	63
Remained at home	42	82
Total	100	196

Includes those accommodated on an occasional respite basis.

Frequent change is a feature of the lives of many teenagers who come into contact with social work services, as they move backwards and forwards between various addresses (see, for example, Triseliotis *et al*, 1995). In a number of cases it was clear that young people had stayed in two or three different places away from home during the six-month follow-up period, including ten per cent who both stayed with friends or relatives *and* were accommodated. Most of these periods away from home were fairly short, as shown in Table 12.2. Nearly two-thirds remained in informal placements for less than one month but 15 per cent were away from home for three months or more, evidence of a substantive rupture with their families.

Table 12.2

Time spent away from home (not in accommodation) (n = 73)

Time away	%	Number
Less than 1 week	38	28
1 to 4 weeks	27	20
More than 4 weeks to 3 months	19	14
More than 3 months to 6 months	11	8
More than 6 months	4	3

Most moved to stay with other members of their families, although over a quarter stayed with friends – either the families of their own friends or, in a few cases, with family friends of their parents.

Table 12.3

Types of informal placement (n = 83)

	%	Number
Grandparent	18	15
Other parent (short-term)	4	3
Other relative	11	9
Both relatives and friends	6	5
Friends	25	21
Homeless hostel	2	2
Not specified	34	28

In total, over one-third (35%) stayed with relatives at some time and nearly one-third (31%) stayed with friends. Grandparents played an important role in providing temporary care during crises. Where parents were separated, young people sometimes shuttled between the two. A few stayed temporarily with the other parent before returning home, but six (3%) moved to live long term with another parent. They were not always happy with arrangements made for them to stay with another parent, as one 13-year-old explained:

Mum sent me to me dad's. It was a week of hell, he does my head in. He drinks too much. No, I just don't like my dad. I'm scared of him because he used to beat me mum.

Some informal placements were arranged by young people or parents themselves and some were arranged by workers. Sometimes young people simply walked out and took themselves elsewhere. This happened in several cases where they were unhappy about a parent's new partner. Where family relationships had broken down, workers were anxious to encourage young people to enter into informal arrangements with relatives or friends rather than to enter care. They took the view that it was better for young people to be in a familiar environment with people they knew, and of course for the agency it was cheaper. Like short-term accommodation, these episodes could give young people and parents in conflict a break and this could lead them to calm down and re-evaluate their relationship. One mother commented:

> I think she thought that life would probably be better by not being here but after three weeks she was coming round more and she kept saying to me: 'That's not my home. This is my home.'

Although some walked out, young people did not always choose to leave. A 15-year-old boy, who had been thrown out of home, explained:

> I went to stay with my nan as I was not getting on well at home with my step-dad and things were difficult with my mum. I had no choice but to go to my nan as there was nowhere else I could go.

While he was away, his support worker offered support to his grandmother and worked with him and his mother on their relationship and on his behaviour. He returned home after a few months.

Some of these arrangements were unstable, with young people walking out or being thrown out of the places they were staying in. These were young people whose behaviour was difficult, so it is not surprising that informal placements were often troubled, and these arrangements put a particular strain on grandparents. Sometimes young people stayed with relatives for a while and were then accommodated once this arrangement broke down, while in other cases they were accommodated first and then moved to friends or relatives when it became clear that a return home was not possible. They could also drift into uncertain and even risky situations, with no plans for a return home, as one mother described:

> It's much the same. She takes herself off all the time, here one day, gone

the next. It's been a lot calmer the last six months because she's not been here. From my point of view she hasn't been any trouble to me but I worry about her, 'cos she's only 14 and I don't know where she's living and I know she's on drugs and drink.

Quite apart from the risks that this girl was currently facing, the implications for the future of such young people are worrying. Other research has highlighted the way in which young people with a history of family problems, which may have led to earlier episodes in care, sometimes drift into homelessness once they reach an age at which social services will no longer offer them a care placement (Pleace and Quilgars, 1999; Biehal *et al*, 2000). Paradoxically, where family support services "succeed" in preventing accommodation when they are under the age of 16, perhaps through encouraging informal arrangements, young people may no longer be able to gain access to support as "children in need" when they are 16 or 17 years old and may join the ranks of the homeless, as did two young people in this study who reported that they had stayed in hostels for the homeless.

Furthermore, in situations where children's needs might be better met through a period of accommodation, encouraging such informal arrangements or supporting them under Section 17 of the Children Act 1989 may effectively deny vulnerable young people entitlement to future support under the provisions of the Children (Leaving Care) Act 2000. Indeed, some workers suggested that their authorities actively wished to avoid accommodating teenagers precisely because of the financial implications for local authorities of this Act.

While informal stays with relatives or friends could be helpful in providing a short period of respite with people known to the young person, some such episodes could result in drift for young people and their future remained uncertain at follow-up. Around one in eight of the sample (25 young people) stayed away for more than one month and a small proportion (6%, 11 young people) had been away from home for more than three months by follow-up. Although these placements were informal and in most cases initiated by the young people or parents, for those away for more than a short period, planning for their future is just as important as for those formally accommodated.

For both, it is important to address the issues of whether or not a young person and parent wish to be reunited, whether it is desirable for this to happen, and if not, what longer-term alternative arrangements should be made. Such informal arrangements should not, therefore, be seen as a panacea, resulting in a rapid withdrawal by social services before such issues are resolved. Where young people stay away for more than a short period of time, careful consideration should be given to plans for their future, particularly when they move to stay with friends rather than relatives.

A further question is whether longer-term stays with relatives should be supported or even formalised. There is some controversy over the role that the state should play in supporting, or perhaps supervising, relative caregivers (Ainsworth and Maluccio, 1998; Hegar and Scannapieco, 1999; Sykes *et al*, 2002). Should informal caregivers be assessed if children stay with them for more than a short period? Should they be supervised or financially supported, or would such strategies lead to net-widening, with the state intruding unnecessarily into family life? As in this study, research in the USA has found that many kinship carers are grandparents. While the formal and informal use of kinship carers is consistent with a policy agenda of promoting family responsibility and reducing the costs of public services, such strategies may place an unfair burden on kinship carers, who tend to be older and less well-off financially than foster carers and to have more health and mental health problems (Ainsworth and Maluccio, 1998). Older people with problems of their own may need support to care successfully for troublesome young people if they remain with them for more than a short period of time.

The outcomes of formal and informal placements

In most cases placement was avoided and work was undertaken with young people and parents to resolve problems within the home. In some cases, however, a period of time spent away from home in a care placement or with friends or relatives could help young people to feel better, through defusing tension and allowing time for cooling off. In a few cases, a move to a longer-term placement removed them for the foreseeable future from an unhappy situation.

The majority of young people who spent time away from home rated their circumstances as "better" at follow-up. All but one (96%) of those who were placed in accommodation at some time felt their circumstances had improved, compared to 73 per cent of those not accommodated.[1] All of those who stayed only in accommodation but nowhere else, and 81 per cent of those who stayed with friends or relatives, or had periods away both in these informal placements and in accommodation, also rated their circumstances as "better" at follow-up, compared to 69 per cent of those who did not stay away at all.[2]

A break could help to resolve situations, in the short term at least, particularly if work was undertaken with young people and parents to repair relationships. However, fewer such disruptive episodes away from home might occur if services with lower thresholds were also available, offering support to families at an earlier stage before difficulties became so severe. Equally, the preoccupation with avoiding accommodation at all costs could occasionally lead to a failure to properly consider young people's long- term needs. In a few cases, a series of episodic interventions appeared to serve agency needs to manage demand and contain costs rather than young people's needs for longer-term support or for placement away from home.

Informal placements with friends or relatives were fairly common, and may have been the preferred option for many young people as well as being cheaper for local authorities. However, not all of the young people were happy with these arrangements. Also, some informal placements persisted for several months without any evidence of a clear plan for the future of these young people.

Summary points

- The majority of placements were either emergency or short-term placements offered as part of a plan for family support. Such short-term placements could offer a helpful break for "cooling off" and were often used as an opportunity for workers to help families to rebuild relationships.

---

[1] Chi-square test, significant at p = .017.

[2] Chi-square test, p = .045.

- Most of the longer-term placements occurred because parents flatly refused to accept their child home, although in a few cases such placements were made due to child protection concerns or young people's severe mental health and behavioural problems.
- Workers often viewed placement as a last resort. They were concerned about the possibly damaging impact of placement on the young people but were also heavily influenced by local policy directives regarding the avoidance of accommodation which, in part at least, derived from a concern with containing the costs of services.
- This pressure to avoid accommodation could sometimes lead to situations where practice was resource-driven rather than needs-led, so that agency needs were prioritised over the needs of children.
- In a few cases, attempts to avoid care at all costs meant that young people experiencing long-term emotional abuse received only brief episodes of intervention, whose principal aim was to resolve the current crisis rather than to consider their longer-term needs.
- Apart from those who were accommodated, almost one-third of the young people moved to stay with relatives or friends, in most cases for less than one month (but 6% remained away for three months or more). Some of these arrangements were unstable and ended when young people walked out or were thrown out.
- Where young people had a history of serious family problems and were likely to need support in the future, the provision of financial support to relative caregivers under Section 17 rather than Section 20 of the Children Act 1989 could leave them without entitlement to future support under the provisions of the Children (Leaving Care) Act 2000.
- Social services often viewed informal placements as a resolution of young people's difficulties, allowing cases to be closed, and there was a general failure to plan for the future of these young people. Although short stays with relatives or friends could be helpful in providing a short period of respite, some informal placements were risky or unstable or could lead to drift.

13 How did the interventions help?

The interaction of any social work service with family histories, motivation, changes within the child's family, the actions of other agencies and the local policy and resource context makes it extremely difficult to tease out the ways in which a specific intervention might be helpful. In this complex and shifting family and service environment, qualitative analysis of case histories can enhance our understanding of the relationship between interventions and outcomes. Through analysis of in-depth interviews and other qualitative material, this chapter attempts to tease out the interaction between risk and protective factors and social work interventions in order to understand how, and in what circumstances, positive outcomes for young people occurred and the circumstances in which interventions were less successful.

Moderating the effects of multiple risk factors

We have seen that numerous risk factors were evident in the lives of the young people in this study. Individual risk factors included hyperactivity and learning disabilities, while family risk factors included conflict and violence between parents, parental depression, ill-health and social isolation, together with financial worries. Only half of the parents were thought (by workers) to show warmth and two-thirds were thought to show little consistency in their parenting, while one-fifth were reported to be harsh in their dealings with their child. Risk factors in the community included detachment from school, through truancy or exclusion, and associating with peers who were thought to exert a bad influence. All of these have been shown to be risk factors for emotional and behavioural problems in children and young people (Farrington, 1996; Buchanan and Ten Brinke, 1998).

Multiple risk factors were evident for almost all of these young people, as over 90 per cent of the families had reported six or more difficulties at referral and 40 per cent of them had reported 11 or more. It is in *moderating* the effects of multiple risk factors for young people and in *enhancing* or *developing* protective factors in their lives that social workers and support workers can play an important role in improving their well-being.

Cases that were more successful

In cases that were "successful", that is, where both parents and young people felt that circumstances had improved, workers had addressed a range of issues, offering 'multi-faceted solutions to multi-faceted problems' (Sinclair and Burton, 1998). Three key elements were usually at play: individual work with young people, support and advice to parents, and some mediation between the two. In a number of cases, some change in the young person's environment, including the school environment, also took place. In most of these "successful" cases, young people appeared motivated to change and parents were willing to try out strategies suggested by workers. Although in a few cases these young people had initially expressed negative or pessimistic views about the possibility of change, they did in fact engage with workers. Either their initial pessimism may have been due to feeling depressed about their circumstances and may have masked an underlying willingness to work on their difficulties, or workers may have been particularly skilled in engaging them – or both.

Work with individual young people

Direct work with young people was undertaken principally by support workers or sessional workers, although some social workers also worked directly with them. It took a variety of forms, depending on the young person's particular circumstances. At the very least, taking young people out of the home and giving them individual attention allowed them the opportunity to talk about their difficulties, to feel listened to and to feel valued. Many workers took the view that the young people had low self-esteem and one of the aims of this individual befriending and support was to build self-esteem and a greater sense of efficacy. This individual attention was particularly important for those from families with chronic, multiple problems, such as parental depression, marital conflict and histories of neglect and abuse, where young people's needs as individuals sometimes became overlooked in the welter of family difficulties.

The building of a positive relationship between workers and young people was crucial in establishing trust, as a platform for further work. This use of the social work relationship was highly valued by many of the young people and was indeed a vital ingredient of work with them, as without it they were unlikely to accept any advice or services. In successful cases, good working relationships with young people were not an end in themselves, but a vehicle for delivering the intervention.

Individual work with young people in many cases included a focus on their behaviour and work on strategies to change that behaviour. Workers in the support teams, in particular, delivered much of this through structured programmes, sometimes involving worksheets and "homework" between sessions. Structured work on anger management was common, as was discussion of boundaries to behaviour and the need to respect them. In effect, in successful cases key elements of the interventions were similar to the cognitive-behavioural strategies that have been found to be effective in other studies, namely help in understanding how a problem manifests itself and the teaching of strategies and skills to cope with this problem (Rutter *et al*, 1998).

Individual befriending, often by sessional workers, was also used as a means of engaging young people in positive activities in the community, such as sport or involvement in clubs, in the hope that this might divert them towards more pro-social peers and build community supports that would continue once the intervention ended. To facilitate improved relations both with parents and with peers, work on social skills was sometimes undertaken too, often in groups.

Work with parents

Engaging parents in changing patterns of communication and interaction within the family was another crucial element. If parents found workers supportive and felt able to accept their interventions, they sometimes felt they could look at the situation afresh. In some cases, just the fact that social workers or support workers had become involved could in itself serve as a catalyst for change. As one parent explained:

> *When social services intervened they made me stop and sort of take one step back and review the situation. We do talk a lot more now.*

The process whereby this parenting support was delivered was important.

Parents who felt that circumstances had changed for the better had, on the whole, felt understood, listened to and involved in decision-making by workers, who appeared to be working in partnership with them. When teenagers have behavioural problems, these are often displayed publicly, so parents may feel ashamed and may fear that they will be criticised for failing as parents. Many of the parents in this study were found to suffer from a degree of depression or anxiety at referral and felt despairing about their ability to control their children. In these circumstances, working in partnership with parents and focusing on strengths rather than failings are likely to be important ingredients in engaging them in productive working relationships.

Parents who feel they have little control over their children and develop a sense of helplessness tend to "give up" and let them go their own way (Coleman, 1997). The more successful interventions helped parents to develop a more authoritative parenting style and a greater sense of perceived control. Work with parents in most cases included advice on strategies for dealing with their child, building their confidence in setting and enforcing boundaries and helping them to improve consistency in their parenting. Sometimes this work was done in a structured way through the use of worksheets or parenting groups and sometimes advice was simply offered in discussion.

Work with parents and young people together was also important, as workers mediated between them, helping them to negotiate boundaries and reframe patterns of communication. Parents and their children were helped to negotiate ground rules that both would find acceptable, a democratic approach that was likely to lead to greater co-operation by the young people. The involvement of a social worker or support worker in this process often helped to legitimise parents' attempts to exert their authority.

Where workers were successful in changing parenting strategies, so that parenting became both more positive and more consistent, this often had an effect on the child's behaviour. Equally, some young people felt that learning to respond differently to frustration could lead to more positive reactions from their parents. The mother of a 13-year-old girl described this process:

[The support worker] *spent a lot of time with her explaining about boundaries and things she can do and can't do. He spent a lot of time with me just going over things, basically, and like helping to get my mind straight. I mean, it has improved considerably. I mean it's still going on now, but we know how to handle it. It's better, and the bits that still need working on, we know how to work on them as opposed to banging our heads against a brick wall.*

Several young people described how intervention both with them and their parents had led to improvement in their relationships:

She is ignoring me when I give backchat and it's making me wary not to give her backchat because she will just ignore me more . . . [The support worker] has made me and mum closer. Like, she gives me cuddles now and again.

The reason we're getting on better now is because I'm realising what I'm doing wrong now, my mum's being alright with me and we're just getting on.

When I kick off at home now my mum sits us down and asks what's caused it and that.

Where workers were successful in engaging young people and parents and were able to build on their motivation to change, interventions which addressed both child behaviour and parenting practices could set in motion a virtuous circle, whereby positive change by the parent reinforced positive change in the child, or *vice versa*, and such changes provided further positive reinforcement to both parent and child.

Changes in the environment

Changes in the home environment also had an important part to play and often these changes had nothing to do with social work staff. Household membership changed during the period of the study for nearly one-fifth (17%) of the young people. This most commonly involved siblings moving in or out, or parents' partners joining or leaving the household. A few young people (3%) also moved to live with their other parent for the foreseeable future, although this was not always by choice.

Siblings or parents' partners, moving in or out, could have positive or negative effects depending on the nature of the young person's relationship with them. For example, one young person was happy that his mother's partner had moved out, another felt more supported when her boyfriend moved in to the family home and others reported that general family conflict had reduced since a sibling they frequently argued with had left. In another case, a mother sent her son to live with a relative some miles away when his offending behaviour intensified and this was successful in reducing his offending through breaking his contact with anti-social friends.

In most cases, the environment changed (usually only for a matter of days or weeks) when young people went to stay with friends, relatives or in residential or foster care. A brief period of respite could at times be helpful in defusing tension in serious conflicts between parents and young people, as sometimes conflicts had become so extreme that one or both needed a breathing space. Such a break could provide the impetus for both to re-evaluate their relationship. If the brief placement away from home was accompanied by rapid intervention by support workers or social workers to negotiate a return and help families agree on the changes that might accompany this, the break could serve as a catalyst for change. Occasional respite arrangements for one or two nights a week were also much appreciated by families, especially by parents of young people with extreme behaviour problems associated with hyperactivity who were under considerable strain.

Young people's behaviour sometimes improved during a period of time spent away from the home environment staying with other relatives,. Several parents also commented on how their children's behaviour had improved after a period in care, and some young people mentioned that they found their time in residential or foster care a positive experience. Longer-term follow-up would be needed to see if such changes were sustained on return to the home environment, although earlier research suggests that they may not be (Farmer and Parker, 1991). Any changes occurring away from home may not persist unless they are reinforced within the home environment, and support teams are well placed to provide this reinforcement.

Interventions by other agencies

Changes in the school environment could also be helpful. A few young people returned to school after a lengthy period of exclusion, while a few others who had special needs moved to special schools offering more intensive support. A lack of adequate alternatives to full-time school was a serious problem for those who were excluded from school and workers sometimes tried to put pressure on education authorities and schools to improve their provision for these young people. Young people were positive about these changes:

> *I'm now in a special school for EBD, which I like. There's two teachers for six kids.*

> *[School's] brilliant, yeah it is. 'Cos I'm just getting more help and that at school.*

More commonly, workers mobilised support from schools. A support worker explained:

> *The barrier that had been in before we actually worked the case was that the school didn't have all the information on what this child had been living with ... So we took mum and helped her to tell the headteacher and that was really helpful with school, they really got on board and they had improvements in how he was behaving at school.*

This appreciation of the young people's wider difficulties could result in schools excluding the young people less readily or simply providing enhanced individual support to young people in school. Teachers could be an important source of support to young people, so ensuring that support was available to them was an important aspect of workers' interventions. In recognition of this, one of the support teams had an education worker in post specifically to work on school-related issues. Several young people spoke of the support they received from particular teachers:

> *Actually I've seen my head of year to speak to him about my problems with my mum. I'd trust him and that. I can talk to him about anything 'cos I think he'd understand, 'cos I'd been to him with my troubles before that.*

Facilitating changes in the school environment could bring a positive chain reaction, breaking links with delinquent peers and potentially building self-esteem. As one parent explained:

Now he's happier in school. Not roaming the streets like he was. Not mixing with the kids he got into trouble with.

Problems in behaviour at school, truancy and exclusion were often a source of stress to parents and a source of conflict between them and their children, so improved school support which helped to diminish these behaviours could contribute to reducing parent–child conflict.

Given the extensive nature of the young people's difficulties, interventions often involved making contact with other agencies too, including health and mental health services, youth offending teams, drug and alcohol abuse projects and voluntary sector projects.

The interaction of positive changes

Just as there was often a productive interplay between changes in parenting style, child behaviour and school provision, changes in other aspects of young people's lives could also be beneficial, although it was unclear whether positive chain effects operated in a single direction or whether changes in different areas of young people's lives all interacted with one another. For example, a mother reported that the social worker had helped her 14-year-old daughter to see that she 'had to live by what my rules are', but also said matters had improved because:

She's not drinking like she was and she's got in with a different group of friends, so that's made it easier.

Rutter and colleagues have suggested that, for young people experiencing multiple adversities, as were most of these young people, multi faceted interventions which reduce stress in different areas of their lives are more likely to be beneficial than those which target one or two risk factors in isolation, particularly as risk factors often interact with and reinforce one another (Rutter *et al*, 1998). In a similar vein, an Audit Commission report (1996) on young people with anti-social behaviour recommended taking a holistic approach which targets all key areas of young people's lives. In this study, such a multi-faceted approach was evident in the most successful pieces of work, irrespective of whether it was delivered by support workers or social workers. These usually involved work with parents on parenting strategies alongside direct work with young people and mediation between the two, as well as liaison with other agencies and, occasionally, mobilising support from the extended family. These interventions also targeted specific problems such as drug or alcohol abuse, a lack of support at school, poor social skills or non-involvement in positive leisure activities, usually through referral to groups or to other agencies.

Although many support workers stated that they focused principally on changing present patterns of interaction and behaviours, in a number of the successful cases workers also paid some attention to dealing with longer-term underlying family problems. Outcomes could be positive even for young people with multiple risk factors if both parents and young people were motivated to work on change and if well-planned and co-ordinated work was undertaken, as the following case examples illustrate.

Abigail, age 13, was reported to have ADHD. She could be abusive and violent at home and at school, was a regular truant and had twice taken an overdose in the months prior to referral. Her mother felt that the support worker had helped them considerably and described the work that she had done:

She gave me discipline back. She went through some ground rules with Abigail and myself and the rules we decide in the house, we did them together. It was what she was happy with and I was happy with.

Partnership working was important, and this parent clearly valued the way the worker kept her fully involved:

The initial meeting was here and I was quite aware of what was going on, what they were going to do with her and how they were going to try and help.

The support worker worked with this parent on strategies for setting and enforcing boundaries, while the social worker arranged for her to attend a 'parents of teenagers' course. The support worker contacted

Abigail's psychiatrist regarding problems with her medication and also worked directly with her on her behaviour and, in particular, on anger management. The building of a relationship with Abigail was central to her success, as she explained:

I know that she enjoyed coming out with me. She fully engaged in the work while I was with her, and the work that I left her in between visits. I think the relationship that we built up helped her to move on.

David, 15, had learning difficulties and had experienced neglect and physical, emotional and sexual abuse in the past, often truanted from school, abused drugs and was involved in offending. His mother had alcohol problems, had experienced domestic violence in the past and suffered from depression. However, there was a positive attachment between the mother and child and the support worker was able to build on this. The support worker described this mother as 'basically, very loving in lots of ways, but she could be very erratic in her responses . . . highly strung, and the slightest falling out led to a full-scale argument between them'.

The work helped the mother to respond more calmly and to prevent conflicts escalating and gave her advice on strategies to deal with his behaviour. Other family members were closely involved with mother and son and often interfered, so the worker met with them to explain the need for a consistent approach between them: 'a consistent campaign of action plan which they all agreed to'.

At the same time, a worker from the Youth Offending Team undertook individual work with David on his behaviour. Positive changes in David's behaviour and the family's parenting style were mutually reinforcing, but it was the quality of the parent–child relationship that allowed this intervention to be successful, as their basically positive relationship made them motivated to work on change.

This family had been known to social services for many years both due to child protection concerns and the previous breakdown in the mother and son relationship. In these circumstances, and with the presence of multiple risk factors, it seems likely that from time to time further work would be needed as one short-term intervention was unlikely to resolve definitively their multiple and long-standing problems.

Cases that were less successful

Those cases where neither the young people nor the parents felt that circumstances had improved were dispersed between the groups using specialist and mainstream services and across all authorities. A key feature in many of these cases was young people's reluctance to engage with workers. In several cases, they refused to meet with the worker at all and a few would even run off as soon as they saw the worker arriving. As another study of adolescents and social work services once commented, unlike younger children they may 'vote with their feet' (Sinclair *et al*, 1995). In other cases workers did manage to see the young people but were unable to strike up a working relationship with them. In a few cases it was clear that young people's distress made them anxious about opening up to a stranger, as the following comments indicate:

> *She worked with me but I don't feel . . . telling people that I don't know about my problems, it doesn't feel right. I felt listened to but I couldn't tell her all the things I'd want to tell her. I know she would have helped me if she'd been able to help me if I'd told her, but I just didn't feel like telling her.* (girl, 13 years)

> *I didn't use to listen to what she was saying 'cos I didn't like having meetings and that and didn't use to listen. She were just making me worse.* (boy, 15 years)

The first of these lived in what the worker described as a 'semi-chaotic household', where she had witnessed domestic violence some years earlier, and had a mother who suffered from depression. This combination of both exposure to domestic violence and maternal depression is thought to be particularly damaging to children, if it results in the mother becoming 'emotionally unavailable' (Hester *et al*, 2000). This girl not only had problems in her relationship with her mother and step-parent, including violent behaviour towards them, but also truanted regularly and constantly said that she wished to leave home. Although at referral she had mentioned that she would like help with managing her anger and stopping her cannabis use, she clearly needed time to build a relationship with the worker. A short-term intensive model of work may not be helpful to wary young people who need time to build trust.

The parents of the second also suffered from depression and the worker considered him to suffer emotional abuse and rejection (by his father) and to have very low self-esteem. This young person engaged in extremely anti-social behaviour, including arson, which had put his family at risk of eviction. He had truanted regularly before being permanently excluded from school and was avoiding engagement with all professionals who tried to help, including the pupil referral unit that he refused to attend and the youth offending team. After breaching his supervision order, he spent a few months in a secure unit, which he found a positive experience. At follow-up his behaviour and relationship with his parents appeared to have improved (but at that point he had only been back in the community for two weeks). Again, this was a young person who needed more time to build trusting relationships with adults in order to engage in work with them – something that is more difficult in short-term interventions and in the context of high turnover rates for social workers. Trust was clearly an issue for some other young people too, who indicated that they feared they would be criticised if they began to talk to workers.

In other unsuccessful cases parents would not engage with workers. There were a variety of reasons for this. Some simply did not see any need for them to talk to workers, as they felt that problems lay solely with their child and did not involve them at all. Others would engage with workers at times of crisis but avoid them at other times, reluctant to engage in any structured work during quieter periods. A few were quite simply rejecting of their children, not prepared to countenance anything other than the child's removal. In a number of cases, both parents and young people were reluctant to engage in any work and often failed to keep appointments. For some families, a reluctance to engage with workers was fuelled by distrust of social services either due to a fear that they would be judged or because of earlier experiences of social workers, sometimes in their own childhoods.

Young people could also be suspicious, such as one boy whose friend had been placed in care 50 miles away and who feared that the same would happen to him. Young people who were reluctant to discuss their difficulties with workers were often equally reluctant to take up services offered to them, which may also have contributed to the lack of success of the (attempted) intervention. Where young people or parents lack motivation to change or are difficult to engage in a working relationship, it may be worth exploring strategies for motivational interviewing (see Buchanan, 1999; Dishion and Kavanagh, 2003).

Continuing involvement with an anti-social peer group was a risk factor that could also operate as a barrier to successful work, particularly if this group was involved in offending or substance misuse. One parent described how involvement with anti-social peers could make young people less motivated to work with the support worker:

I don't think he wants to change. He's at that age – all his friends are off the rails and he wants to be like them.

The particular nature of family difficulties could also make it more difficult to promote positive changes. In one case, for example, a 14-year-old boy felt so upset about his mother's renewed relationship with a man who had been violent towards her (even though this man did not visit the home) that he withdrew into himself in anger and distress, feeling that everything was hopeless:

I don't care any more, because mum is seeing him again and I think she's being stupid. I don't like it, he's winning all the time after all the things he did.

In a few cases, the root difficulty appeared to be young people's mental health problems, where the professionals most likely to help were mental health services rather than social services. In a number of cases, chronic child or parent mental health problems, or other long-term difficulties such as serious marital conflict or domestic violence, appeared to result in entrenched problems for the child and family. It appeared that short-term interventions were only successful in making some impact on these situations of chronic difficulty where family members showed a strong commitment to one another and were particularly motivated to work towards change. In a few cases, a particular combination of child and parent difficulties were associated with particularly entrenched problems, as in a small sub-group of young people reported to suffer from ADHD who had also witnessed domestic violence within their families.

Comparing barriers to success for specialist and mainstream services

A lack of resources was highlighted as a problem both by support workers and by social workers offering a mainstream service. Both felt that the lack of accommodation resources was a hindrance, which made it hard for them to offer respite care to families in crisis, or on an occasional basis as a support to families under extreme stress. They would also have liked more groups and clubs to be available for young people so that they could involve them in activities in the community. Similarly, social workers' lack of time for work with families was a problem for those using both types of service. This could lead families to feel let down and could even make them hostile to social services.

However, the lack of resources for family support was clearly a far greater problem for social workers who were unable to refer families to a specialist support team. Social workers offering a mainstream service complained of a lack of time to undertake adequate direct work with families themselves and a lack of support staff to assist them in offering a family support service. The demands of child protection work were overwhelming, leaving them with little time for preventive work even though they would have liked to devote more time to this. Several social workers commented on their frustration at not being able to undertake more therapeutic work with families. They felt that the workload pressures that often restricted their role to the predominantly administrative functions of case management with these families limited what they could achieve.

Where only mainstream services were offered, some parents complained of social services' reluctance to intervene before a serious crisis occurred, or of the fact that they closed the case after only a brief contact. Parents in the two authorities without support teams commented:

Their resources are so very stretched and they deal with priority cases only – but surely the non-priority cases will become priority cases because of the non-intervention. They are dealing with their priorities

195

and they do not see our son as a priority. It's not fair they put their budget first. If they had helped us two years ago this situation would not have happened.

I'm not bothering with social services no more. I've got no time for them and I think the facilities that they say they offer should be improved, because it is always they have run out of funding, they can't afford to do this or they can't afford to send nobody out and I'm sick of hearing it. I've heard it all my life.

The fact that a support team existed at all in some authorities meant that families in those authorities were more likely to receive a family support intervention, as this was the whole *raison d'etre* of these services, whereas area social workers had many other demands on their time.

The duration of interventions

There were a number of cases where intervention by social workers or support workers had initially led to positive changes in child behaviour, parenting and parent–child relationships but the situation had deteriorated rapidly once workers withdrew. This raises the issue of whether, for some families, short-term interventions may be just too short. Time-limited work has long been advocated to improve motivation and concentrate the mind, although undoubtedly it also owes its continuing popularity to budgetary considerations (Reid and Epstein, 1972). For families with chronic and severe problems, however, short-term intensive work may not in itself be sufficient, as other studies in both Britain and the USA have also found (Szykula and Fleischman, 1985; Nelson *et al*, 1988; Besharov, 1994; Schuerman *et al*, 1994; Cleaver and Freeman, 1995; Biehal, 2000).

While short-term intensive services may be enough for some families in crisis, where problems are chronic and severe an infrastructure of longer-term services may be needed, offering less intensive support, as needed, to both young people and parents. Such secondary preventive services would operate with lower thresholds than current services and could offer help to families in need at an earlier stage, before difficulties reach crisis point. More intensive support could then be available from specialist support teams on an occasional basis, if crises recurred, to reassess the situation and help to stabilise it. However, it is important that episodic intervention of this kind nevertheless retains a wider focus on the longer-term welfare of the child rather than concentrating on the short-term goal of placement prevention.

Summary points

- Cases that were more successful were usually those where:
  - interventions were multi-faceted, including individual work with young people, support and advice to parents and mediation between the two;
  - workers addressed multiple difficulties;
  - young people (especially) and parents were motivated, or became more motivated, to work towards change.
- Cases that were less successful tended to be those where:
  - young people or parents could not be successfully engaged in the work and either refused to see the worker or showed no motivation to change patterns of behaviour or interaction;
  - involvement in an anti-social peer group persisted;
  - young people's mental health difficulties or parents' marital conflict were chronic and severe;
  - short-term interventions were the sole, or principal, service offered to families experiencing chronic and severe difficulties.
- building positive relationships with young people was an important vehicle for delivering interventions, such as work on strategies to change behaviour and improve family relationships.
- supportive relationships with parents and a focus on strengths were a vehicle for encouraging parents to attempt strategies to develop a more authoritative and consistent parenting style and a greater sense of perceived control.
- worker mediation and help in reframing patterns of communication, often alongside individual work with young people and parents, could lead to a virtuous circle where positive changes were mutually reinforcing.
- positive changes in the young person's environment could also be helpful, e.g. at school, in household membership or place of residence.

14 Working with adolescents

What has changed in work with teenagers?

Research since the early 1980s has highlighted the dearth of services working in ways appropriate to families with teenagers. With the development of support teams in the last 15 years or so, this situation has changed for the better. There are now some excellent services in place working in age-appropriate ways, which are much appreciated by young people and parents. Some of these specialist services are targeted exclusively at older children and teenagers, while others are offered to all age groups but nevertheless work predominantly with children age 11 or above. Specialisation enables these teams to develop skills and confidence in working with this older age group.

What has not changed is that it is still very difficult for families to receive a family support service before they reach crisis point. Thresholds for receiving a service remain high, as we can see from the severity of difficulties of the majority of the young people in this study, all of whom had multiple problems. Although specialist services are now available, they are offered mainly to those with the highest levels of need. In all authorities, but especially in those that did not have specialist support teams, families complained of their difficulties in obtaining a family support service.

Family support: a low priority service?

Decisions about rationing are intrinsic to the provision of public services and no doubt contributed to the past failure to provide adequate support services to families with teenagers, prior to the development of support teams. Currently, a number of factors appear to intersect to influence decisions about the allocation of resources to family support. The perennial problem of managing limited resources is now complicated by the demand for councils with social services responsibilities to meet a range of performance indicators set by central government, including those set out in the *Quality Protects* objectives and the *Performance Assessment Framework* indicators (DH, 1998a and 2002a). Despite the policy imperative towards refocusing services in such a way as to give greater priority to family support, family support services do not constitute a key element in the measurement of social services' performance. The performance of children's services is principally measured by indicators relating to child protection, children looked after and children leaving care. This centralisation of service priorities at national level makes it likely that local provision will be targeted on those services used as the key benchmarks for local authorities' performance. At the same time, professional concerns about protecting children at risk and anxiety about the public scrutiny of child protection decisions when things go wrong also lead to a situation where family support services are accorded a lower priority.

As a result, it remains difficult for families with older children and teenagers to obtain a family support service. Although such a service is more likely to be offered in authorities that have specialist support teams, nevertheless the majority of families who do receive this service are those whose difficulties have become so severe that they are considered to be at risk of family breakdown. In these authorities, it is anticipated that the provision of community-based support services to these families will lead to some reduction in the use of residential and fostering services, which are more expensive.

The picture is one of beleaguered social services holding back the tide of demand for a limited service, which is made even more limited by the national shortage of social workers. In this context, both managers and social workers become preoccupied with gate keeping the limited service available and with the diversion of families who request support. In this respect, agency needs to contain demand sometimes appear to be prioritised over children's needs for support.

These findings are consistent with the observations of the Laming Inquiry, which pointed to major deficiencies in the implementation of the Children Act 1989 (DH, 2003b). The Laming Report contends that the provisions of the Act for both family support and for child protection investigations, which sought to ensure an appropriate response to the differing needs of children, are being used as a means of rationing access to services. This has led to the family support provisions, under Section 17 of the Act, being regarded as having low priority.

The strengths of support teams

In view of these pressures to contain demand for family support services, at the most basic level the existence of support teams means that at least some families with older children will receive a family support service, precisely because resources for family support have been ring-fenced. Not only do specialist teams have the opportunity to develop skills in direct work with teenagers, specialisation also enables them to build links with other local agencies offering services to teenagers.

For most teams, case management functions were carried out by area social workers who retained case responsibility, allowing support team staff to spend more time on direct work with families. Support workers seemed to be better able to engage young people in working with them than area social workers, perhaps because of their more intensive contact with them and their specialist skills in work with older children. Most support workers had many years of experience in working with older children, often in residential settings, and had a wide range of skills. However, given the contraction of the residential sector in recent years, such a pool of experienced staff will not be available to staff these teams in the long term. In view of this, and the severity of the difficulties of the families the teams work with, in the longer term it will become important to appoint staff with professional social work qualifications.

The teams made good use of structured resources for work on behaviour and parenting, but their success in using these methods appeared to be grounded in more traditional social work skills in the use of relationships to promote change. Their more intensive contact with families, an informal, participative style and a strengths-based approach helped them to build these good working relationships as a platform for the more structured work they undertook. Their mainly short-term interventions focused on bringing about concrete changes in behavioural performance, helping to change both young people's behaviour and parenting skills, and they appeared to be frequently successful in these tasks.

Crucially, most young people and parents were satisfied with the service they received and perceived the support teams to be helpful. They felt that they were listened to and involved in decision-making. Families were more likely to report that support workers had helped to improve their situation than social workers. However, since in many cases social workers had devolved much of the direct provision of therapeutic help to support teams, this is perhaps not surprising. The service should be seen as one comprising the efforts both of support workers and social workers, who often undertake different roles in the provision of the service as a whole.

Comparing outcomes

Changes in child and family functioning

At six-month follow-up, many of the families using both specialist and mainstream services showed considerable improvement, according to standardised measures of children's emotional and behavioural difficulties and quality of life, family functioning and parents' mental health. Families also reported a substantial overall reduction in the severity of child behaviour problems. Analysis of change in respect of specific problems reported at referral also showed that positive change had occurred in between one-third to over one-half of all cases for each problem reported. Change was more likely on issues within the family environment (behaviour at home, parent–child communication, relationships and problem-solving). In particular, there was a reduction in child violence towards parents and in running away for nearly two-thirds of those young people initially reported to engage in these behaviours. However, behaviour outside the home showed less improvement. There was little evidence of change in problems at school, although the proportion truanting decreased considerably. There was also little improvement in offending behaviour.

Although the support team service and the mainstream social work service differed in many respects, there was no significant difference in extent of change between the groups using the two different types of service. However, the specialist teams appeared to be working with a somewhat more difficult group, who were more likely to have long-term problems, severe emotional and behavioural difficulties, to have experienced abuse in the past and to have had recent contact with mental health and educational psychology services. So although the *degree* of change was similar for the two groups, the support teams achieved this change with a group that included proportionately more young people with longer-term and severe difficulties.

It is difficult to derive clear-cut findings on the effectiveness of the specialist service when, for ethical and practical reasons, it was not possible to compare support teams to a "no-service" alternative. Also, the complex and shifting multi-agency environment in which services for children are delivered and the impact of informal support from relatives and friends also make it hard to tease out the effects of just one team's work. For example, changes in relation to the school environment often triggered changes in other aspects of the young people's lives. Equally, the severity of family difficulties is influential, as positive change is harder to achieve in families with chronic and severe problems than in those experiencing acute but more recent stress. Young people and parents' motivation to change was another key element and was closely related to their willingness to engage in work with support workers and social workers.

The interaction of this multiplicity of factors may influence the outcomes that *any* type of social work service may achieve. What did not appear to influence outcomes to a significant extent, however, were the precise components of the service offered. If families were offered a service, were prepared to engage with workers and were motivated to change (or were encouraged by workers to become more motivated), then matters improved in many cases.

Worker skills in engaging families and providing therapeutic help appeared to be more important than the precise nature of the service offered. Families who were prepared to engage with workers made good use of either type of service. In essence, family support services helped to bring about positive changes in both child and family functioning irrespective of whether they were delivered by support teams or mainstream social work teams, but in the absence of a specialist service families were less likely to receive any support of this kind. However, it should be borne in mind that, due to sampling problems, the comparison sample in this study was relatively small, which may have made it difficult to detect possible differences between the two groups.

Preventing placement

Although one-quarter of the young people entered care at some point during the six-month follow-up period, most of these placements lasted less than four weeks. Only eight per cent of the sample were expected to remain looked after in the long term. In authorities where no support team service was available, young people using a mainstream social work service were twice as likely to enter care placements as those referred to support teams. They were also nearly five times more likely to enter care placements that were anticipated to be long term. The support teams therefore appeared to be more effective in preventing placement than mainstream services and, indeed, placement prevention was one of their principal objectives.

However, service outcomes of this kind are strongly influenced by system factors such as local policies on placement and the availability of residential and foster placements. Decisions about placement are, at the very least, influenced as much by the availability of placements as by the circumstances and needs of the child. Most of the support teams had been set up following the closure of children's homes, whose residential staff had been redeployed as support workers. In these authorities, the new support service was therefore provided in the context of a reduction in placement resources, which in itself was likely to bring about a decrease in placement rates. Nevertheless, while these policy and resource factors clearly had an impact on placement rates, the support teams also played an important role in preventing placement through their provision of an alternative, community based service to families.

A more fundamental issue was the apparent fixation among workers in both the support teams and the mainstream social work teams with avoiding placement at all costs. This derived partly from practice concerns regarding the potentially damaging effects of care and partly from local policy directives regarding the need to avoid placement. These concerns led to a presupposition that placement was invariably damaging, should be resisted whenever possible and should only be used as a last resort. Yet evidence from this study shows that a short-term placement as part of a plan for family support was often helpful to families under stress, helping to defuse tension and providing time for cooling off before the young person stabilised again at home.

The fixation with avoiding placement also led to a failure to consider the longer-term needs of a small number of children experiencing severe emotional abuse, needs which may potentially have been better met through placement in long-term foster care than through repeated episodic interventions that focused single-mindedly on keeping them at home. Agency concerns with reducing the use of placement sometimes led to situations where practice was resource driven rather than needs led, so that agency needs were prioritised over children's needs. Although such strategies may be effective in reducing expenditure in the short term, this may be at the expense of meeting the longer-term needs of children. In addition, individual agencies' preoccupation with containing their own costs in the short term, whether by failing to provide a placement, a school place or a mental health service, might potentially lead to greater social and financial costs to society in the long term, such as increased use of mental health or criminal justice services.

Limitations to the study

It is possible that this study's failure to detect any greater effectiveness on the part of the specialist teams in bringing about changes in child and family functioning was due to its methodological limitations. It was only possible to identify a relatively small control group, half of which came from a single local authority in which a high level of service was available – and this service was not dissimilar to the specialist service. The service received by this half of the control group was perhaps closer to that provided by the specialist teams than to the mainstream service provided in the other two authorities from which the control group was drawn, which may possibly have skewed the results.

The failure to detect a difference in the effectiveness of the two services may also be due to another limitation of the study, arising from its quasi-experimental design. Despite efforts to sample equivalent groups, there were some clear differences between them, with the experimental group containing a higher proportion of young people with chronic and severe difficulties than the control group. If the specialist teams were indeed working with a higher proportion of young people with long-term and serious difficulties, it would be harder for them to achieve more positive outcomes than mainstream services working with proportionately fewer young people with this level of difficulty. Nevertheless, it remains equally possible that the specialist support teams were no more effective in bringing about positive changes in child and family functioning than mainstream services.

Implications for policy and practice

The impact of abuse, neglect and domestic violence

Although concerns about abuse and neglect are more common in relation to younger children, who may be more physically vulnerable, the evidence from this study suggests that these issues are of continuing importance in work with older children and adolescents. Research in the USA has shown that the abuse of adolescents is not always recognised as such, and adolescents may display the effects of abuse through troubled or troublesome behaviour (Rees and Stein, 1997). We have seen that social workers had had past concerns about abuse in respect of one-third of the young people in this study and over one in ten were considered to have experienced past neglect. At the time of referral, workers considered that over half of the young people had recently experienced abuse or neglect. Emotional abuse was the most common form, mentioned in respect of one-third of the young people in the study; nearly one-fifth were considered to experience neglect and more than one in ten had recently experienced physical abuse.

The parents of 43 per cent of the young people had experienced domestic violence either recently or in the past, and some of the young people had witnessed this violence. Some continued to be troubled by these experiences even many years after they had occurred. Those children with experience of domestic violence were more likely to have severe emotional and conduct problems at referral. Domestic violence clearly has continuing effects on some children and the effects of abuse may be evident in behaviour such as self-harm, depression, running away and offending (Rees and Stein, 1997). There was also a clear association between high scores on the SDQ for emotional problems, which may develop as a result of these difficult family experiences, and young people's violence to their parents. Over half were reported to be violent to parents and over two-thirds were violent to others. Clearly many of these young people had difficult histories and complex needs. The continuing impact of both past and current abuse, neglect and domestic violence demonstrates the importance of providing a range of family support services to older as well as younger children.

Providing an infrastructure of less intensive services

Since the late 1980s there has been an increasing focus on parenting, with an emphasis on parental responsibility evident in the Children Act 1989, the Crime and Disorder Act 1998 and the Anti-social Behaviour Act 2003. The concern with disruptive behaviour by older children and teenagers at school and in the community and the increasing focus on parental accountability for the actions of their children has led to the introduction of parenting orders and anti-social behaviour orders. Alongside the more punitive policies associated with the Crime and Disorder Act, the Children Act 1989 proposed family support as a proactive service to families and the subsequent Children Act 2004 has highlighted the importance of universal services to support families.

Since the change of government in 1997, there has been a big increase in the provision of family support services, for example, through the growth of charities such as the National Family and Parenting Institute and Parentline Plus, but a national mapping of family services has found that services often do not place enough emphasis on preventive work with families (Henricson *et al*, 2002). Also, the majority of family services are aimed at families with younger children, for example, those funded under the Sure Start and Children's Fund initiatives and the emphasis in the Children Act 2004 continues to be on services to support families with younger children.

Although the behaviour of teenagers causes much concern, there are few comparable services to support parents and young people at an early stage, before difficulties become more severe. There may, perhaps, be an assumption that if services are targeted at younger children, fewer problems will emerge in adolescence. Yet even in the context of preventive services for younger children, support services will continue to be needed for older children in difficulty and their parents.

Findings from this study suggest that intervention earlier in the development of problems is also important. As the Treasury spending review highlighted in 2002, in relation to family services in general, most activity is focused on work with families in crisis or in acute stress rather than on prevention and the early identification of need (HM Treasury, 2002). As we have seen, service provision was often triggered by demands for a child to be removed and occasionally by parental threats that they might harm their children if no help was provided. The provision of a service at an earlier stage, before problems reach crisis point, may prevent the escalation of difficulties for some, or even many, young people. Such services may have a positive effect not only on the welfare of these young people but also on their behaviour at school and in the community, leading to wider benefits to society beyond the realm of individual families.

The need for a continuum of family support services

For those young people with severe difficulties and high levels of need, the short-term, intensive service provided by support teams was often effective in helping families to resolve crises and in providing them with strategies for addressing their difficulties in the future. Given the multiple and often long-term difficulties of these young people and parents, it is likely that crises will re-occur and that some may need further interventions of this kind from time to time. Specialist support teams therefore have an important role to play in providing these intensive family support services for families with severe difficulties.

However, perhaps fewer families would reach crisis point if this intensive service were located in an infrastructure of less intensive services providing support to teenagers and their families. Also, given the high proportion of young people in this study with emotional and behavioural difficulties, disabilities or impairments, mental health problems or serious health problems, it is clear that some families are likely to need continuing support. For example, for young people with ADHD, problems are unlikely to disappear after a short period of intensive work, although there may be moderate improvement. Families experiencing long-term stress are likely to benefit from less intensive support over a longer period to help them cope with such stresses.

Specialist services, such as support teams, should therefore form part of a continuum of support services for children and families. These should include less-intensive services offering advice and support to parents and children before problems become severe, as well as services to encourage and support vulnerable children to become engaged in age-appropriate local clubs and activities, as the support workers and sessional workers in this study tried to do. These less intensive services should be multi-professional, involving health, mental health, education and youth work services, as well as voluntary agencies offering parenting skills groups or volunteer befriending services for young people. Social services, with their expertise on family work, should retain a key role in this inter-agency framework.

The first five of the core standards set out in the *National Service Framework* and the objectives of the *Every Child Matters: Change for Children* programme could, through their emphasis on early intervention and support to families, provide a rationale for the development of family support services. These initiatives, together with the Children Act 2004, also focus on the greater integration of services for children. Closer inter-agency and inter-disciplinary working may help to resolve situations where social services become involved in supporting families whose difficulties have been intensified by the failure of education departments to provide a school place or appropriate specialist resource, or the failure of mental health services to provide a timely service. Universal services are less likely to be perceived as stigmatising and families under stress may be more willing to take up a family support service if it is delivered within a framework which provides universal services, such as day care, education and health services, as well as services targeted at families in difficulty. To enhance access to more specialist services, there could be some integration of these within a framework of universal services, for example, through the development of Children's Trusts. However, Children's Trusts are in their early stages and it is unclear what models might develop and whether they will indeed succeed in delivering more responsive services.

The use of placement
The proposed service continuum for children's services should range from low-level support to families at one end, via more intensive support such as that provided by support teams, to a range of placement resources at

the other end. As well as longer-term placements for the small number of children who need them, the creative use of short-term placements as an element of family support provision would be a valuable service for those experiencing severe stress. These might include emergency and planned short-term residential services such as those developed in Northshire, with work with parents and children undertaken both during and after placement. Regular respite care, such as the single overnight stays with foster carers once a month over a period of several months provided by a small number of support care fostering schemes around the country, might also be a valuable resource (Aldgate and Bradley, 1999). In Sweden a more broadly-based model of support care has been developed, known as the contact family service. This scheme links families with a contact person or family, who undertake a range of activities with the child, help the parent with parenting tasks and offer occasional respite care overnight (Andersson, 2003). Support care or contact family services may relieve family stress and may prevent family breakdown in the long-term. Where family breakdown does occur, treatment foster care schemes providing intensive intervention with both children and parents might lead to the successful rehabilitation of more children with their families, but these have yet to be evaluated in a British context (Baker and Chamberlain, 1997).

Family support and placement should not be seen as competing alternatives. Instead, and consistent with the Children Act 1989, placement should be seen as one form of family support that can help to ensure that children remain with their families in the long term.

The role of social workers

Social workers had fewer opportunities than support workers for direct therapeutic work with families as much of their time was taken up with case management. Some social workers mentioned their frustration at not being able to make greater use of their professional skills in working directly with families because much of their time was spent on tasks they viewed as bureaucratic, which they typically described as 'making sure that all the right boxes are ticked'. Other research has also found that social workers now have few opportunities for undertaking therapeutic work and, in particular, work on family support (Macdonald and

Williamson, 2002). Such work is increasingly being located in specialist teams, yet these are mostly staffed by people without professional social work qualifications and, in most cases, without training in therapeutic work. In authorities where support teams were available, social workers viewed them as a valuable resource that could provide the direct therapeutic work that they themselves had little time to offer.

Given their level of training and their experience with children and families, there is some indication that the professional skills of social workers were often under-exploited. A few support workers who were professionally qualified as social workers said that they had joined support teams precisely because these gave them more opportunities for what they viewed as "real" social work. Restricted opportunities for the therapeutic work that many view as professionally more satisfying may be one factor contributing to the current shortage of social workers.

The duration of interventions

Support teams offered brief, intensive interventions that often helped to bring about changes in parenting style and young people's behaviour. Where successful, these short-term interventions often helped to set in train a virtuous circle, in which improved child behaviour and more consistent parenting were mutually reinforcing, leading to a reduction in family stress. These interventions helped to defuse tension and resolve family crises. However, while time-limited, task-centred support may be helpful for those experiencing acute crises, particularly if problems have emerged relatively recently, short-term work may not be ideal for every family. For families with multiple and long-term problems it may be unreasonable to expect that short-term interventions can bring lasting change, as other studies of parenting support have also suggested (Tunstill and Aldgate, 2000; Ghate and Ramella, 2002; Macdonald and Williamson, 2002).

We have seen that some children in this study had received a series of episodic interventions over a number of years to deal with immediate crises, with little evidence of a considered assessment of their longer-term needs. The pressure on social workers to achieve a steady turnover of cases, particularly in the context of the national social worker shortage and the rapid turnover of social workers, militates against taking a longer-term view of the needs of children outside the care system. Equally, consistent long-term support to children may be hard to provide in agencies which find themselves obliged to rely heavily on agency staff due to difficulties in recruitment. However, for some children living with their families, long-term support may be needed, even though this is currently out of fashion. For example, for older children experiencing emotional abuse, the co-ordination of longer-term help may be needed to support them at home, if assessment indicates that remaining at home is in their best interests.

Supporting families, preventing breakdown

The findings from this study suggest that an ecological approach, targeted at the different domains of their lives, is most likely to be helpful in social work with young people. Given the multiple risk factors for the young people in this study, change was only likely to occur if workers intervened at the level of the individual, the family, the peer-group and the school.

While motivation was a mediator of positive change, having long-term difficulties appeared to function as a moderator, which made positive outcomes less likely to occur. The building of supportive relationships with young people and parents also functioned as a mediator of change. The old-fashioned social work skill of using relationships was a crucial factor, with these relationships used not as an end in themselves but as a platform for focused work. Skilful interventions by support workers and social workers enhanced protective factors in the young people's lives, for example, by giving parents strategies for more effectively setting consistent boundaries and reinforcing good behaviour, or by helping to ensure greater integration in school and engagement in pro-social leisure activities.

Although it has been difficult to arrive at any clear conclusion as to whether support teams are more effective than mainstream services, it is clear from this study that they are highly valued by families and that the circumstances of children and families receiving both types of family support service often improve dramatically. However, where family support services are not ring-fenced, it is hard for families to gain access to a service before problems become severe.

Specialist support teams offer a valuable service targeted at those with high levels of need. This intensive service should be located within a continuum of services, offering less-intensive help to families at an earlier stage or as a follow-up service. Multi-professional services could offer an ecological approach to service provision, intervening in different areas of young people's lives to address the multiplicity of difficulties which intersect in the lives of these young people. This approach could co-ordinate interventions to address risk factors at the level of the child, the family, the school and the local community, as necessary. Help that is more or less intensive could be offered in each of these areas, as appropriate. It is clear from this study that many parents of "difficult" teenagers and many teenagers themselves would welcome such help and our evidence suggests that, where skilled help is offered and parents and young people are motivated to change, many may benefit from it. Since teenagers sometimes externalise their difficulties and manifest them in the form of difficult behaviour outside the home, as well as within it, such help may be of benefit to the wider community too.

Appendix 1

Scores on outcome measures at referral

Outcome measure (n)	Perspective	Support team group Mean (SD)	Mainstream group Mean (SD)	Mean difference (95% CI)	p-value
Well-being[1] (175)	Young person	54.68 (25.68)	51.89 (25.68)	−2.79 (−10.50–4.92)	0.476
GHQ-12 (202)	Parent	6.47 (3.72)	8.14 (3.79)	−1.67 (−2.81–5.26)	**0.004**
FAD (209)	Combined	2.38 (0.50)	2.35 (0.50)	0.03 (−0.18–0.13)	0.740
Severity of difficulties (176)	Young person	10.02 (5.08)	11.33 (5.43)	−1.32 (−2.99–0.36)	0.122
Severity of difficulties (123)	Parent	16.97 (5.20)	17.80 (5.50)	−0.83 (−2.44–0.78)	0.311
SDQ (177)	Young person	19.44 (5.08)	17.67 (4.92)	1.77 (0.16–3.38)	**0.032**
SDQ (202)	Parent	23.64 (5.77)	23.79 (6.11)	−0.15 (−1.95–1.65)	0.866

[1]Based on the Lancashire Quality of Life Profile (Huxley *et al*, 1996).

Change in outcomes between referral and follow-up

Outcome measure (n)	Perspective	Support team group Mean (SD)	Mainstream group Mean (SD)	Mean difference (95% CI)	p-value
Well-being (99)	Young person	13.74 (26.28)	12.60 (21.11)	0.12 (−11.52–11.76)	0.983
GHQ-12 (135)	Parent	−2.99 (4.77)	−3.68 (3.79)	0.69 (−0.849–2.22)	0.377
FAD (141)	Combined	−0.19 (0.47)	−0.05 (0.57)	−0.14 (−0.32–0.04)	0.137
Severity of problems (99)	Young person	−2.88 (5.10)	−3.33 (5.51)	0.45 (−1.97–2.87)	0.711
Severity of problems (136)	Parent	−5.06 (6.92)	−4.95 (8.06)	−0.11 (−3.05–2.83)	0.939
SDQ (101)	Young person	−3.46 (6.29)	−2.56 (4.64)	−0.90 (−3.62–1.81)	0.512
SDQ (134)	Parent	−3.05 (5.34)	−2.38 (5.10)	−0.67 (−2.65–1.32)	0.507

Differences between the groups which were statistically significant at the 5% level are shown in bold. Scores for the two groups were compared using the independent samples T-Test.

Appendix 2

Interventions delivered to families receiving different types of service[1]

Focus of help	Elements of the intervention	Per cent of users of mainstream service (n = 44)	Per cent of users of specialist service (n = 132)
Practical help	Practical help/services	30	35
	Financial/material help	25	22
	Help with housing problems	18	13
	Advice about benefits	41	57
	Advocacy with other agencies	39	54
Young person's behaviour	Strategies for parent	55	87
	Strategies for young person	50	79
	Work on drug or alcohol problems	0	27
	Young person's social skills	34	59
	Sexual behaviour puts self/others at risk	18	24
Emotional problems (child)	Emotional problems	46	79
	Mental health problems	5	16
Family relationships	Mediation	57	82
	Improving communication	64	89
	Focus on underlying causes of problems	57	83
Parenting capacity	Work on marital difficulties	16	30
	Support to improve parental care	9	44
	Mental health problems	7	13
	Work on drug or alcohol problems	5	8
	Mobilising informal social support	30	37

[1] Differences between the groups which were statistically significant at the 5% level are highlighted in grey.

References

Ainsworth, F. and Maluccio, A. N. (1998) 'Kinship care: false dawn or new hope?', *Australian Social Work* 51(4).

Alderson, P., Brill S, Chalmers I., Fuller, R., Hinkley-Smith, P., Macdonald, G., Newman, T., Oakley, A. Roberts, H. and Ward, H. (1996) *What Works? Effective Social Interventions in Child Welfare*, Barkingside: Barnardo's.

Aldgate, J. and Bradley, M. (1999) *Supporting Families through Short-Term Fostering*, London: The Stationery Office.

Aldgate, J. and Tunstill, J. (1995) *Making Sense of Section 17. Implementing Services for Children in Need within the Children Act 1989*, London: HMSO.

Alexander, J. and Parsons, B. (1982) *Functional Family Therapy*, Monterey, CA: Brooks Cole.

Andersson, G. (2003) 'Evaluation of the contact family service in Sweden', in Katz, I. and Pinkerton, J. (2003) *op. cit.*

Audit Commission (1994) *Seen But Not Heard – Co-ordinating Community Child Health and Social Services for Children in Need within the Children Act 1989*, London: HMSO.

Audit Commission (1996) *Misspent Youth*, London: The Audit Commission.

Baker, J. A. and Chamberlain, P. (1997) 'Family connections: a treatment foster care model for adolescents with delinquency', *Journal of Child and Family Studies*, 6(2), pp. 267–69.

Bank, L., Marlowe, J. H., Patterson, G. R. and Weinrott, M. R. (1991) 'A comparative evaluation of parent training interventions for families of chronic delinquents', *Journal of Abnormal Child Psychology*, 19, pp. 15–33.

Barlow, J. (1999) 'What works in parent education programmes', in Lloyd, E. (ed.) *Parenting Matters. What works in parenting education?* Barkingside: Barnardo's.

Barlow, J. and Parsons J. (2002) *Group-based Parenting Programmes for Improving Emotional and Behavioural Adjustment in 0–3 year old Children (Cochrane Review)*, Oxford: Cochrane Library Issue 3.

Bates, B. C., English, D. J. and Kouidou-Giles, S. (1997) 'Residential treatment and its alternatives: a review of the literature', *Child and Youth Care Forum*, 26(1), pp. 7–61.

Bath, H. I., Richey, C.A. and Haapala, D. A. (1992) 'Child age and outcome correlates in intensive family preservation services', *Children and Youth Services Review*, 14(5), pp. 389–406.

Bath, H. I. and Haapala, D. A. (1993) 'Intensive family preservation services with abused and neglected children: an examination of group differences', *Child Abuse and Neglect*, 17, pp. 213–225.

Batty, D. (2002) 'Social exclusion: the issue explained', *The Guardian*, 15/01/2002.

Bebbington, A. and Miles, J. (1989) 'The background of children who enter local authority care', *British Journal of Social Work*, 19(5), pp. 349–68.

Berridge, D., Beecham, J., Brodie, I., Cole, T., Daniels, H., Knapp, M. and MacNeill, V. (2002) 'Costs and consequences of services for troubled adolescents: an exploratory, analytic study', Luton: University of Luton.

Berry, M. (1997) *The Family at Risk. Issues and trends in family preservation services*, Columbia: University of South Carolina Press.

Besharov, D. J. (1994) 'Looking beyond 30, 60 and 90 days', *Children and Youth Services Review*, 16(5–6) pp. 445–52.

Biehal, N. (1993) 'Changing practice: participation, rights and community care', *British Journal of Social Work*, 23, pp. 443–58.

Biehal, N., Clayden, J., Stein, M. and Wade, J. (1995) *Moving On: Young people and leaving care schemes*, London: HMSO.

Biehal, N., Clayden, J. and Byford, S. (2000) *Home or Away? Supporting young people and families*, London: National Children's Bureau.

Biehal, N. and Wade, J. (2000) 'Going missing from residential and foster care: linking biographies and contexts', *British Journal of Social Work*, 30, pp. 211–25.

Bone, M. and Meltzer, M. (1989) *OPCS Survey of disability in Great Britain: Report 3 – Prevalence of disability among children*, London: HMSO.

Borduin, C. M. (1999) 'Multisystemic treatment of criminality and violence in adolescents', *Journal of the American Academy of Child and Adolescent Psychiatry 1999*, 38(3), pp. 242–49.

Bowlby, J. (1951) *Maternal Care and Mental Health*, Geneva: WHO.

Brannen, J. (1996) 'Discourses of adolescence: young people's independence and autonomy within families', in Brannen, J. and O' Brien, M. M. (eds) *Children and Families. Research and policy*, London: Falmer Press.

Brodie, I., Berridge, D., Ayre, P., Barrett, D., Burroughs, L., Porteous, D. and Wenman, H. (1998) *Family Support for Adolescents: An evaluation of the work of the Adolescent Community Support Team*, Luton: University of Luton.

Bronfenbrenner, U. (1979) *The Ecology of Human Development. Experiments in nature and design*, Cambridge, MA: Harvard University Press.

Brosnan, R. and Carr, A. (2000) 'Adolescent conduct problems', in Carr, A. (ed.) *What Works for Children and Adolescents? A critical review of psychological interventions with children, adolescents and their families*, London: Routledge.

Brown, J. (1998) *Family and Adolescent Support Service*, London: National Institute of Social Work.

Buchanan, A. (1999) *What Works for Troubled Children?* Ilford: Barnardo's.

Buchanan, A. and Ten Brink, J. (1998) 'Measuring outcomes for children: early parenting, conflict, maladjustment, and depression in adulthood', *Children and Youth Services Review*, 20(3), pp. 251–78.

Bullock, R., Randall, J. and Weyts, A. (2000) *Social Work Effectiveness: Evaluating the contributions of social workers to interventions with children in need*, Dartington: Dartington Social Research Unit.

Burchard, J. D. and Clarke, R. T. (1990) 'The role of individualized care in a service delivery system for children and adolescents', *The Journal of Mental Health Administration*, 17, pp. 48–60.

Byles, J., Byrne, C., Boyle, M. and Offord, D. (1988) 'Ontario child health study: reliability and validity of the general functioning subscale of the McMaster Family Assessment Device', *Family Process*, 27(1), pp. 97–104.

Cantril, H. (1965) *The Pattern of Human Concern*, New Brunswick, New Jersey: Rutgers University Press.

Carpenter, J. and Dutton, J. (2003) *Outcomes and Costs of Therapeutic Family Support Services for Vulnerable Families with Young Children. Report to the Department of Health*, Durham: University of Durham.

Clarke, J. (1996) 'After Social Work?', in Parton, N. (eds) *Social Theory, Social Change and Social Work*, London: Routledge.

Clarke, J., Gewirte, S. and McLaughlin, E. (2000) *New Managerialism, New Welfare?*, London: Sage.

Clarke, R. T., Schaefer,M., Burchard, J. D. and Welkowitz, J. W. (1992) 'Wrapping community-based services around children with severe behavioural disorder: an evaluation of Project Wraparound', *Journal of Child and Family Studies*, 1, pp. 241–61.

Cleaver, H. (2000) *Fostering Family Contact*, London: The Stationery Office.

Cleaver, H. and Freeman, P. (1995) *Parental Perspectives in Cases of Suspected Child Abuse*, London: The Stationery Office.

Cleaver, H., Unell, I. and Aldgate, J. (1999) *Children's Needs – Parenting Capacity*, London: The Stationery Office.

Cliffe, D. with Berridge, D. (1991) *Closing Children's Homes. An end to residential child care?*, London: National Children's Bureau.

Cohen, E. M., R. G. and Yates, G. I. (1991) 'HEADSS: A psychosocial risk assessment instrument: implications for designing effective programs for runaway youth', *Journal of Adolescent Health*, 12, pp. 539–44.

Cole, T., Sellman, E., Daniels, H. and Visser, J. (2002) *The Mental Health Needs of Young People with Emotional and Behavioural Difficulties*, London: The Mental Health Foundation.

Coleman, J. (1997) 'The parenting of adolescents in Britain today', *Children & Society*, 11(1), pp. 44–52.

Coleman, J. C. and Hendry, L. B. (1999) *The Nature of Adolescence*, London: Routledge.

Collishaw, S., Maughan, B., Goodman, R. and Pickles, A. (2004) 'Time trends in adolescent mental health', *Journal of Child Psychology and Psychiatry*, 45(8), pp. 1350–62.

Colton, M., Drury, C. and Williams, M. (1995) *Children in Need: Family support under the Children Act 1989*, Aldershot: Avebury.

Coote, A. (2005) 'But does Sure Start work?', *The Guardian*, 19/01/2005.

Cox, A. D. (1997) 'Preventing child abuse: a review of community projects 1: intervening on processes and outcomes of reviews', *Child Abuse Review*, 6, pp. 243–56.

Dagenais, C., Begin, J., Bouchard, C. and Fortin, D. (2004) 'Impact of intensive family support programs (IFPS): a synthesis of evaluation studies', *Children and Youth Services Review*, 26, pp. 249–263.

Danziger, S. and Waldfogel, J. (2000) *Investing in children. What do we know? What should we do? CASE Paper 34*, London: London School of Economics.

Department for Education and Skills (2003) *Every Child Matters*, London: DfES.

Department for Education and Skills (2004a) *Every Child Matters: Change for Children*, London: DfES.

Department for Education and Skills (2004b) *Statistics of Education: Outcome indicators for looked after children*, Twelve months to 30 September 2003. London: DfES.

Department for Education and Skills (2005) *Children Looked After by Local Authorities, Year ending March 31st 2004*, London: DfES.

Department for Education and Skills/Department of Health (2004) *National Service Framework for Children's, Young People's and Maternity Services. Core Standards*, London: DfES/DoH.

Department of Health (1995) *Child Protection Messages from the Research*, London: HMSO.

Department of Health (1996) *Focus on Teenagers. Research into Practice*, London: HMSO

Department of Health (1998a) *The Quality Protects Programme: Transforming Children's Services, LAC (98) 28*, London: Department of Health.

Department of Health (1998b) *Modernising Social Services*, London: Department of Health.

Department of Health (2000a) *Framework for the Assessment of Children in Need and their Families*, London: The Stationery Office.

Department of Health and National Statistics (2000b) *Key Indicators Graphical System*, London: Department of Health/NationalStatistics.

Department of Health and National Statistics (2001b) *Social Services Performance Assessment Framework Indicators, 2000–2001*, London: National Statistics.

Department of Health (2002a) *Social Services Performance Assessment Framework Indicators 2001–2002*, London: National Statistics/Department of Health.

Department of Health (2002b) *Children in Need 2001. National Results*, London: Department of Health.

Department of Health (2002c) *Children looked after by local authorities year ending 31 March 2001 England*, London: Department of Health.

Department of Health (2003a) Integrated Children's System, *http://www.children. doh.gov.uk/integratedchildrenssytem/about.htm*.

Department of Health (2003b) *The Victoria Climbié Inquiry*, Norwich: The Stationery Office.

Department of Health and Social Security (1985a) *Review of Child Care Law*, London: HMSO.

Department of Health and Social Security (1985b) *Social Work Decisions in Child Care*, London: HMSO.

Department of the Environment, Transport and the Regions (1998) *Modernising Local Government – Improving Local Services through Best Value*, London: DETR.

Dishion, T. J. and Andrews, D. W. (1995) 'Preventing escalation in problems behaviours with high-risk young adolescents: immediate and 1 year outcomes', *Journal of Consulting and Clinical Psychology*, 63, pp. 538–48.

Dishion, T. J. and Kavanagh, K. (2003) *Intervening in Adolescent Problem Behaviour: A family-centered approach*, New York: Guilford Press.

Dore, M. M. (1991) *Family-based Mental Health Services Programs and Outcomes*, Philadelphia: Philadelphia Child Guidance Clinic.

Dunleavy, P. and Hood, C. (1994) 'From old public administration to new public management', *Public Money and Management*, July–September pp. 9–16.

Elander, J. and Rutter, M. (1996) 'Use and development of the Rutter Parents' and Teachers' Scales', *International Journal of Methods in Psychiatric Research*, 6, pp. 63–78.

Epstein, N. B., Baldwin, L. M. and Bishop, D. S. (1983) 'The McMaster Family Assessment Device', *Journal of Marital and Family Therapy*, 9(2), pp. 171–80.

Fanshel, D. and Shinn, E. B. (1978) *Children in Foster Care. A longitudinal investigation*, New York: Columbia University Press.

Farmer, E. and Owen, M. (1995) *Child Protection Practice – Private risks and public remedies*, London: HMSO.

Farmer, E. and Parker, R. (1991) *Trials and Tribulations*, Norwich: The Stationery Office.

Farrington, D. (1996) *Understanding and Preventing Youth Crime*, York: Joseph Rowntree Foundation.

Fawcett,B., Featherstone, B. and Goddard, J. (2004) *Contemporary Child Care Policy and Practice*, Basingstoke: Palgrave Macmillan.

Feldman, L. K. (1991) *Assessing the Effectiveness of Family Preservation Services in New Jersey*, New Jersey: Division of Youth and Family Services, Bureau of Research, Evaluation and Quality Assurance.

Fisher, M. (1983) *Speaking of Clients*, Sheffield: University of Sheffield.

Fisher, M., Marsh, P. and Phillips, D. (1986) *In and Out of Care*, Batsford/British Agencies for Adoption and Fostering.

Flynn, R., Ghazal, H., Legault, L., Vandermeulen, G. and Petrick, S. (2004) 'Use of population measures and norms to identify resilient outcomes in young people in care: an exploratory study', *Child and Family Social Work*, 9(1), pp. 65–80.

Fogelman, K. E. (ed.) (1983) *Growing up in Great Britain: Collected papers from the National Child Development Study*, London: Macmillan.

Fox-Harding, L. M. (1991) *Perspectives in Child Care Policy*, London: Longmans.

Fraser, M., Pecora, P. and Haapala, D. (1991) *Families in Crisis: The impact of intensive family preservation services*, New York: Aldine de Gruyter.

Fraser, M. W., Nelson, K. E. and Rivard, J. C. (1997) 'Effectiveness of family preservation services', *Social Work Research*, 21(3), pp. 138–53.

Frost, N. (1997) 'Delivering family support: issues and themes in service development', in Parton, N. (eds) *Child Protection and Family Support*, London: Routledge.

Frost, N. (2002) 'A problematic relationship? Evidence and practice in the workplace', *Social Work and Social Sciences Review*, 10(1), pp. 38–50.

Frost, N., Johnson, L., Stein, M. and Wallis, L. (1996) *Negotiated Friendship: Home-Start and the delivery of family support*, Leicester: Home-Start UK.

Fuller, R. (1989) 'Problems and possibilities in studying preventive work', *Adoption and Fostering*, 13(1), pp. 9–13.

Gardner, R. (1992) *Supporting Families: Preventative social work in practice*, London: National Children's Bureau.

Gardner, R. and Manby, M. (1993) 'The Children Act and family support: a crisis of values', *Adoption and Fostering*, 17(3), pp. 20–5.

George, V. (1970) *Foster Care*, London: Routledge and Kegan Paul.

Ghate, D. and Ramella, M. (2002) *Positive Parenting: The National Evaluation of the Youth Justice Board's Parenting Programme*, London: Youth Justice Board for England and Wales.

Gibbons, J. (1990) *Family Support and Prevention: Studies in local areas*, London: HMSO.

Gibbons, J. (1991) 'Children in need and their families: outcomes of referral to social services', *British Journal of Social Work*, 21, pp. 217–27.

Gibbons, J., Conroy, S. and Bell, C. (1995) *Operating the Child Protection System*, London: HMSO.

Gibbs, A. (2001) 'The changing nature and context of social work research', *British Journal of Social Work*, 31, pp. 687–704.

Gibbs, I. and Sinclair, I. (1992) 'Consistency: a pre-requisite for inspecting old people's homes?', *British Journal of Social Work*, 22, pp. 535–50.

Giddens, A. (1998) *The Third Way. The Renewal of Social Democracy*, Cambridge: Polity Press.

Gilligan, R. (2001) *Promoting Resilience: A resource guide on working with children in the care system*, London: BAAF.

Glass, N. (2001) 'What works for children – the political issues', *Children and Society*, 15(1), pp. 14–20.

Glass, N. (2005) 'Surely some mistake?', *The Guardian*, 05/01/2005.

Greenfields, M. and Statham, J. (2004) *Support Foster Care. Developing a short-break service for children in need*, London: Institute of Education, University of London.

Goldberg, D. (1978) *Manual of the General Health Questionnaire*, Windsor: The Bradford Medical Library, NFER Publishing Company.

Goldberg, D. and Huxley, P. (1992) *Common Mental Disorders. A Bio-social Model*, London: Routledge.

Goldberg, D. and Williams, P. (1988) *A User's Guide to the General Health Questionnaire*, Windsor: NFER-Nelson.

Goldberg, D. P., Gater, R., Sartorius, N., Ustun, T. B., Piccinelli, M., Gureje, O. and Rutter, C. (1997) 'The validity of two versions of the GHQ in the WHO Study of Mental Illness in General Health Care', *Psychological Medicine*, 27, pp. 191–97.

Goldson, B. (2000) 'Children in need or young offenders? Hardening ideology, organizational change and new challenges for social work with children in trouble', *Child and Family Social Work*, 5, pp. 255–65.

Goldstein, J., Freud, A. and Solnit, A. (1973) *Beyond the Best Interests of the Child*, New York: Free Press.

Goodman, R. (1997) 'The Strengths and Difficulties Questionnaire: A research note', *Journal of Child Psychology and Psychiatry*, 38(5), pp. 581–86.

Gordon, D., Parker, R. and Loughran, F. (2000) *Disabled Children In Britain: A re-analysis of the OPCS Disability Survey*, London: The Stationery Office.

Gordon, D., Arbuthnot, J., Gustafson, K.E. and McGreen, P. (1988) 'Home-based behavioural systems family therapy with disadvantaged juvenile delinquents', *The American Journal of Family Therapy*, 16(3), pp. 243–55.

Graham, J. and Bowling, B. (1995) *Young People and Crime*, London: The Home Office.

Haapala, D. A. and Kinney, J. M. (1988) 'Avoiding out-of-home placement of high-risk status offenders through the use of intensive home-based family preservation services', *Criminal Justice and Behaviour*, 15(3), pp. 334–48.

Hardiker, R., Exton, K. and Barker, M. (1991) *Policies and Practices in Preventive Childcare*, Aldershot: Avebury.

Hegar, R. L. and Scannapieco, M. (1999) *Kinship Foster Care – Policy, Practice and Research*, New York: Oxford University Press.

Henggeler, S. W., Melton, G. B. and Smith, L. A. (1992) 'Family preservation using multisystemic therapy: an effective alternative to incarcerating serious juvenile offenders', *Journal of Consulting and Clinical Psychology*, 60, pp. 953–61.

Henggeler, S. W., Melton, G. B., Brondino, M. J., Scherer, D. G. and Hanley, J. H. (1997) 'Multisystemic family therapy with violent and chronic juvenile offenders and their families: the role of treatment fidelity in successful dissemination', *Journal of Consulting and Clinical Psychology*, 65, pp. 821–33.

Henricson, C., Katz, I., Mesie, J., Sandison, M. and Tunstill, J. (2002) *National Mapping of Family Services in England and Wales – a consultation document. Executive summary and consultation questions*, London: National Family and Parenting Institute.

Henricson, C. and Roker, D. (2000) 'Support for the parents of adolescents: a review', *Journal of Adolescence*, 23, pp. 763–83.

Hester, M., Pearson, C. and Harwin, N. (2000) *Making an Impact: A reader*, London: Jessica Kingsley.

Heywood, J. (1978 – first published 1959) *Children in Care. The development of the service for the deprived child*, London: Routledge and Kegan Paul.

HM Treasury (2002) *Pre-Budget Report*, London: HM Treasury.

Holman, B. (1988) *Putting Families First: Prevention and childcare*, Basingstoke: Macmillan.

House of Commons Health Committee (1998) *Children Looked After by Local Authorities, Second report of the House of Commons Health Committee*, London: The Stationery Office.

House of Commons Social Services Select Committee (1984) *House of Commons Second report from the Social Services Select Committee on Children in Care (Short Report)*, London: HMSO.

Howe, D. (1994) 'Modernity, postmodernity and social work', *British Journal of Social Work*, 24, pp. 513–32.

Howe, D. (1996) 'Surface and depth in social work practice', in Parton, N. (eds) *Social Theory, Social Change and Social Work*, London: Routledge.

Huey, S. J., Henggeler, S. W., Brondino, M. J. and Pickrel, S. G. (2000) 'Mechanisms of change in multisystemic therapy: reducing delinquent behaviour through therapist adherence and improved family and peer functioning', *Journal of Consulting and Clinical Psychology*, 68(3), pp. 451–67.

Humphreys, C. and Mullender, A. (undated) *Children and Domestic Violence*, Dartington: Research in Practice.

Huxley, P., Evans, S., Burns, T., Fahy, T. and Green, J. (2001) 'Quality of life outcome in a randomized controlled trial of case management', *Social Psychiatry Psychiatric Epidemiology*, 36, pp. 249–55.

Huxley, P., Evans, S. and Gately, C. *et al* (1996) *The Lancashire Quality of Life Profile*, London: Health Services Research Department, Institute of Psychiatry, King's College, University of London.

Jack, G. and Stepney, P. (1995) 'The Children Act 1989-protection or persecution? Family support and child protection in the 1990s', *Critical Social Policy*, 43, pp. 26–39.

Joughin, C. (2003) 'Cognitive behaviour therapy can be effective in managing behavioural problems and conduct disorder in pre-adolescence', *What Works for Children Group: Evidence Nugget*, whatworksforchildren.org.uk/docs/Nuggets.

Katz, I. and Pinkerton, J. (2003) *Evaluating Family Support. Thinking internationally, thinking critically*. Chichester: Wiley.

Kinney, J. M., Madsen, B., Fleming, T. and Haapala, D. (1977) 'Homebuilders: keeping families together', *Journal of Clinical and Counseling Psychology*, 43, pp. 667–73.

Kolvin, I. (1990) *Continuities of Deprivation? The Newcastle 1000 Family Study*, Aldershot: Gower.

Landis, J. and Koch, G. (1977) 'The measurement of observer agreement for categorical data', *Biometrics*, 33, pp. 159–74.

Lethem, J. (2002) 'Brief solution focused therapy', *Child and Adolescent Mental Health* 7, 4, pp. 189–92.

Lindsey, D. (1994) 'Family preservation and child protection: striking a balance', *Children and Youth Services Review*, 16(5–6), pp. 279–94.

Lindsey, D., Martin, S. and Doh, S. (2002) 'The failure of intensive casework services to reduce foster care placements: an examination of family preservation studies', *Children and Youth Services Review*, 24(9/10), pp. 743–55.

Lister, R. (2003) 'Investing in the citizen-workers of the future: transformations in citizenship and the state under New Labour', *Social Policy and Administration*, 37(5), pp. 427–43.

Littell, J. H. (2005) 'Lessons from a systematic review of the effects of multisystemic therapy', *Children and Youth Services Review*, 27(4), pp. 445–63.

Littell, J. H. and Schuerman, J. R. (1999) 'Innovations in child welfare', in Biegel, D. E. (eds) *Innovations in Practice and Service Delivery across the Life Span*, New York: Oxford University Press.

Littell, J. H. and Schuerman, J. R. (2002) 'What works best for whom? A closer look at intensive family preservation services', *Children and Youth Services Review*, 24(9/10), pp. 673–99.

Little, M. and Mount, K. (1999) *Prevention and Early Intervention with Children in Need*, Aldershot: Ashgate.

Little, M., Axford, N. and Morpeth, L. (2004) 'Research review: risk and protective factors in the context of services for children in need', *Child and Family Social Work*, 9(1), pp. 105–17.

Lloyd, E. (2000) 'Changing policy in early years provision and family support', *NCVCCO Annual Review Journal*, 2.

Macdonald, G. (1999) 'Social work and its evaluation: a methodological dilemma?', in Williams, F., Popay, J. and Oakley, A. (eds) *Welfare Research: A critical review*, London: UCL Press.

Macdonald, G. and Williamson, E. (2002) *Against the Odds. An evaluation of child and family support services*, London: National Children's Bureau/Joseph Rowntree Foundation.

Macdonald, G. and Roberts, H. (1995) *What Works in the Early Years?*, Ilford: Barnardo's.

Maluccio, A. N. and Fein, E. (1983) 'Permanency planning: a redefinition', *Child Welfare*, 62(3), pp. 195–201.

Maluccio, A. N. (1998) 'Assessing child welfare outcomes: the American perspective', *Children and Society*, 12(3), pp. 161–68.

Maluccio, A. N. and Anderson, G. R. (2000) 'Future challenges and opportunities in child welfare', *Child Welfare*, 79(1), pp. 4–9.

Maluccio, A. N. and Whittaker, J. K. (1997) 'Learning from the 'family preservation' initiative', *Children and Youth Services Review*, 19(1–2), pp. 5–16.

Marsh, P. and Triseliotis, J. (1993) *Prevention and Reunification in Child Care*, London: Batsford.

McAuley, C., Knapp, M., Beecham, J., McCurry, N. and Sleed, M. (2004) *Young Families under Stress. Outcomes and costs of Homestart Support*, York: Joseph Rowntree Foundation.

McAuley, C. (1999) *The Family Support Outcomes Study*, Belfast: Queen's University.

McIvor, G. and Moodie, K. (2002) *Interchange 77: Evaluation of the Matrix Project*, University of Stirling: Social Work Research Centre.

McKey, H. R., Condelli, L., Ganson, H., Barrett, B., McConkey, C. and Platz, M. (1985) *The Impact of Headstart on Children, Families and Communities. Final report of the Headstart Evaluation, Synthesis and Utilization Project*, The Headstart Bureau. Administration for Children Youth and Families, Washington DC: US Department of Health and Human Services.

Meezan, W. and McCroskey, J. (1993) 'Outcomes of home based services: effects on family functioning, child behaviour and child placement' (Unpublished paper: University of Southern California School of Social Work) cited in Littell, J. H. and Schuerman, J. R. (eds) *A Synthesis of Research on Family Preservation and Family Reunification Programs*, Chicago: Westat Inc., in association with James Bell Associates and the Chapin Hall Center for Children, University of Chicago.

Meezan, W. and McCroskey, J. (1996) 'Improving family functioning through family preservation services: results of the Los Angeles experiment', *Family Preservation Journal*, pp. 9–29.

Meltzer, H. (2000) *The Mental Health of Children and Adolescents in Great Britain. Summary Report*, London: National Statistics.

Meltzer, H. (2001) *Children and Adolescents who try to Harm or Kill Themselves*, London: National Statistics.

Meltzer, H., Harrington, R., Goodman, R. and Jenkins, R. (1999) *Children and Adolescents who try to Harm, Hurt or Kill Themselves*, Newport: National Statistics.

Minuchin, S. (1974) *Families and Family Therapy*, London: Tavistock.

Mount, J., Lister, A. and Bennun, I. (2004) 'Identifying the mental health needs of looked after young people', *Clinical Child Psychology and Psychiatry*, 9(3), pp. 363–82.

National Statistics (2003) *Census 2001 National Report for England and Wales*, London: The Stationery Office.

Nelson, K., Emlen, A., Landsman, M. and Hutchinson, J. (1988) *Family-based Services: Factors contributing to success and failure in family-based welfare services*, Iowa City: University of Iowa.

Newburn, T. (2001) 'What do we mean by evaluation?', *Children & Society*, 15(1), pp. 5–13.

Newman, T. and Blackburn, S. (2002) *Transitions in the Lives of Children and Young People: Resilience factors. Interchange 78*, Edinburgh: Scottish Executive Education Department.

Newman, T. and Roberts, H. (1997) 'Assessing social work effectiveness in child care practice: the contribution of randomized controlled trials', *Child Care Health and Development*, 23(4), pp. 287–96.

Oakley, A., Mauthner, M., Rajan, L. and Turner, H. (1995) 'Supporting vulnerable families: an evaluation of Newpin', *Health Visitor*, 68(5), pp. 188–91.

Oakley, A., Rajan, L. and Grant, A. (1990) Social support and pregnancy outcome, *British Journal of Obstetrics and Gynaecology*, 97, pp. 155–62.

Oliver, J., Huxley, P. and Bridges, K. *et al* (1996) *Quality of Life and Mental Health Services*, London: Routledge.

Oliver, J., Huxley, P. and Priebe, S. *et al* (1997) 'Measuring quality of life of severely mentally ill people using the Lancashire Quality of Life Profile', *Social Psychiatry Psychiatric Epidemiology*, 32, pp. 76–83.

Packman, J. (1975) *The Child's Generation*, Oxford: Blackwell.

Packman, J., Randall, J. and Jaques, N. (1986) *Who Needs Care? Social Work Decisions about Children*, Oxford: Blackwell.

Packman, J. (1993) 'From prevention to partnership: child welfare services across three decades', *Children and Society*, 7(2), pp. 183–95.

Packman, J. and Hall, C. (1998) *From Care to Accommodation*, London: The Stationery Office.

Packman, J. and Jordan, B. (1991) 'The Children Act: looking forward, looking back', *British Journal of Social Work*, 21, pp. 315–27.

Parker, R. (1966) *Decisions in Child Care*, London: Allen and Unwin.

Parker, R. (1980) *Caring for Separated Children*, London: Macmillan.

Parker, R. (1990) *Away from Home*, Barkingside: Barnardo's.

Parton, N. (1991) *Governing the Family. Child care, child protection and the state*, London: Macmillan.

Parton, N. (1996a) 'Child protection, family support and social work: a critical appraisal of the Department of Health research studies in child protection', *Child and Family Social Work*, 1, pp. 3–11.

Parton, N. (1996b) 'Introduction', in Parton, N. (ed.) *Social Theory, Social Change and Social Work*, London: Routledge.

Parton, N. (1997) 'Child protection and family support: current debates and future prospects', in Parton, N. (ed.) *Child Protection and Family Support*, London: Routledge.

Parton, N. and O'Byrne, P. (2000) *Constructive Social Work*, Macmillan.

Pecora, P., Fraser, M., Nelson, J., McCroskey, J. and Meezan, W. (1995) *Evaluating Family-Based Services*, New York: Aldine de Gruyter.

Pecora, P. J., Fraser, M. W. and Haapala, D. A. (1991) 'Client outcomes and issues for programme design', in Wells, K. and Biegel, D. (eds) *Family Preservation Services*, Newbury Park, CA: Sage.

Pitts, J. (2001) *The New Politics of Youth Crime*, Dorset: Russell House Publishing.

Platt, D. (2004) 'The Children Bill and what it means for childrens services'. Speech to the Inter-Agency Group conference, July 2004. London: Commission for Social care Inspection.http://www.csci.org.uk/about_csci/speeches/iag_conference_15_07_04.doc

Pleace, N. and Quilgars, D. (1999) 'Youth homelessness', in Rugg, J. (eds) *Young People, Housing and Social Policy*, London: Routledge.

Prout, A. (2000) 'Children's participation: control and self-realisation in late modernity', *Children and Society*, 14, pp. 304–15.

Rees, G. and Stein, M. (1997) 'Abuse of adolescents', *Children and Society*, 11, pp. 63–70.

Rees, S. (1979) *Social Work Face to Face*, New York: Columbia Press.

Reid, W. and Epstein, L. (1972) *Task-Centred Casework*, New York: Columbia University Press.

Ridenour, T. A., Daley, J. G. and Reich, W. (1999) 'Factor analyses of the Family Assessment Device', *Family Process*, 38(4), pp. 497–510.

Rohner, R. P. (1986) *The Warmth Dimension: Foundations of Parental Acceptance-Rejection Theory*, Beverly Hills, CA: Sage.

Rowe, J., Hundleby, M. and Garnett, L. (1989) *Child Care Now*, London: Batsford/BAAF.

Rowe, J. and Lambert, L. (1973) *Children Who Wait*, London: Association of British Adoption and Fostering Agencies.

Rutter, A., Giller, H. and Hagell, A. (1998) *Antisocial Behaviour by Young People*, Cambridge: University of Cambridge Press.

Rutter, M. (1979) 'Protective factors in children's responses to stress and disadvantage', in Bruner, J. and Garten, A. (eds) *Primary Prevention of Psychopathology*, Hanover NH: University Press of New England.

Rutter, M. (1987) 'Psychosocial resilence and protective mechanisms', *American Journal of Orthopsychiatry*, 57, pp. 316–31.

Rutter, M. and Smith, D. (eds) (1995) *Psychosocial Disorders in Young People and Their Causes*, Chichester: Wiley.

Rutter, M., Tizard, J. and Whitmore, K. (2002) *Education, Health and Behaviour*, London: Longman.

Safe on the Streets Research Team (1999) *Still Running. Children on the streets in the UK*, London: The Children's Society.

Scholte, E. M. (1992) 'Prevention and treatment of juvenile problem behaviour. A proposal for a socio-ecological approach', *Journal of Abnormal Child Psychology*, 20, pp. 247–62.

Schuerman, J., Rzepnicki, T. and Littell, J. (1994) *Putting Families First: An experiment in family preservation*, New York: Aldine de Gruyter.

Schwartz, I. M., Au Claire, P. and Harris, L. J. (1991) 'Family preservation services as an alternative to the out-of-home placement of adolescents: the Hennepin County experience', in Wells, K. and Biegel, D. E. (eds) *Family Preservation Services*, California: Sage.

Scott, S. (1998) 'Fortnightly review: Aggressive behaviour in childhood', *British Medical Journal*, 316, pp. 202–206.

Scott, S. and Sylva, K. (2002) *The 'SPOKES' project: Supporting Parents on Kids' Education*, Report to the Department of Health, Oxford: Department of Education Studies, University of Oxford.

Secretary of State for Social Services (1974) *Report of the Committee of Inquiry into the Care and Supervision Provided in Relation to Maria Colwell*, London: HMSO.

Sinclair, I. (2000) 'Methods and measurement in evaluative social work', ESRC Theorising Social Work Research Seminar Series, www.elsc.org.uk/socialcareresource/tswr/seminar6/sinclair.htm.

Sinclair, I. and Gibbs, I. (1998) *Children's Homes: A Study in Diversity*, Chichester: Wiley.

Sinclair, I., Wilson, K. and Gibbs, I. (2000) *Supporting Foster Placements. Report to the Department of Health*, York: Social Work Research & Development Unit.

Sinclair, R. and Burton, S. (1998) 'Avoiding the snakes, strengthening the ladders: preventive services for adolescents', in Utting, D. (ed.) *Children's Services Now and in the Future*, London: National Children's Bureau.

Sinclair, R., Garnett, L. and Berridge, D. (1995) *Social Work and Assessment with Adolescents*, London: National Children's Bureau.

Sinclair, R., Hearn, B. and Pugh, G. (1997) *Preventive Work with Families. The role of mainstream services*, London: National Children's Bureau.

Sloper, P. (1999) 'Models of service support for parents of disabled children. What do we know? What do we need to know?' *Child Care, Health and Development*, 25(2), pp. 85–99.

Smith, T. (1996) *Family Centres and Bringing up Young Children*, London: HMSO.

Social Services Inspectorate (1997) *Responding to Families in Need. Inspection of assessment, planning and decision-making in family support services*, London: The Stationery Office.

Statham, J. (2000) *Outcomes and Effectiveness of Family Support Services. A research review*, London: Institute of Education.

Statham, J. (2003) *Evidence base for children in special circumstances (Report to the National Service Framework working group)*, London: Thomas Coram Research Unit.

Statham, J., Dillon, J. and Moss, P. (2000) 'Sponsored day care in a changing world', *Children and Society*, 14, pp. 23–36.

Statham, J., Holtermann, S. and Winter, G. (2001) *Supporting Families: A comparative study of outcomes and costs of services for children in need*, London: Thomas Coram Research Unit, Institute of Education, University of London.

Statham, J. and Holtermann, S. (2004) 'Families on the brink: the effectiveness of family support', *Child and Family Social Work*, 9(2), pp. 153–66.

Staudt, M. and Drake, B. (2002) 'Intensive family preservation services: where's the crisis?', *Children and Youth Services Review*, 24(9/10), pp. 777–95.

Stein, M. and Carey, K. (1986) *Leaving Care*, Oxford: Blackwell.

Stevenson, O. (1996) 'Emotional abuse and neglect: a time for reappraisal', *Child and Family Social Work*, 1(1), pp. 13–8.

Stiffman, A. (1989) 'Physical and sexual abuse in runaway youths', *Child Abuse and Neglect*, 13, pp. 417–26.

Sykes, J., Sinclair, I., Gibbs, I. A. and Wilson, K. (2002) 'Kinship and stranger foster carers: how do they compare?', *Adoption and Fostering*, 26(2), pp. 38–48.

Szykula, S. and Fleischman, M. (1985) 'Reducing out of home placements of abused children: two controlled field studies', *Child Abuse and Neglect*, 9, pp. 277–83.

Thoburn, J., Wilding, J. and Watson, J. (2000) *Family Support in Cases of Emotional Maltreatment*, London: The Stationery Office.

Thorpe, D., Smith, D., Green, C. and Paley, J. (1980) *Out of Care*, London: Allem and Unwin.

Trasler, G. (1960) *In Place of Parents*, London: Routledge and Kegan Paul.

Triseliotis, J., Borland, M., Hill, M. and Lambert, L. (1995) *Teenagers and the Social Work Services*, London: HMSO.

Tunstill, J. (1992) 'Local authority policies on children in need', in Gibbons, J. (ed.) *The Children Act and Family Support: Principles into Practice*, London: HMSO.

Tunstill, J. (1996) 'Family support: past, present and future challenges', *Child and Family Social Work*, 1(3), pp. 151–58.

Tunstill, J. and Aldgate, J. (2000) *Services for Children in Need. From Policy to practice*, London: The Stationery Office.

Van Den Berg, J. E. (1993) 'Integration of individualized mental health services into the system of care for children and adolescents', *Administration and Policy in Mental Health*, 20, pp. 247–57.

Vernon, J. and Fruin, D. (1986) *In Care: A study of social work decision-making*, London: HMSO.

Walby, C. and Colton, M. (1999) 'More children – more problems?', *Community Care*, 15–21 July, pp. 26–7.

Walker, S. (2002) 'Family support and the role of social work: renaissance or retrenchment?', *European Journal of Social Work*, 5(1), pp. 43–54.

Wells, K. and Whittington, D. (1993) 'Child and family functioning after intensive preservation services', *Social Service Review*, 67(1), pp. 55–83.

West, D. J. and Farrington, D. P. (1973) *Who Becomes Delinquent?* London: Heinemann.

Whittaker, J. K. and Maluccio, A. N. (2002) 'Rethinking 'Child Placement': a reflective essay', *Social Service Review*, March 2002, pp. 108–33.

Widom, C. S. and Ames, M. A. (1994) 'Criminal consequences of childhood victimisation', *Child Abuse and Neglect*, 18(4), pp. 303–17.

Williams, F. (2004) 'What matters is who works: why every child matters to New Labour. Commentary on the DfES Green Paper *Every Child Matters*', *Critical Social Policy*, 24(3), pp. 406–27.

Wolfe, D. A., Jaffe, P., Wilson, S. K. and Zak, L. (1985) 'Children of battered women: the relation of child behaviour to family violence and maternal stress', *Journal of Consulting and Clinical Psychology*, 53(5), pp. 657–65.

Woolfenden, S., Williams, K. and Peat J. (2003) 'Family and parenting interventions in children and adolescents with conduct disorder and delinquency aged 10–17 (Cochrane Methodology Review)', *The Cochrane Library,* 4.

Yuan, Y. T., McDonald, W. R., Wheeler, C. E., Struckman-Johnson, D. and Rivest, M. (1990) *Evaluation of AB 1562 in-home care demonstration projects*, Sacramento, CA: Walter R. McDonald and Associates, Inc. Cited in Lindsey *et al.* (2002) op. cit.

Yuan, Y. T. and Struckman-Johnson, D. L. (1991) 'Placement outcomes for neglected children with prior placements in family preservation programs', in Wells, K. and Biegel, D. E. (eds) *Family Preservation Services: Research and evaluation*, Newbury Park, CA: Sage.

Index

Compiled by Elisabeth Pickard